To Peggy Whitmer,
With Best Wishes,
Best of Gretta
12/14/01

Gwen Knight Lawrence

"I was truly moved while reading the histories of these impressive women. I was struck not only by the challenges of their lives, but the parallels of their lives to mine and many of my peers—the struggle to be accepted into an integrated school of nursing; the added stress we experienced in our efforts to succeed in a setting in which we were not welcomed; the supports we received throughout our careers that enabled our professional mobility. In the various communities in which we have resided throughout this country, we have been "the minority" and sometimes seen as a deviant force, an irritant, persons who challenge the status quo. No wonder we have sometimes chosen to band together, for mutual sustenance and renewal of spirit. I applaud all of these women and am proud to have them as my sisters."

Hilda Richards, Ph.D.
President, National Black Nurses Association

"Lois Price Spratlen has performed an important and admirable community service in bringing together the experiences of the twenty-six registered nurses and recording them for posterity. Virtually all of the accounts successfully illustrate the crucial nexus between personal determination, familial support and professional success for all of these women. Theirs is a story of courage, tenacity and triumph. It should be read and remembered."

Quintard Taylor, Ph.D.
Scott and Dorothy Bullitt
Professor of American History
University of Washington, Seattle, WA

"The stories that are recorded in this book reflect the lives, words, ideas and images of a group of 26 African American Nurses in a specific geographic area. Yet, they have far reaching implications for nurses throughout the country. Although the themes and nuances in many of the critical events are most familiar to African American Nurses, they are not unfamiliar to other nurses, in America and beyond these borders. Furthermore, I believe that this book will serve as an illuminating resource for anyone in quest of a better understanding of the importance and challenges of diversity."

Rhetaugh Graves Dumas, Ph.D., RN, FAAN
Former President, American Academy of Nursing
Former President, National League for Nursing
Life Member, National Black Nurses' Association
Member, American Nurses' Association

"Readers of this book will be well rewarded. It is a revealing and inspiring testament to a group of Black women who persevered through economic hardship, racism, gender bias, and often personal tragedy to help shape a new world of respect and opportunity for themselves and succeeding generations working in health care. I think this a wonderful contribution, and look forward to using it in classes."

Michael Honey, Ph.D.
Professor of African American, Labor and Ethnic Studies and American History
University of Washington, Tacoma, WA
Harry Bridges Chair of Labor Studies
University of Washington, Seattle, WA
Author of the prize-winning *Southern Labor and Black Civil Rights* (1993).

African American Registered Nurses in Seattle

The Struggle for Opportunity and Success

Lois Price Spratlen

Peanut Butter Publishing
Seattle Washington

Copyright © 2001 Lois Price Spratlen

All rights reserved.

Cover design by David Marty Designs
Cover art by Gwendolyn Knight Lawrence
Text design by Precise Productions

No part of this book may be reproduced or utilized in any form or by any means, electronic or mechanical, including photocopying and recording, or by any information storage and retrieval system, without permission in writing from the author.

05 04 03 02 01   5 4 3 2 1

ISBN: 0-89716-906-9

First Printing April 2001
Printed in the United States

Published by Peanut Butter Publishing
Seattle, Washington

Peanut Butter Publishing
Seattle Washington

Dedication

This book is dedicated to the 13 nurses who founded Mary Mahoney Registered Nurses Club (MMRNC), now Mary Mahoney Professional Nurses Organization (MMPNO). Their organizational vision, values and sense of discovery continue to serve as the foundation on which our organization rests and provide the impetus for continuous growth and development.

Anne Foy Baker

Celestine Hodge Thomas

Sadie Haynes Berrysmith Wallace

Katie Stratman Ashford

Juanita Alexander Davis

Gertrude Robinson Dawson

Ira Gordon

Maxine Pitter Davis Haynes

Mary Marshall Davis Hooks

Mary Turner Stephens Lanier

Mary Martyn

Rachel Suggs Jones Pitts

Ernestine Rutledge Williams

Knowing our legacy—undistorted by others and documented by those who lived it—correctly aligns you and me and our children in the continuing struggle to fully claim our dignity in all areas of life.

Dr. Maya Angelou

Acknowledgements

Developing this book from interviews to final editing has been a labor of love, one that has enriched my life immeasurably. A major reason for that enrichment has been the assistance I sought and received from many individuals. I am gratified to acknowledge each individual's contribution.

To the 26 registered nurses who agreed to my interviewing them and to my using their words as the basis for these narratives, I extend my deepest thanks. The book could not have existed without their willingness to recall, candidly and in great detail, their life experiences. (Two nurses whose photographs are included without narratives died before I could interview them, and no family members were found to supply the needed information.) Even after their interviews, each of these nurses and their family members remained available to supply any additional information needed to complete their stories. I appreciate everyone's generous cooperation.

Through the Provost's Office at the University of Washington, I received financial support that provided two research assistants for this project: Marni Aaron and Lisa Nagaoka. Marni completed several writing projects before working with me on this book. Several interviews were completed with her assistance. She later transcribed these tapes before completing her master's degree in Urban Planning and leaving the project.

Lisa Nagaoka accompanied me during 20 interviews and transcribed them. She also did library research related to African American nurses and analyzed the data she had gathered. Before I completed the final interviews, she finished a Ph.D. in Anthropology.

Thelma Pegues, a nurse who is featured in the second half of this book, read each story and offered commentary. She brought to the manuscript her shared experience and historical perspective, having worked as a nurse's aide at Harborview Hospital in the late 1940s when many of the nurses who founded Mary Mahoney Registered Nurses Club were employed there.

Tiffany McClain, a college student majoring in African American literature at Mount Holyoke College, eagerly critiqued these stories and made helpful suggestions for improvements.

Among the several services rendered by Louise Cutter Davis were the typing and editing of multiple drafts of each story, scanning all photographs, and ferreting out sometimes arcane information. An example of the latter service is her obtaining details about which railroad lines served various areas of the United States 50 or more years ago. She has shown a steadfast level of interest in completing this book that matches my own.

Spencer G. Shaw, Professor Emeritus of the School of Library and Information Science, University of Washington, used his expertise as a library educator and as a storyteller to critique each story and recommend changes that might better capture and hold a reader's attention.

Joycelyn Moody, Black feminist scholar and faculty member in the Department of English, University of Washington, critiqued the stories, placing them within the context of a larger body of writings by African American female scholars from various disciplines. She recommended and I accepted her suggestion to organize this book into two major parts. She also made editorial suggestions.

Eugene Smith, Associate Professor Emeritus of English, University of Washington, edited all these stories, using his considerable expertise to reduce their length while retaining the themes, descriptions and voice of each nurse. He has remained available and interested in every phase of this book's development until it was ready to be delivered to the publisher.

As publisher, one of Elliott Wolf's valuable services was to assign Eugene Smith as editor. I thank him for his role in making this professional relationship possible, and for his early encouragement to write this book.

Gwendolyn Knight Lawrence created the image that appears on the cover of this book. After learning that this book is focused on African American registered nurses, she decided to entitle this image "we are one." We are joined together by a single thread which is our shared humanity.

Acknowledgements

Susan Neff, Assistant Ombudsman, University of Washington, has efficiently managed the day-to-day operations of the Ombudsman's office, thus enabling me to balance my responsibilities as Ombudsman with the demands of writing. She continues to be an important resource person in this office.

Thaddeus H. Spratlen remains my loyal supporter through many years of marriage and authorship. He was helpful with many tasks involved in writing this book, not the least of which was to help achieve a balance in our family life during the several years required by this writing project.

To each of these individuals I express my sincere appreciation.

Table of Contents

Acknowledgements vii

Introduction 13

Part I
Founding Members of Mary Mahoney
Registered Nurses Club (MMRNC) 17

Helping, Healing, Heeding a Calling
Anne Foy Baker 19

Nursing: A Satisfying Career
Celestine Hodge Thomas 29

An Effective Leader and a Spirit-Filled Christian Caregiver
Sadie Haynes Berrysmith Wallace 43

From Selma to Seattle—Racial Signs Down,
Segregation Still Around
Katie Stratman Ashford 55

A Daughter of Pioneers and a Determined Nurse
Maxine Pitter Davis Haynes 67

Nursing: The Journey from Pediatric Patient
Through a Professional Career
Mary Scott Marshal Davis Hooks 82

Inspired by a Pioneering Spirit to Become a Nurse
Juanita Alexander Davis 91

Turning Obstacles into Opportunities
Gertrude Robinson Dawson 102

A Quiet Spirit in a Comforting Caregiver
Mary Turner Stephens Lanier 112

A Colored Girl Who Became a Professional Nurse
Rachel Suggs Jones Pitts 117

A Caring and Compassionate Nurse
Ernestine Rutledge Williams 129

Ira Gordon 137

Mary Martyn 138

Part II
 Members of Mary Mahoney Professional Nurses Organization
 (MMPNO) for At Least One Quarter of a Century 139

A Long Road and a Late Entry into Nursing
Leola Sarah Fobbs Lewis 141

Love, Learning, and Living Life As My Mother Taught Me
Thelma Jacobs Pegues 149

A Nurse and a Community Activist
Willa Theresa White Lee 161

A Spirit of Hope and Determination
Verna Ward Hill 169

A Nurse Anesthetist
Frances Workcuff Fraizer Demisse 182

Education: A Pathway to Self-Development and Service to Others
Frances Jefferson Terry 192

A Sense of Place, Person, and Promise
Lois Price Spratlen 204

An Advocate for Children, Families, and Community Change
Elizabeth Moore Thomas 215

Seattle's First African American School Nurse
Shirley Williams Ticeson Gilford 227

Public Health: "The Right Place for Me"
Gwendolyn Harden Browne 239

A Professional Journey: In and Out of Community
Mary Lee Pearson Bell 250

A Nurse in Public Schools, the U.S. Air Force Reserve,
and Overseas Mission Programs
Muriel Grace Softli 264

Excellence and Achievement Across Three Generations
Vivian Odell Booker Lee 277

Rising Above Circumstances to Become a Professional Nurse
Rosa Dell Young 289

A Vision of Self-Sufficiency Through Service to Others
Wilma Jones Gayden 298

Afterword 311

References 318

Appendix 321

Introduction

This book is about a group of pioneering African American registered nurses in Seattle, Washington, who in 1949 formed the Mary Mahoney Registered Nurses Club (MMRNC). They did so to celebrate the legacy of their heroine and initially as a means of supporting one another to meet the challenges associated with being in a new community. Through this organization they received the needed assistance to survive and succeed as professional nurses in their places of employment in Seattle.

Mary Eliza Mahoney was the first Colored graduate nurse in the United States. In 1879, she received a diploma in nursing after completing a sixteen-month program of study in the New England Hospital for Women and Children in Boston, Massachusetts. She went on to become the first Colored registered nurse in America. Because of these achievements she is credited with opening the field of nursing to Negroes in the United States. Mary Eliza Mahoney enjoyed a long and distinguished career in nursing before her death in 1926 at the age of 81.

Throughout this book I use varied racial references: Colored, Negro, Black and African American. They are appropriate descriptions for particular times in our history. Each is considered to be equally respectful of us as a people.

Focus and Content of This Book

Life stories of 26 African American registered nurses form the narrative content and focus of this book. Two nurses are pictured without narratives, Ira Gordon and Mary Martyn. No family members or friends were found to share needed information to develop a story about them. (If any readers have information about these nurses, please contact the author.)

These stories reflect day-to-day events that occurred in the life of each nurse. Descriptions are provided of developmental challenges, varied obstacles and triumphs, lessons learned, failed love affairs and deaths of significant friends and family members. Embedded within these stories are gems of wisdom, hope, courage, and humor, which can enrich the life of each reader while reflecting the reality of each nurse's struggles and successes.

It is apparent in their stories that family members, neighbors, religious participation, natural intelligence and school performance combined to make a significant foundation for these nurses' career aspirations. The availability of these resources reinforced the values that were learned in the home, at church and at school. Though most of these nurses attended racially segregated public schools and were restricted to participation in racially segregated social organizations, they realized in early childhood that they wanted to become professional nurses even though most of them did not see or know Negro nurses.

Twenty-two of the featured nurses were born in Southern states. Two nurses, Maxine Pitter Davis Haynes and Juanita Alexander Davis, were natives of Seattle, Washington. The remaining two nurses, Frances Workcuff Fraizer Demisse and Muriel Grace Softli, were from Montana and New York, respectively. Regardless of the region of the country from which they came, all 26 nurses shared similar experiences. All were subjected to racial discrimination and segregation in education, organizational affiliation and employment.

During the 1940s, over one-half of these registered nurses attended racially segregated schools of nursing in the South which did not have alumnae associations. Since 16 Southern state associations denied membership to Negroes, MMRNC founders from the South could not become members of the American Nurses Association (ANA) which only granted membership to state associations. Individual memberships were not available to Negroes until 1948. In 1908 the National Association of Colored Graduate Nurses (NACGN) was founded, 12 years after ANA and continued to exist until 1951, three years after individual memberships in ANA were finally available to Negroes.

Introduction

In the area of employment, Negro nurses who arrived in Seattle during the 1940s were mainly limited to employment at Harborview Hospital (a county operated facility). During the mid-1940s, Providence Hospital employed one member of MMRNC, Maxine Pitter Davis Haynes. One nurse, Juanita Alexander Davis, was also hired in the public health department to work in the clinic serving patients who came to this facility for health care services. In the face of these and other limitations, Negro professional nurses continued to pursue opportunities to provide care in any facility where they could find employment. Such was their dedication to their chosen profession.

This book is organized in two parts, followed by an Afterword. The first three founders' stories are presented based on their critical role in identifying and bringing together the other 10 founders. All other stories are sequenced in the order of individuals' birth dates. Part One includes the stories of 11 of the 13 founding members of MMRNC. These nurses' performance in the workplace provided a foundation for the success of other African Americans who came after them. These 13 nurses were trailblazers and pathfinders in hospitals, clinics and in their communities. Part Two includes the professional nurses who came after the founders and joined this organization during the 1950s-1970s. It is evident that nurses in this group benefited from the professional efforts of our founders. They had greater access to educational and employment opportunities than was available to our founders. Shifts in racial attitudes as well as shifts in attitudes towards women's public work also account for some of these recent opportunities. It is now our collective responsibility to work for greater access and opportunities for future nurses and for students from other fields of endeavor who desire to pursue personal and professional development in any discipline.

The Afterword provides a place where these 26 personal stories can be viewed from a selected historical, socio-cultural, and theoretical perspective. The contributions which this broadened perspective make to understanding can be described and discussed from a social relationship and group development point of view.

African American Registered Nurses in Seattle

The History of MMRNC

The history of MMRNC is told through the stories of nurses who are represented in this book. Their narratives cover a period from the time of their births in the early 1900s through their careers and retirement, into the 1990s.

MMRNC was established on July 9, 1949. Thirteen founding members attended this meeting. This organization came into being because these nurses recognized the values of organizational affiliation to promote their professional development. Initially these nurses provided intellectual, social and familial support to one another. Later they decided to reach out to the Seattle community to provide scholarship support for the recruitment of new members into the health care profession. In order to develop greater public awareness of the existence of this organization, members participated in candle light services in various churches in the community. Still later these nurses organized preventive health programs related to hypertension, sickle cell anemia and diabetes for residents of their communities. These organizational efforts served the needs of residents of the community and they motivated some new registered nurses to join this organization.

In 1987, MMRNC was renamed Mary Mahoney Professional Nurses Organization (MMPNO). This latter name reflected the need for all members to possess or acquire some education and training as professional nurses. At the time of the name change, several members were seeking to make membership in MMPNO available to licensed practical nurses. Since the needs and challenges of professional nurses differ in amount and kind from those of licensed practical nurses, the membership voted to continue its struggle for success as a professional nurses' organization.

This book documents and describes the struggles, obstacles and challenges that these registered nurses faced as the first African American nurses to practice in Seattle. Their inspirational stories are preserved for the benefit of posterity.

Part I

Founding Members of Mary Mahoney Registered Nurses Club (MMRNC)

Founding Members
Pictured standing left to right: Mary Martin, Ira Gordon, Mary Davis Hooks, Ernestine Williams, Gertrude Dawson, Maxine Pitter Haynes, Rachel S. Pitts and Katie Ashford. Seated left to right: Anne Foy Baker, Sadie Berrysmith Wallace, Juanita Davis and Celestine Thomas. Not shown: Mary Lanier. (Photographed by Chester Berrysmith).

Helping, Healing, Heeding a Calling

Anne Foy Baker

Anne Foy Baker refers to her practice of nursing as a *calling*. She likens her understanding of being called to one's life work to the expression used by men in her youth as "being called to the ministry."[1] Her career path in pursuing this calling is instructive, for it reveals a pattern that is evident in most of the nurses' experiences that are represented in this book. Essentially, when Negro nurses worked in the South in segregated situations, there were opportunities to be appointed to leadership and administrative roles. In desegregated treatment settings in the North, such opportunities were generally more difficult for Negroes to obtain.

Childhood Influences

Anne recalls, from a very early age, the visits made to her home by the public health nurse. With 11 children in Anne's family, the nurse came rather often to check on their immunizations and general health status in relation to entering and returning to public school. She remembers the very special feeling she had while the nurse was present in their home and the long-lasting, positive effects associated with the nurse's visits.

Born to Juliet Pierce Foy and Eddie Foy on December 15, 1914, in Greensboro, North Carolina, she was the second child and first daughter in their family. Nine other children were later born to this couple. They were sufficiently close in age that all 11 children, consisting of five boys and six girls, were present in the home for several years.

---
[1] *Ministry* has its roots in Latin, defined as a form or kind of service. Service is integral to the definition of *nursing*; thus both the ministry and nursing share service as a dimension of their meaning.

Her father always worked two jobs both as an ordained Methodist minister and as a postal worker. He worked in the post office five days each week, but he was a minister all the time. In addition to Sunday services, he practiced his ministry on weekends, holidays, and evenings. Anne vividly recalls his visits to neighbors' homes, hospitals, pool halls, and wherever he was needed to spread the word of the Lord. Observing and being part of the nurse's home visits and her father's calling led Anne to understand nursing as her calling. Since there were no women ministers in Greensboro, Anne would not have thought of becoming a minister nor would schoolteachers or community leaders have encouraged her to do so.

As a postal worker and minister, Anne's father earned enough money so that her mother did not work outside the home. In her housewife and mother role, she had nearly total responsibility for the management of their home and family and was, Anne recalls, well organized and very attentive to the family. The family lived in the same house in Greensboro for most of their lives, where there was always enough food to eat and clothes were handed down in the family until they were no longer usable. As soon as they were old enough, all the children worked at something to earn money. Anne recalls that the one thing her father had them do often was to bring their shoes to him for inspection. He would place in line those 11 pairs of shoes to determine which would be half-soled, which needed to be replaced with new shoes, and which could go without anything but a bit of shoe polish. He seemed to really like this fatherly task, and the children also enjoyed the ritual of their father's shoe inspections.

Singing was one of their major forms of family entertainment. For as long as Anne can remember, the home had a piano and organ, both of which her mother played and tried to teach each child to play. She recalls being more interested in playing ball than in learning music; so, she never learned to play either instrument very well. Even today she enjoys group singing that she hears over the radio and TV.

All of the Foy children had an opportunity to attend a vocational school or college. At least four of the children remained in Greensboro while attending North Carolina Agricultural and Technical University. Her father used to walk to the Bursar's office to pay their college bill, always paying something even when he could not pay the entire bill. Money and its management were topics that were openly discussed in the Foy family. Whenever children worked, they were encouraged to use some proportion of their money for tithing.

Ten of the 11 children were practicing professionals or skilled workers until retirement. Only one brother was a "ne'er do well." Today, Anne (age 84), her two remaining sisters, Hattie (74) and Cordia (68) and one brother, Joseph Daniel (76), continue to follow the practice of giving generously to the church and Sunday school. Currently, the three sisters live together in Greensboro and are still members of the church in which they were baptized as children. Anne's brother, Joseph, died in August 2000 in his home in Kansas City, Missouri.

During these years in Greensboro, life was simple, safe, and generally quite predictable. The Foy children grew up, of course, without television. Work, church, and school were the center of activities in their home. Singing, listening to the radio together in winter, and sitting on the front porch in summer during the evening while children played together were well-established forms of entertainment for adults and children.

Completion of Nursing Program

In 1940, when Anne graduated from James B. Dudley High School, she decided to join a high school friend and pursue nursing, then a three-year diploma program, at Piedmont Sanatorium in Burkeville, Virginia. The first 18 months involved work to obtain a certificate in the management of tuberculosis patients. Afterward, students from both Piedmont and Hampton Institute pursued a clinical affiliation in medical/surgical, pediatric, obstetrics/gynecology, and other areas at St. Philip Hospital in Richmond, Virginia. All enrolled students completed the same program of study for the purpose of developing competence in all clinical areas of nursing. At that time nursing schools, particularly in the South, but also in many Northern states, were segregated by race. The number of places where Negroes who desired professional nursing degrees could study was small (Hine, 1985). This helps to explain why there were students from several different colleges and hospital programs concentrated at St. Philip.

At this hospital, Negro patients were treated, and Negro student nurses received their clinical training. White students obtained their clinical experience and White patients received care at the Medical College of Virginia, St. Philip's parent institution. Though the two institutions were in close proximity, they were generally as separate as night and day physically and operationally. Administratively, the dean of the Medical College of Virginia was also the dean of St. Philip, but this relationship was not very evident to students.

Even during the early 1950s, however, Negro and White students attended some theory courses together. When it was time for clinical practice, it was separate and very unequal. Differences in physical facilities and equipment were great and distressingly visible. As an example, only several thicknesses of newspaper protected sheets and mattresses on some Negro patients' beds, while beds for White patients had rubber sheets. Linens and other supplies were chronically in short supply throughout St. Philip. The nursing arts manual for Negro students contained suggestions for improvising or making substitutions—from bed linens to medical and surgical equipment. When Negro student nurses shared information about conditions in St. Philip with White students, they learned that these conditions did not exist at MCV. Nursing was truly a form of improvisational art in this setting.

Negro teachers principally taught clinical education and training at Burkeville, teachers whom Anne viewed as just as interested in preparing excellent nurses as those at Richmond. Both hospitals had a similar organizational structure with supervisors, head nurses, and a director of nursing. At St. Philip some Negro nurses served in these important leadership roles and thereby gained experiences that might not have been available in the non-segregated setting. In retrospect, Anne feels that she benefited immeasurably from their investment in her education and professional development.

Entry into the Profession and Marriage

After graduation, Anne stayed on at St. Philip to gain experience as a professional nurse, with an appointment as 3:00-to-11:00 supervisor of the operating room in St. Philip which was quite an honor for a recent graduate. She also needed to prepare to take state board

Helping, Healing, Heeding a Calling

examinations to become a tuberculosis technician and to become a registered nurse. She passed both the first time she took them and became a registered nurse, working in Richmond, Greensboro, Baltimore, and New York City.

By managing her money well, she was able in 1944 to take a trip with her sister and niece to Seattle. It was during this trip that Anne met the man, Albert R. Baker, who eventually became her husband. Though he was more than twice her age, she found him to be one of the kindest and most wonderful men she had ever known. "Age did not matter for we were in love," she says. After a three-year-long courtship by letter, on June 12, 1947, they were married by a Justice of the Peace in Seattle. Anne said she moved right into Albert's home on the very day she returned to Seattle from Greensboro, but she did so as his wife and not as people often do today— by living together before marriage. "I got off the train and we went directly to the Justice of the Peace to be married."

Anne Foy Baker in 1949 shortly after the founding of Mary Mahoney Registered Nurses Club. (Photo courtesy of Gil Baker)

For the first 18 months following their marriage, Anne enjoyed the status of a new bride, working only as a volunteer for the Red Cross of Seattle. Even before marriage, Anne had already established communication with a Piedmont schoolmate, Celestine Thomas, who worked at Harborview Hospital. Along with their husbands, they established a close friendship.

Formation of Mary Mahoney Registered Nurses Club

Eventually Anne, feeling the need to become more involved with practicing nurses, asked Celestine Thomas to get the names and telephone numbers of as many local Negro nurses as she could. From a list of 10, Anne invited each to attend a meeting in her home. All accepted. She explained that she thought they needed to come together as a group, though she wanted to leave it to the group to decide what their objectives should be. Even though most of these nurses were employed at Harborview, they did not know each other very well, since they worked on different shifts and different floors of the hospital. Most were also relatively new to Seattle.

Before the first meeting occurred, Celestine reminded Anne that Negro nurses were eligible to be members of the National Association of Colored Graduate Nurses (NACGN). They also recognized that the American Nurses Association (ANA) at that time was taking steps to offer individual membership to Negro nurses. Inspite of these developments, Anne felt that a local Negro nurses' organization was also needed in order to address the concerns, interests and needs of local RNs.

On July 9, 1949, 13 Negro nurses assembled at Anne Foy Baker's home to establish the Mary Mahoney Registered Nurses Club. They chose the name in honor of the first Colored registered nurse in America, Mary Eliza Mahoney. Their main order of business was to tell their personal and selected professional stories to one another. They also decided to hold monthly meetings in the home of each nurse. Meetings were scheduled for 5:00 p.m. on the first Saturday of each month, a time that enabled the largest number of members to attend. Now, 50 years later, meetings of the organization continue to occur monthly, not in members' homes but at Group Health Hospital's conference room on Capitol Hill in Seattle.

Soon after the first meeting the organization's Constitution and By-laws were developed. A copy of the first Constitution and By-laws appears in the Appendix of this book.

It was Anne's vision and leadership that led to the development of the Club's aims: (1) concern for the continuing professional development among these members; (2) recruitment of new members to the profession; and (3) community outreach, the primary way to raise awareness within the community of problems and challenges which were unique to Negro nurses in their work life. Focusing on these aims, members joined together to engage in collective actions that were socially appropriate and professionally relevant to their mission. They used the church and other social and civic organizations such as Young Women's Christian Association, Phillis Wheatley Club, and local sororities, as settings for public education and for engaging in fund-raising efforts in the community.

Helping, Healing, Heeding a Calling

A Life-Changing Accident

In November 1949, just two years and five months after their marriage and only four months after the founding of MMRNC, Anne and her husband were in an automobile accident. He was killed and Anne received very serious injuries which made it impossible for her to attend his funeral. Indeed, she did not remember seeing the obituary until it was found by Celestine Thomas' husband, Lawrence, who was searching for items that could be used in this book. A copy of this obituary was sent to Anne in 1999.

Anne remained in the hospital following the accident for some weeks. While in the hospital and after she had returned to her home in Seattle, members of MMRNC provided nursing care, arranging their schedules so that she could have 24-hour care. All of the money which the insurance company paid for nursing care was donated to Anne. Once Anne was well enough to travel, her parents came to Seattle and carried her back with them to North Carolina.

Anne remained in Seattle for only five months after founding MMRNC. However, the remaining 12 nurses continued to meet and sustain the organization. Among the founding members, six are now deceased: Katie Ashford, Ira Gordon, Mary Lanier, Mary Martyn, Sadie Berrysmith Wallace and Celestine Thomas. Two of the founders are inactive and the remaining four are active members: Gertrude Dawson, Maxine Haynes, Mary Davis Hooks and Rachel Pitts. Anne has continued to support this organization financially and emotionally for more than 50 years. In 1996 she was made an emerita member of Mary Mahoney Professional Nurses Organization.

The 1987 organizational name change from Mary Mahoney Registered Nurses Club to Mary Mahoney Professional Nurses Organization was prompted by a desire on the part of some members to propose that this local professional organization merge with the National Black Nurses Association. Since NBNA consists of both professional graduate and licensed practical nurses, some members thought that the new name would appropriately reflect MMPNO's membership-eligibility requirement. This change is still the subject of periodic debate.

African American Registered Nurses in Seattle

Later Career Experiences

Following her return to the East Coast and her recovery from the accident, Anne worked as head nurse on the 3:00-11:00 p.m. shift at the Medical College of Virginia. Some level of desegregation had occurred there since Anne was a student during the 1940s; she was in charge of all surgery cases at St. Philip and MCV when she worked in Richmond in the 1960s. When she worked at Johns Hopkins Hospital in Baltimore from 1962 to 1965, she lost her supervisory role, serving only as staff nurse, although by this time she had over 20 years of professional nursing experience in a variety of treatment settings. At base Anne had more leadership roles in the Southern hospitals than she had in the North. This pattern has been observed in the careers of other nurses represented in this book and in the larger profession. In racially segregated treatment settings, it was considered natural to have Negro registered nurses serve in leadership roles. This was not the case for Negro nurses in predominantly White treatment settings. Neither patients nor other White nurses would likely be accepting of the Negro nurses' leadership during that period in American history.

After returning to Greensboro in 1968, Anne worked as a staff nurse in College Health Services at A & T College, interacting daily with enrolled students. She served as a role model and caregiver to students, many of whom were away from their families for the first time. Drawing upon her family experiences and others acquired in the process of living, she influenced most who knew her to value health, personal and professional development, and community service. She often made personal loans to students, counseled students' parents, and spoke to college administrators on students' behalf. Her intensity of involvement with students and her outreach to their parents are consistent with Anne's conceptualization of her practice of nursing as her calling, ministering to the soul and psyche of those whom she touched. In this educational environment she served individuals and the institution by helping, healing, and heeding the call to nursing.

In addition to being a founder of Mary Mahoney Registered Nurses Club (now Mary Mahoney Professional Nurses Organization), Anne founded another organization in Greensboro

Helping, Healing, Heeding a Calling

that provides health and related social services to local residents of a nursing home. First called the St. James Nursing Center Auxiliary, it concentrated on geriatric patients who lacked adequate resources for managing daily life, attempting to improve the quality of life for residents. Anne mobilized members of her church and other members of the community to provide bedspreads, bed clothing, and toilet items for residents. They also organized social activities and a structured visitation program. Sometime during the 1980s this nursing center closed, but not before members of the auxiliary voted to change their name to the Anne Foy Baker Support Group (AFBSG) in honor of Anne's leadership.

Anne Foy Baker in 1988 seated in the living room of her home in Greensboro, NC. (Photo taken during the author's visit with Anne)

Shortly before the nursing center closed, Anne learned about an urban ministry that provided meals to homeless persons in shelters and in other churches throughout the city. She established a collaborative relationship with this group through which AFBSG continues to serve the needy alongside their White colleagues. Once again, Anne used her philosophy of nursing to help, heal, and answer a calling.

Anne in Later Life

Over 20 years ago, Anne retired from college nursing; however, former students continue to remain in contact with her through cards, letters, and telephone calls. When students whom Anne befriended return to the campus, they often include a visit to her home, enabling her to be a continuing, significant presence in the lives of those with whom she worked and served long ago.

Since January 1998 Anne has been bedridden. Some of her immobility problems are associated with the injuries she sustained in the 1949 automobile accident. However, Anne remains in phone contact with friends and anyone else who calls, writes, or sends messages to her through other people.

Anne's lifetime of helping, healing, and answering the call to nursing is exemplary, spent in service to others in response to the call to enter nursing which she received as a very young girl growing up in Greensboro. This calling remains as vivid to her today as it was over 50 years ago. Despite infirmities, Anne has organized a telephone prayer and visitation program for members of her church and other community residents who desire to be part of this fellowship. Anne's outlook on life and concern for others reflect great strengths and a compelling resolve to continue helping, healing, and heeding her calling in nursing and in her life! Her ministry is a continuous practice of nursing as a service and truly caring profession.

Nursing: A Satisfying Career

Celestine Hodge Thomas
(1919-2000)

Celestine Hodge was born on November 3, 1919, in Pocahontas, Mississippi, to parents who were farmers. She spent her first 13 years helping with various chores in the field and in the home. At a very early age she decided that there had to be an easier way to earn a living than by farming. Fortunately, her father wanted his girls to have an education, and he, along with Celestine's mother and maternal grandmother, encouraged her "to get an education and be somebody."

One of nine children born to Lulu Kelly Hodge and John Wesley Hodge, she was the first daughter and the fourth child in the family. Her three oldest brothers in order of their births were West Ernest, Linwood, and Chrisler. The five younger siblings in order of their births were Lester, Augusta, Sasarine, Fred Lewis, and Willie T. In addition to these nine children, her maternal grandmother, Margaret Johnson Kelly, lived in the home and played a significant role in Celestine's and Sasarine's development.

Learning the Value of Work and Education

"My grandmother used to tell us stories about slavery and how difficult it was even for her, although not a slave, to get the opportunity to learn how to read and write. There were no public schools for Negroes. Many churches tried to establish schools, but it was hard to find teachers for these schools." Her grandmother was taught how to read by "a White lady." Through her grandmother's stories, she realized just how much her parents and grandmother wanted her to get an education.

Farming demanded hard physical labor six days a week. Her father, along with his three older sons, raised hogs, cows, chickens, cotton, and many kinds of vegetables. Everyone who was old enough to perform any task worked. Young children started off carrying fresh water to those who were working in the field. Everyone moved up to more challenging chores as they progressed in age. All of the children had their own beds, but they shared rooms. Since there were only two girls, the two of them were always in the same room and liked being together.

Their mother and grandmother, along with the two girls, were principally responsible for cooking, cleaning, canning, and managing the home; however, when Celestine was about 10 or 12 years old, she worked in the field. She admits that she liked to talk; so, her father often separated her from her younger brother, Lester, as they got older, because their father wanted less talk and more work from them.

"My mother was a very smart woman," she said. She worked with the home-extension agent, Miss Luckett, and helped other women in the area learn how to can and preserve vegetables and meat. Miss Luckett not only visited their farm often but later helped Celestine identify the nursing school that she attended. Whenever Miss Luckett came to their farm, it was a social occasion because other women from the neighborhood came to learn. They often stayed and visited with one another after Miss Luckett finished teaching.

Her father only had a third grade education. "But my dad could do anything. I saw him build a fence, install a roof on the barn, lay bricks, and make a leather hinge from old shoes. He was one of the most successful Negro farmers in our area." The older sons learned how to farm from their father.

Farm chores were completed very early on Sunday morning in order for the entire family to attend the local Baptist church together. Her mother taught Sunday school, her father encouraged everyone to thank God for giving them another week of life, and her grandmother enjoyed teaching others to read the Bible. The children sang in the choir and learned how to pray from the adults.

Public schools were segregated in Mississippi and Negro children could attend the first eight grades in Pocahontas; however, grades nine-12 were not available to Negro children. Celestine went to live with relatives in Jackson, Mississippi, to attend high school. Her happiest memories of public school were of the time that she spent in Cedar Grove Elementary School. There, she was taught by teachers who were members of the community. She recalled being in school plays and especially the yearly event of "winding the May pole." Later in life, she could even see the colors of crepe paper attached to the top of the pole before they started the winding process. These public school and Sunday school experiences were pleasant and filled with fun.

When she left her family to go to Lanier High School, she was sad about leaving but understood this was the only choice available to her. Prior to moving to Jackson, she had not had much contact with the relatives with whom she would live, but "They took me in and treated me very well." The high school was large and attended by Negro children from many areas of Mississippi. She did not like living away from home and looked forward to weekends when she often returned for family visits. At Lanier High she met Lawrence Thomas, who years later became her husband. Also, she often participated in activities with Lawrence and other teenagers in the school. "But Lawrence and I were not boyfriend and girlfriend; we were just good friends," she insists. Neither expected to marry the other. In 1940 she and Lawrence graduated from high school, after which she returned to the family farm and he went into the army; however, they kept in touch through letters.

The Urge to "Be Somebody"

She was uncertain what she would do with her life, but she became more convinced than ever that she needed to find something satisfying to pursue. She'd seen her father laying bricks when he built the cistern in their yard. She felt that she could lay bricks, too, but when she told her father of her interest in becoming a bricklayer, he immediately rejected that idea. "My father had warped ideas about what was girls' and boys' work. It was OK for me to plant and help harvest food from the garden, but I was never expected to build anything or help with farm repairs. I had a cousin, Willie Mae, who was an auto mechanic, but my father would never have allowed me to become one," she says. Early in life, her father had told her he wanted her to become a nurse. "My mother wanted me to be a school teacher, and my grandmother just wanted me to be somebody." Meanwhile, her mother regularly volunteered her babysitting services for other families' children. There was also a good bit of childcare needed by her younger brothers and sister.

Although studying to become a school teacher would have been convenient at nearby Jackson State College, she knew this was not the profession for her. She also knew that she definitely wanted to leave home. These desires coincided, with the help of Miss Luckett. During one of her visits, Celestine mentioned her interest in getting information about nursing. She knew that her father would be happy for her to become a nurse and that she would find nursing a satisfying career. When she suggested going to Tuskegee Institute in Alabama, which she thought had a school of nursing, Miss Luckett said she thought the school was having some financial problems but she would get back to her with details. Shortly thereafter, Miss Luckett presented information about Piedmont Sanatorium School of Nursing in Burkeville, Virginia, and none about Tuskegee.

Leaving Home to Begin Nursing Training

What a deep sense of joy she had when she had written and mailed the letter stating her interest in being admitted to Piedmont Sanatorium to study nursing! She still recalls her enormous sense of satisfaction from completing this task. Furthermore, she had no doubt that her father would pay for her educational expenses, since both parents wanted her to pursue her own professional dream. As she got information about travel from Pocahontas to Burkeville, she found herself becoming more frightened about leaving home, traveling by bus and train to this far-away and unknown place. However, her desire to leave home exceeded her fear of traveling, so she completed her plans to depart.

Entering Piedmont Sanatorium in 1941, she was among 13 or 14 other Negro students. Since all had had a rural life in the South, they readily got to know one another and felt comfortable together. Celestine formed very close ties with several of her classmates and remained in touch with them for many years after they graduated.

Piedmont had a three-year diploma program which included the first 18 months there and the last 18 on affiliation at St. Philip Hospital in Richmond, Virginia. Associated with the Medical College of Virginia, St. Philip treated Negro patients, while the Medical College treated Caucasian patients. Sometimes, when patients were alone or unconscious, it was difficult to tell by looking at them to which hospital they should be assigned. "Most of the instructors were White; clinical instructors were Negro and White."

Being at Piedmont was one of the happiest times of her life. Accustomed to hard work in the field at home, she realized that giving nursing care had a spiritual aspect that often created in her similar feelings to those aroused by attending church with her family. She also loved the Piedmont method of teaching, which included much patient contact and hands-on experience. She especially liked the nursing-arts class when she got to be the patient. Recalling, years later, the bed baths and back rubs that students gave to one another while they learned the art of nursing filled her eyes with pleasure. Also, at Piedmont Sanatorium in 1941, she met Anne Foy (who later married and became Anne Foy Baker), the night supervisor. Their paths crossed again when, in 1943, Celestine went to St. Philip and found that Anne had transferred there to do medical-surgical nursing. (Later Anne became the evening supervisor in the operating room at St. Philip and the Medical College of Virginia.)

At the time she was in nursing school, the principal method for treating patients with tuberculosis consisted of isolating or quarantining the affected patient. Thus, the sanatorium existed to provide bed rest and a nutritious diet and to teach patients how to manage their sputum. Nurses provided this health teaching. Other treatments included surgery when tuberculosis was localized in the kidney or some portion of the lung and common use of streptomycin. Maintaining a calm atmosphere for patients was also central to treatment and nursing care. Celestine enjoyed this quiet, clean, and serene atmosphere.

Most patients were confined entirely to the hospital, with stays ranging from a few months to several years. Major kinds of diversion consisted of listening to the radio, records, reading books, and playing cards, which were activities in which nurses regularly participated along with patients. Some patients could go to the chapel where religious leaders from various denominations regularly came to provide services.

Nurses lived in a home where life was similar to that of patients, although only radio and records were available to them. There was no television. Going into town to shop was the most exciting activity for her and other nurses. Nurses could also attend religious services in the chapel.

At the conclusion of the first 18 months of their program, each nurse took an examination. Those who passed were certified tuberculosis nurses and went to Richmond to complete the 18-month affiliation at St. Philip. While there, Negro student nurses lived in residences next door to Caucasian nurses. At St. Philip, students completed medical, surgical, obstetrics and gynecology, pediatrics, and orthopedic nursing which contained theoretical content and clinical experiences. Instructors were Negro and Caucasian. For some subjects Negro and Caucasian students attended classes together, but nursing care was segregated with Negro student nurses caring for Negro patients and Caucasian student nurses caring for Caucasian patients. Caucasian medical doctors, interns, and residents worked in both hospitals.

At St. Philip Celestine became aware of her real nursing skills. Never having had experience working with children, she loved her pediatric rotation; however, the obstetric/gynecology rotation convinced her that this was the service for her. The opportunity to work with mothers and their newborn infants made her see "the birth of a baby as a real miracle." The joy that this event usually brought to the mother made work on this service one of her most satisfying experiences.

Another experience brought great pleasure to her. It was a surprise visit from Lawrence Thomas, her high school friend. "He just showed up one day." The visit, though brief and unplanned, encouraged her to take this relationship more seriously than she had previously. She was working a split shift the day he visited on a three-day pass. They had gone to a movie, but they did more talking than watching. He needed to get back on the bus for the return ride to Camp Butner in North Carolina; so, they agreed to stay in touch. Lawrence's army uniform had made him seem more mature, and, from then on, she began to think that marriage might be in their future.

She especially enjoyed being in Richmond, the largest city in which she had ever lived. Going to movies, to church, and shopping

Nursing: A Satisfying Career

were new and exciting big-city activities for this country girl. The capping ceremony that climaxed this three-year program in 1944 remains for Celestine the most memorable. It was not just the capping itself but, also, receipt of a Florence Nightingale lamp which she kept track of for many years and a nursing cape, which she also treasured. Before and during the graduation exercises, with her parents present only in spirit, she realized that she had satisfied the childhood dream of becoming a graduate nurse, further anticipating that she would also become a registered nurse. This optimism was based upon her having achieved good grades and on her instructors' helpfulness and supportiveness.

Finding Employment

Following graduation Celestine returned to Jackson, feeling a deep sense of satisfaction to be returning to a place so close to her hometown. The relatives with whom she had lived while attending high school were still there, proud of her accomplishments and welcoming her return. Her parents, too, were delighted to have her return to Pocahontas for visits. The reason for coming to Jackson was to seek employment. She does not recall how she happened to apply at the Sally Harris Clinic in Jackson, but just stopping in to inquire about employment possibilities led to a job offer. The clinic, owned and operated by a Negro general practitioner, performed frequent Caesarean sections, as well as abortions, which she found objectionable. Indeed, her displeasure with participating in any activity related to abortions eventually led her to resign, but, before leaving the clinic, she passed state board examinations. She had also had some excellent nursing experiences and enjoyed practicing as a professional in a community where she occasionally saw individuals she had known before and who often told her how proud they were of her accomplishments.

A Move to Seattle and New Employment

During her years in nursing school, her sister, Sasarine, met and married a man in the Navy and moved to Seattle. Knowing that "our mother wanted us girls to be together," Celestine joined her in May

1945. Since her husband was often away from home, Sasarine was thrilled to have her sister with her. Before coming, Celestine had looked for job opportunities in hospitals in the area and had identified (in the *American Journal of Nursing*) Harborview as the place to go first. When she called the nursing supervisor, Miss Glenn, a few days after she arrived, she expected to make an interview appointment; instead the interview occurred on the phone and included a job offer which required working evenings in general medicine. The shortage of nurses made the supervisor eager to hire her. "On the medical-surgical floor there were lots of older patients and I enjoyed caring for them," she recalls.

Typically, in the 1940s nurses were not always provided a comprehensive orientation to the service on which they worked. Celestine's orientation consisted only of being told the locations of the pharmacy, central supply, and linen closet. As for reactions to her skin color, some nurses were nice and others ignored her. A few were unkind; however, kindness predominated. She was also fortunate to get a regular evening shift, especially when new nurses were often assigned split shifts.

Socially, the sisters discovered how discrimination worked in a variety of locations such as housing, employment, and restaurants. When they entered certain restaurants, for example, instead of orally denying service as soon as they entered the door, a staff member allowed Negroes to sit down, but no one would come to offer service. Soon the sisters knew where to go to eat and be treated with respect. Celestine concluded that discrimination operated differently in Seattle than in Mississippi, which had signs for Colored and Whites. Seattle had no such signs; rather, Negroes were expected to know where they were and were not welcomed.

Marriage and Motherhood

Soon Celestine began to feel more comfortable about being in Seattle, partly because she and Lawrence continued their courtship through letters. He told her that, when he was discharged, he planned to come to Seattle. This happy prospect made her think they would surely soon be married. Indeed, in late September Lawrence was discharged from the army and on November 5, 1945, they were

Nursing: A Satisfying Career

married. They found a home in White Center housing projects where they remained for about five years. Lawrence found work, first, at the Port of Embarkation and later as a merchant seaman. Finally, while working at Bethlehem Steel Company, he was admitted to the University of Washington, where he planned to be a business major. Since the G. I. Bill would pay for school expenses, he was confident that he could work full-time and attend college part-time. But in 1947 they had their first son, Larry, an event that required significant changes in their lives with her working part-time and with him dropping out of school. They willingly made these changes to care for their son.

Prior to her marriage, Celestine had been reassigned to the obstetrics/gynecology service and continued to work the regular evening shift. After her son's birth, she began working part-time only on weekends, first in obstetrics/gynecology and then in the outpatient clinic. When childcare duties became somewhat less demanding, she returned to full-time work and was promoted to assistant supervisor, a position that was less satisfying than previous staff and charge nurse positions had been. One reason was that whenever she proposed changes, her supervisor regularly rejected them and then, later, made the same proposals as if they were her own ideas. This happened so frequently that Celestine stopped making proposals, although she never confronted the supervisor about this aspect of her behavior. Whenever she felt especially discouraged about her work situation, she found satisfaction in the responses that patients and several of the doctors shared with her about her care-giving practice. These expressions of appreciation kept her going to work so that she never gave up entirely.

Helping to Found Mary Mahoney Registered Nurse Club

Anne Foy reappeared in her life in 1947, having moved to Seattle to marry Albert Baker. She and her husband became good friends with Celestine and her husband. It was part of the reason for Anne's asking her, in 1949, to help her and Sadie Berrysmith to organize a professional nurses' organization for Negro nurses in the Seattle area. Since there were so few hospitals where Negro nurses could find employment, Sadie and Celestine could contact nearly every Negro nurse in Seattle to ask them to join the group. On July 9, 1949, 13 nurses gathered together to establish the Mary Mahoney Registered Nurse Club. By being instrumental in establishing this group, Celestine felt that she had met the expectations of her parents and grandmother.

Later in 1949, she met Mary Davis Hooks and Katie Ashford. They befriended one another and began meeting outside of the workplace. This friendship led to Celestine's being called "Tommie," a nickname that all the nurses in the hospital and other providers also began using. Whether or not the nickname had anything to do with it, she determined, after working in Harborview for less than a year, that she knew whom to trust and with whom to limit her contacts. With regard to patients, she found that, on the obstetrics/gynecology floor, people were generally very accepting of her care. When anticipating the arrival of a baby, most patients focused on that event and less on her racial/ethnic identity. "Back then people had concerns about whether their baby was healthy or not, so these concerns assumed priority. There were no ultrasound or other technologies to allay apprehension and anxiety that mothers experienced."

Celestine Hodge Thomas in 1959.

One of her most unpleasant experiences at Harborview concerned the hanging of Dr. Martin Luther King's picture in a clinical service area in the mid-1970s. The administration's request that the picture be removed and subsequent action sparked a crisis among African American and other providers of similar persuasion. One administrator elected to resign rather than carry out the picture-removal request. Celestine's son, Wayne, recalls that there was a press conference and media coverage about this incident. He said, "I helped my mother write the remarks that she made during that event." She later interviewed over 200 employees at Harborview regarding their feelings about the racial climate there and documented that African

Nursing: A Satisfying Career

American employees felt there was discrimination in the hospital and clinics. One of the most positive outcomes associated with this incident was the decision by employees and management to establish the Minority Affairs Committee to recommend changes in policies to management. Celestine remained active in this group until she retired.

In 1951 the National Association of Colored Graduate Nurses disbanded after it became possible to become members of the American Nurses Association. Two nurses from NACGN came to meet with members of Mary Mahoney Registered Nurses Club to encourage them to join ANA, and some MMRNC members did.

Between 1950 and 1951, Celestine and Lawrence had two more sons, Gregory and Wayne. Their three sons certainly filled their lives with joy, enhanced by their joining the Peoples Institutional Baptist Church and becoming active members. Beginning in 1950 and

Celestine in 1958 with her family as a "den mother". She served in this role for eight years.

continuing through 1968, Celestine and other members of Mary Mahoney organized regular candlelight services in churches throughout Seattle, using these occasions to educate the community about the existence of the organization. She especially enjoyed organizing and scheduling these events because they allowed her to merge the religious with secular life in socially appropriate ways.

In 1968 members of Mary Mahoney organized their first professional workshop, inviting nurses from all of the colleges and universities in the Puget Sound area. Celestine took pride in helping make this a successful event since it represented one of the first times that faculty from schools of nursing in the area attended an educational function organized by this group.

Filling a Professional Empty Place

In 1974, when Celestine had been employed at Harborview Hospital for nearly 30 years, she realized that something significant was missing in her work life. While she enjoyed the work and her positive relationships with most of her patients and with many of her colleagues, work was not as satisfying as it had once been. She knew in her heart of hearts that she needed a change. She ended these thoughts by praying to God for help, never mentioning these thoughts to anyone at work. Within weeks, Dr. Russell Dejong, chief of obstetrics/gynocology, asked her if she wanted to become an obstetrics/gynecology nurse practitioner. Though she had always believed in the power of prayer, this represented one of the most direct relationships between prayer and opportunity she had ever experienced.

On second thought, maybe this offer was designed to relieve her of her assistant supervisory role; nevertheless, she decided that, no matter what the motivation, she would accept this offer to receive further education and training. After discussing it with Lawrence, she accepted. "At first I thought I was too old. Then, when Dr. Dejong pointed out that not all of our patients were young, I thought it was OK for me to try to learn again."

She learned that she was one of seven women selected to participate in this six-month, full-time program, offered at Pacific Medical Center (the former Marine Hospital in Seattle). There, as the only African American nurse, she met nurses from other hospitals in the Puget Sound area. They studied together and helped one another, making it one of the most positive adult-learning experiences of her life. It reminded her of the time when she was a student at

Piedmont Sanatorium, where students had studied and worked together as a team.

Upon her return to Harborview Outpatient Clinic, she was designated as Women's Healthcare Specialist. In this new and expanded nursing role, she taught women to do breast self-examinations, completed pap smears, and taught classes on childbirth. She also provided patient counseling related to abortions. Although she was never fully comfortable with the abortion issue, "I made myself do this because so many of our patients could not afford or did not want to have a baby." She acquired greater self-confidence and enjoyed increased personal and professional satisfaction in her work. "I've had patients say to me, 'I'm glad you are a woman and you're going to examine me.' I never had one patient refuse my care."

She became so interested in promoting breast-cancer prevention and other preventive practices that she started a breast-self-examination program in her church. She was surprised and disappointed to learn that women in her church were unwilling to take off their Sunday clothes and hats to learn how to do breast self-examinations; however, she did not give up on this preventive idea. Later offering this program during the week, only a few women took advantage of this service. Eventually the program was discontinued.

Retirement and Alzheimer's Disease

For five years, she worked full-time as a Women's Healthcare Specialist, until 1980, when she decided to retire. A very nice retirement reception marked a major transition in her professional life. Now she would have time to devote to her grandchildren and to engage in other activities she never had enough time for before. At her retirement reception she told colleagues, "I had an opportunity late in my professional career to serve patients in a role that I never even considered when I graduated back in 1944. My entire life was enriched by this experience."

Lawrence continued to work full-time until 1983, when he, too, decided to retire. From 1983 until 1996, they were nearly inseparable, increasing their work in the church and traveling. Locally, she became active in Sound Heart and in the Christian Crusaders Club and Queen Esther Circle at her church. She also worked as a volunteer at the Central Area Senior Activities Center, where she and Gertrude Dawson regularly offered rummage-sale items to seniors and others who attended activities at the Senior Center. Together, they raised several hundred dollars for donations to the Center and to Mary Mahoney Professional Nurses Organization scholarships.

Celestine Hodge Thomas in 1994. She served as the 2nd Vice-President at the time this photo was taken.

In 1996 Celestine developed Alzheimer's disease and steadily declined in subsequent years. Lawrence remained her primary caregiver. In late March 2000, I stopped by to visit and entered the home at a time when he was feeding her ice cream. He said to me, "Fifty-five years ago I took a vow to love and care for Celestine in sickness and in health. I intend to honor that pledge for as long as I can." He remains committed to MMPNO. The demands for her care, however, usually prevented him from attending fund-raising events sponsored by this organization. In regular telephone contacts, he was consistently pleasant and optimistic about the future throughout the final period of her life.

Before Alzheimer's robbed Celestine of her mental faculties, she had many opportunities to recognize that nursing had brought her real satisfactions in important areas of her life which included family, organizational affiliation, and the community. She undoubtedly followed the guidance of her maternal grandmother, "to be somebody."

On September 26, 2000, Lawrence called to inform me of Celestine's death. He asked and I agreed to write her obituary. During this conversation it seemed appropriate to convey to him the fact that he had truly honored the pledge—*till death us do part*—which he made to Celestine 55 years ago.

An Effective Leader and a Spirit-Filled Christian Caregiver

Sadie Haynes Berrysmith Wallace
(1921-1998)

Sadie Haynes' birth to Leona and Algin Haynes on April 1, 1921, in Silver City, Mississippi, was met with joy and thankfulness rather than as a prank, which is usually associated with April Fool's Day in America. Her sister, Rosie, was born in 1924. Both girls learned the meaning of work from an early age as they played near where their parents were working.

Their mother, Leona, worked as a domestic, cleaning the houses of better-off White people in their community. When she was not working outside of the home, she worked in the field with her husband who raised cotton and corn, as well as a vegetable garden which also required a lot of work. While working as a farmer, Algin spent some of his time perfecting his skills as a cook. Since his teenage years, he had dreamed of becoming a cook on the railroad.

Facing the Realities of Racial Segregation

Like many other Negroes, until they were in their 30s, Sadie and Rosie faced the harsh realities of total racial segregation which meant very limited opportunities in all areas of life. During their early childhood, the public schools were available for education from grades one through six and only White students could attend the community high school. After Sadie had completed sixth grade in Silver City, Leona and Algin moved the family to Jackson, Mississippi. Following this move, Algin was hired as a cook on the Illinois Central Railroad with a run from New Orleans to Chicago. His increased income meant that Leona no longer needed to work outside of the home, but being a fulltime homemaker also entailed not seeing her husband for weeks at a time. She sincerely missed having Algin at home.

For him, however, the new job had several assets. While he worked very hard as a cook, this job was much less strenuous than farming. He also enjoyed receiving a regular salary and other benefits not usually available to farmers. Seeing parts of the country that he had never seen before added an element of adventure to his work. Further, a strong level of camaraderie developed among the Negroes who worked on the railroad lines. It was a feeling he had never experienced as a farmer.

Sadie entered Jackson's Lanier High School in 1937, where she met many Negro children who had left their families in distant parts of Mississippi in order to obtain a high school education. Among them were Celestine Hodge and Lawrence Thomas, who graduated in 1940, one year ahead of Sadie. Eventually, they would meet again in Seattle, Washington.

Choice of a Nursing Career

Following graduation, Sadie met Ellen Hughes, a cousin of her mother's, who was the first Negro nurse to graduate from Mississippi State Charity Hospital in Jackson. She then went to Kentucky to study midwifery, returned to Mississippi, and practiced as a midwife with a local doctor. Sadie was impressed with Ellen's accomplishments, and in 1942 Sadie, too, was admitted to the MSCH School of Nursing. Convinced that she wanted to become a registered nurse, she never regretted this choice of a career.

Following the three-year-diploma program of the basic nursing course, students learned by practicing on the clinical wards with experienced registered nurses. These close mentoring relationships enabled students to

Sadie Haynes while she was a student at Mississippi State Charity Hospital, Jackson, Mississippi, 1942-1945.

An Effective Leader and a Spirit-Filled Christian Caregiver

develop excellent clinical skills and professional competencies. However, since the hospital was segregated by race, all Negro students cared for Negro patients who came with complex problems and diseases. Sadie later recalled, "We cared for some of the sickest patients I ever saw. Many of them were nursed back to health, but we also lost many young patients, too." The benefit for her and other student nurses was that they received excellent training.

In 1945, having completed all requirements and having received her diploma in nursing, Sadie worked for a year at MSCH; meanwhile, she studied and passed state board examinations. In summoning up the feelings associated with that experience, she said, "I am proud that I made the second highest scores on state boards and that a student in my class made the highest scores that year." This is one of her most important professional accomplishments.

A Move from Mississippi to Washington

She also read ads in the *American Journal of Nursing*, one of which was from Seattle's King County (now Harborview) Hospital. She called the director of nursing and was hired over the telephone. The impetus for this call was a childhood friend, whose aunt lived in Seattle and who had traveled to Seattle some months earlier to visit the aunt and decided to stay. Her assessment of job opportunities was favorable. Sadie reasoned that, if jobs were so easy to get, it should be possible to obtain employment before she left Mississippi. The response to her telephone interview was therefore not entirely a surprise. She was extremely excited and eager to leave Mississippi once she knew she had a job.

Since her father worked for the railroad, he was able to get her a pass for the trip, which took three days. The excitement of anticipation about leaving the South helped her enjoy the trip, although the train had separate cars for Colored and Whites. When she reached Seattle in January, 1947, she was surprised and happy to observe no signs on drinking fountains or restrooms that indicated they were for Colored or Whites. This initial contrast with the South was both striking and welcome.

For the first six months Sadie lived with her friend in her aunt's apartment; later she moved to Harborview Hall, across the street from Harborview Hospital. She enjoyed having her own room and being so close to her place of work. Another early experience which pleased her was seeing Lelia Duffel, the first Negro student admitted to the University of Washington's School of Nursing, one of the few nurses she had met. At that early point in her career, she thought the "Lord had really blessed me."

Finding Deeply Satisfying Work

First assigned to the medical geriatrics ward at Harborview, she was never given an orientation to this service, but "The White nurses were so very nice that they were almost patronizing." At that time, not many nurses wanted to work in geriatrics, but Sadie considered it a "blessing" to be able to provide care to all patients on her ward including post-polio patients. She says, "My reward was being able to give services to relieve the aches, pains, and discomforts of these patients." After being on the ward for a short period, Sadie realized that she was expected to manage as many as 40 patients with the help of one licensed practical nurse and one orderly. To give the quality of care she desired to provide, she worked many hours overtime, although no overtime pay was given: "When I worked overtime, it was considered that I was inefficient." Since most nurses did not want the stigma of being labeled "inefficient," few nurses complained about their working conditions. One way that Sadie adapted to this double bind was to define her mission: "to give unselfishly of my service to the sick and the afflicted." Later on in her career Sadie defined this as "doing God's work." She felt filled with the spirit and pleased with her circumstances. She was out of the South, single, living close to the hospital, loving her work, and knowing that she was a very good nurse. She regularly thanked God for all of "my blessings."

 She also attended church as often as possible. Raised a Methodist, she began attending Seattle's First AME Church. Since she often worked on weekends, it was a real treat to have one weekend off per month when she could attend church. During those weeks when she could not attend, she regularly prayed and read her Bible, convinced that she gave her best care to patients when she ministered to her own spirit.

An Effective Leader and a Spirit Filled Christian Caregiver

Marriage and a Sense of Community

A friend introduced Sadie to Chester Berrysmith, a porter on the Great Northern Railroad line with a run from Spokane to St Paul, Minnesota. Occasionally, he, too, attended services at First AME Church. Shortly after their meeting, they began their courtship. Prior to his migrating to the Pacific Northwest, he was an elementary school principal in Louisiana. In Seattle, however, he got a job on the railroad, requiring his relocation to Spokane, although he was also a photographer and had a small studio in Seattle. In January, 1949, Sadie and Chester were married. At the time of their marriage, Chester had two sons, Don and Fredrohl, who, during their teen years, worked as orderlies at Harborview on the floor with their stepmother, Sadie.

"We were married in Spokane where I knew no one. Chester arranged to get the marriage license and he made arrangements with the minister to marry us. A friend of his also stood with us. We were married in the evening and the next morning, Chester left for St. Paul and I returned to Seattle and went to work in the evening."

Following her marriage, she reestablished her relationship with her high school friends, Celestine and Lawrence Thomas, who were members of Peoples Institutional Baptist Church. She felt a sense of community with people in this church and specifically with the Thomas family. Work continued to be a significant and satisfying challenge and the place where she spent most of her time.

Reaching a High Level of Nursing Care

After working in geriatrics for about two years, she felt that she had demonstrated her competence as a registered nurse but also realized that the quality of care being provided to patients could be improved. She used her own initiative to bring about the desired change. She remembers, "Way back then, I established a standard of care for assessing all patients on this service, which included weighing each patient and completing a test of urine along with the standard temperature, blood pressure, pulse, and respiration. We were able through this routine assessment to identify several undiagnosed patients with high blood sugar, who were later diagnosed as diabetics." Though nurses generally waited to have doctors give orders about the kind of tests each patient should receive, Sadie felt sufficiently certain about the level of nursing care these patients needed (and she could deliver) that she instituted these services. This assessment protocol was later adopted by all nurses who worked on the geriatrics ward. Neither the nursing supervisor nor any of the doctors ever acknowledged that she had established this standard for assessing patients, but, as usual, Sadie quietly went about giving the highest quality of care she could provide to all of her patients and never mentioned to anyone that she established this assessment protocol.

She also had several encounters with doctors who were less than complimentary. One new intern who was with an attending physician with whom she had had a long and excellent relationship asked Sadie if she knew how to give a return-flow enema. This attending physician was quick to chastise this intern, saying, "Don't you ever ask her that kind of question again. She has taught me some of the things that I will be teaching you." Sadie was so happy about the attending physician's reaction that she rededicated herself to working even harder to demonstrate her nursing skills.

On another occasion, she had a patient admitted to her service whom she recognized as having a case of pemphigus, a serious skin disease characterized by vesicles and bullae on the skin and mucus membrane. The intern on duty did not know what was wrong with this patient; so, Sadie told the intern what she thought it was. Even though her diagnosis was correct, the doctor never acknowledged the accuracy of her diagnosis. She took silent pride, therefore, in reading the chart some days later and learning that her diagnosis was correct. This was evidence that "In those days nurses were not supposed to make a diagnosis."

She realized that, even though she performed at a very high level as a registered nurse, few people ever really gave any recognition to her or other Negro nurses. Harborview had no Negro head nurses. The only change in Sadie's professional status during these years occurred when she was made charge nurse on evenings. This represented for her a less than subtle form of internal discrimination: "Negro nurses were not promoted. Most Negro nurses worked evenings, nights, or a split shift, and we worked more than our share of weekends and holidays." In spite of these conditions, she knew that life in Seattle was better than what she had experienced in

An Effective Leader and a Spirit Filled Christian Caregiver

Mississippi. Most of all, she appreciated several of the attending physicians at Harborview, who conveyed through their behavior more than through words just how much respect they held for her.

From the time she began work in 1947 through 1966, Sadie remained on the medical geriatrics ward. "There were always at least one or two White nurses who were very kind to me," she recalls. Although they didn't spend a lot of time with her, each conveyed a regard for her in different ways. For example, they sometimes offered Sadie help when they had finished their own work or asked her to join them for a break or a dinner meal.

The Founding of Mary Mahoney Registered Nurses Club

In July, 1949, Celestine Hodge Thomas and Anne Foy Baker asked her to attend a meeting they were organizing to introduce Negro nurses to one another. Agreeing, on July 9, 1949, she became one of the 13 charter members of Mary Mahoney Registered Nurses Club. Thrilled to meet so many fellow nurses, she was elected vice president of the new organization. The group also decided to schedule monthly meetings and to establish a rotation pattern for hosting each meeting. Another decision that especially pleased her was that each meeting began and ended with prayer.

The organization had met only four times when Anne Foy Baker, the president, and her husband, Albert, were involved in an automobile accident. Albert was killed and Anne was critically injured. The members of MMRNC organized themselves and provided private nursing care to Anne throughout the entire period of her recovery. Eventually, Anne's parents came to be with her in Seattle. Although her father was able to remain for a only a short time, her mother remained until Anne could travel with her mother back to her hometown of Greensboro, North Carolina. The effect of this experience on interpersonal and organizational relationships among members of MMRNC was positive, enabling them to develop extremely strong emotional bonds with one another.

Sadie who was now president of MMRNC, a leadership role she thoroughly enjoyed, proposed that the club begin awarding scholarships to students. Her suggestion accepted, all members began helping to raise money for this purpose. In an effort to increase the community's awareness of the existence of MMRNC, she also proposed that candlelight services be scheduled in various churches in the area to introduce this new organization to other members of the community. These services continued for several years after the club was established.

Deeper Involvement in Church Activities

In late 1949, Chester Berrysmith arranged to be assigned a new and shorter run on the railroad, between Seattle and Portland and sometimes to Canada. Even on this shorter route, he often felt tired and overworked, which lead him to seek another line of work. Since photography continued to bring him great joy, he took several pictures of members of MMRNC, including the picture of the 12 of 13 founding nurses that appears after the introduction to this book. (This picture has appeared in local newspapers and exhibits that have traveled throughout the state.) His eventual departure from railroad work, however, began in the mid-1950s, when he began studying to become a Methodist minister. That process made the relationship between him and Sadie even stronger than it had been, as she began seriously studying the Bible. The two of them spent many hours together discussing Biblical concepts and principles. She continued to seek ways to integrate religious principles into her nursing practice, most obviously in her attitude to overtime nursing work. "After learning more about the Bible and God's work, I did not resent my long hours of service that I gave to patients. I realized that I was carrying out the will of God."

While caring for Anne Foy Baker, she realized the marked difference in caring for a patient with whom one could pray versus caring for patients for whom she offered silent prayers. This experience convinced her that, at some time in her life, she would integrate a more overt spirit-filled approach to her nursing care. Yet, she knew that this was not the time to do so; that had to wait until retirement from Harborview. Through volunteer work in the community, she was able to include spirituality as a dimension of her care for family members, friends, and others in the community who asked for her services.

An Effective Leader and a Spirit-Filled Christian Caregiver

Becoming a Mother

On February 27, 1950, Sadie and Chester had their first child; three others followed during the years between 1950 and 1963. The children in order of their births are Guy in 1950, Betty in 1953, Celestine in 1957, and Chester Jr. in 1963. (Celestine, Chester, and Don Berrysmith make their home in the Puget Sound area. Betty lives in the Bay area of San Francisco and Guy lives in Martinez, CA. Fredrohl, her stepson, is deceased.) Following each pregnancy and birth, Sadie took a leave of absence but returned to work. During this period, her nursing skills increasing, she seldom worked overtime hours, and she won the respect and admiration of several nurses, doctors, and patients. In 1966, she requested and was granted a transfer to the surgical recovery-room service.

Becoming a Minister's Wife, Then Losing a Husband

She was delighted when Chester completed his studies for the ministry and was assigned to serve at First AME in Seattle under the tutelage of the senior pastor. After two years, he was assigned to Bailey AME Church in Everett, Washington. During this period they began to tithe. "We voluntarily gave one-tenth of our earnings to the church and I continue to do so today."

Bailey AME Church was a small congregation in a very rundown building. Chester put his heart, mind, and soul into building this congregation, succeeding in bringing in new members and raising enough money to buy land for a new church. He worked with these dedicated members until there was a plan for the new building, but in 1966 he was diagnosed with pancreatic cancer. He lived to see the foundation poured for the new church before his death in 1967.

Continuation of a Nursing Career in an Outpatient Clinic

Sadie continued to work fulltime after her husband's death, with the continuing help of her mother, who, during the early 1950s, had moved to Seattle after separating from Sadie's father. Her mother had managed the children since 1953, when Betty was born; her presence was a great source of strength and help. Work and home life therefore went extremely well, even as a single parent. Many members of Bailey AME Church also served as a source of dependable love and emotional support.

Following Chester's death, Sadie realized that she preferred to give nursing care to patients who were on a medical ward. She enjoyed talking with patients and their families. In the surgical recovery room, by contrast, there was limited communication, as patients received but did not participate actively in their own care. Being a float nurse, therefore, seemed more attractive. Her request to move to the outpatient clinic was granted. She served in this role for two years before being assigned to work in the ophthalmology clinic fulltime with Dr. Milem.

Her new work responsibilities in ophthalmology were quite different, consisting of working only the day shift and assuming more management responsibilities than she had ever had before. She was promoted to nurse coordinator, the equivalent of being a head nurse. Dr. Milem conveyed in words and deeds his deep admiration and respect for her clinical skills and directly helped her increase her administrative competence. Within a relatively short time, they worked together in a very effective and satisfying manner. "He knew I could do just about everything to keep that clinic running smoothly and I did. We were a great team," she says. These were some of the happiest years of her professional life.

Remarriage and Retirement

On the home front things were going well, too. The children were performing well at home, school, and church. Also, Sadie had been introduced to George Wallace; they began dating and, on December 21, 1974, they were married.

Her fulltime work in the outpatient ophthalmology clinic continued until 1977, as she enjoyed a high level of satisfaction at work and at home. Dr. Milem and most of his patients appreciated her high quality of nursing care and she loved having every weekend off. She was pleased as well that her MMRNC colleagues, Celestine Thomas and Mary Davis Hooks, also worked in the outpatient clinic during the time that Sadie worked there. They, too, achieved the status of nurse coordinator in their respective clinics and they enjoyed seeing one another and being together.

An Effective Leader and a Spirit-Filled Christian Caregiver

In 1977 after 30 years of professional practice, Sadie retired. "My last seven years of work were the most enjoyable ones of my professional career. I knew most of the doctors in the outpatient department. The nurses and other staff people demonstrated their respect for me. The patients just really appreciated the care that I gave them. I really looked forward to going to work, but I also wanted to be home."

Sadie entered retirement at a time when she still had a great deal of energy to work. She devoted herself to her church where she participated in Bible study and the women's missionary circle. On her own initiative, Sadie ministered to the sick and provided prayer counseling for anyone who contacted her for spiritual guidance. She became active in the Urban League of Seattle and remained active in MMPNO.

After six golden years of retirement, spent with her new husband and her children with whom she was in close contact, she was diagnosed with cancer of her left breast, necessitating surgery and chemotherapy. During the recuperative process, she wanted to speak in her own voice about matters of importance to her. Most of all she was thrilled that she had just had her first grandchild, Alexis Tiana Berrysmith.

She was pleased that she had come to Seattle to work at Harborview Hospital at the time she did. She knew she brought to this job some of the best skills of any nurse in that hospital. Regardless of skills and abilities, Negro nurses did not have access to opportunities for promotion and advancement that White nurses enjoyed.

Sadie felt that she had lived a life that was pleasing in God's sight. Since early childhood she knew that she had followed the wishes and expectations of her parents. She remained as emotionally close to her sister, Rosie, as they had been in childhood.

"Chester and I enjoyed a love that certainly must have been arranged in heaven." Their children turned out to be successful adults and her grandchild, Alexis, brought her enormous joy. Meeting George was the icing on her cake of life. She had never planned to remarry and remained surprised that she had met and loved two wonderful men in this lifetime.

Sadie's only regret is that she "failed to work hard enough to obtain a baccalaureate degree in nursing." She was happiest about becoming a nurse coordinator in the ophthalmology clinic, with Dr.

Sadie Haynes Berrysmith Wallace in 1994 during her 17th year in retirement.

Milem's help. In 1995 Sadie was totally surprised to learn that the members of Bailey AME had voted to name the fellowship hall in her honor. The thought of this honor brought her true joy each time it crossed her mind.

Asked if she had any thoughts about nursing that she wanted others to know about, Sadie said, "I want to see more men enter nursing and become involved in MMPNO. Also, I want to see our group give more attention to the spiritual aspect of nursing than they usually do." (At a recent MMPNO Executive Board meeting, I recommended that one of several interest groups become the Bible study group. This proposal was voted on and approved).

Sadie's abiding faith in God permeated virtually all areas of her life. It included a spiritual component in her delivery of nursing care. Her family and home life responsibilities were met through her own efforts and with God's help.

In MMPNO she used a low-keyed manner to ensure that a spiritual element was included in organizational activities. She even interpreted her diagnosis of cancer as God's plan for her. "I never asked God, 'Why me?'"

From Selma to Seattle—Racial Signs Down, Segregation Still Around

Katie Stratman Ashford
(1919-1996)

For the first 25 years of her life (1919-1944), Katie Stratman resided in Selma, Alabama, and Atlanta, Georgia, where conditions appeared very similar. Lynchings were reported in newspapers, and signs for Colored and White facilities were on many public buildings, on water fountains and restrooms. Public accommodations were very restricted for Negroes; housing and educational institutions were almost totally segregated by both law and by practice.

In spite of, or perhaps because of, these conditions, Katie developed a very strong sense of self-determination and was highly motivated to assume a professional role. She observed that many Negroes worked in jobs as janitors, garbage collectors and domestics, but she also recognized that schoolteachers served in very visible roles in public school and at church. She wanted to be more like this latter group. Reinforcing this desire was the value of education stressed at her home, school, and church. She absorbed and embraced the idea that development through education would improve the life chances for every Negro in America and was therefore the key to personal and group success.

Born to Become Educated

Born in Selma on January 20, 1919, Katie, the first of two daughters born to Flossie Jackson Stratman and Joseph Stratman, Jr., recalls that both her grandfather (Joseph Stratman, Sr.) and her father were small businessmen, delivering ice, the grandfather full-time and her father working after school and during the summer. Her grandfather's role-modeling had a powerful influence on her as she watched him deliver large blocks of ice to the homes within and outside of their immediate neighborhood and observed how much respect both Negro and White families accorded him. He frequently stressed the value of getting an education to Katie and her sister, Josephine. That value recieved additional emphasis from their parents, whose expectation was that both girls would attend college. Further reinforcement came from public school and Sunday school teachers, from her father's having been valedictorian of his public school class, and from her mother's attending a private school.

As one of the first steps in their educational plan for their children, the family enrolled Katie in the Selma University School (SUS), a private high school and junior college combined, one of the first of its kind for Negro students. Since many families felt that the public school education provided to Negro children during these years was inferior to the education given to Selma's White students, parents of some financial means sent their children to this college-preparatory school. This was their way of trying to correct systemic inequality.

From kindergarten through the 10th grade, Katie attended Clark School. She entered and completed the 11th and 12th grades at SUS in 1938. Her neighbor, Mary Marshall, later to become Mary Marshall Davis Hooks, another nurse profiled in this book, also attended SUS during the years that she was there. They lived across the street from one another and remained close in their personal and professional lives until Katie's death in 1996.

Upon graduating, she learned that it would not be possible for her to pursue a career in music at Fisk University in Nashville, Tennessee, even though she had studied the piano since she was seven years of age. This had been a long-time dream of hers, but her financial resources were not sufficient for her to realize this dream. Instead, she decided to pursue a career in nursing, the next best option. Once in nursing school, she could work in order to reduce some expenses. In 1941, she therefore entered Grady Hospital School of Nursing in Atlanta, Georgia, for a three-year diploma program and immediately found Atlanta to be just as segregated as her hometown. The residences where nurses lived were located in one single block, but White students lived on one side of the street in buildings labeled "White only," with Negroes in "Colored only" buildings across the street. The invisible dividing line was distinct and uncrossable.

The hospital was also segregated by race: Negro students served Negro clients and White students their own group. Only White doctors served the medical needs of both client groups. Administrators of the Nursing School went so far as to have different yet similar uniforms for Negro and White nurses. Negro students wore pink and White students wore blue uniforms, both covered with white bibs and aprons. These students were never encouraged to recognize or have any contact with one another.

Katie became aware of the different working conditions, pay differentials at Grady Hospital for Negro and White nurses, and separate and unequal care given Negro patients. Professional Negro nurses were paid $90.00 per month while their White counterparts with equivalent educational backgrounds received $150.00 per month. Not only were there signs for Colored and White, the physical facilities were markedly different, with rats and roaches visible in the hospital and nurses' residences frequented by Negroes.

The practice of using signs to perpetuate racial segregation was so effective that Katie never remembers hearing anyone tell Negro nurses not to be friendly towards White nurses. Yet, she does not recall a single time when she or any other Negro nurse had anything to say to a White nursing student. According to her, Negro and White students could enter through the same door of a store in their neighborhood, but that was the closest they came to having direct contact with one another.

Instructional offerings were segregated, although White doctors and nurses provided theoretical instruction to both Negro and White students with the same books and the same content. Instruction was given on different days and at different times and places according to race. Negro students received clinical instruction from Negro nurses, most of whom were Grady graduates who worked in the hospital with Negro patients. Katie's best memory of this racial separation is the strong personal interest that their Negro clinical instructors showed in their development; they encouraged them to study and work together in order to successfully complete the nursing program. As a result, she judged the quality of education at Grady to be excellent. She felt well prepared to compete with any nurse in the country when she graduated in June 1944. Her confidence in her knowledge led her to take state-board examinations in August and to leave for Seattle to join her mother before receiving her results. True to her expectations, in October 1944, she learned that she had passed her boards.

During her second year while she was a student at Grady and mindful of her sister's educational aspirations, she suggested that Josephine, who wanted to become a home economics teacher, should enroll at Clark College, a four-year institution, in Atlanta. Following through on this suggestion, Josephine entered Clark in 1943 to pursue a baccalaureate degree in home economics. On parallel tracks in their respective educational endeavors, they resumed the close and supportive bond they had enjoyed in earlier years, returning to Selma in December 1943, for the Christmas holidays and to be with their mother, Flossie.

Katie Stratman in 1944 after graduating from Grady Hospital School of Nursing in Atlanta, Georgia.

Soon thereafter, Flossie divorced Joseph and took a train trip to Los Angeles. While traveling, she met Collie Livingston, a merchant seaman based in Seattle. They maintained a courtship through letters for over a year. He had asked Flossie to marry him shortly after they met, but she delayed her acceptance until after Christmas when she had adequate time to tell Katie and Josephine about the new love in her life. The girls were happy that their mother had found this person to marry. So, in January 1944, Flossie left Selma to marry Mr. Livingston in the Bush Hotel in Seattle.

Thus, even before completing her nursing program, Katie knew that she would soon migrate to Seattle.

A Journey West

Her decision to move West brought some help from the newlyweds, who had moved into a temporary housing project at 13th and Yesler. Flossie worked in the Bremerton shipyard and Collie continued to work as a merchant seaman. They talked with a Seattle Urban League representative who went door-to-door asking residents in the project if they had relatives in the South with college degrees. He encouraged them to write and invite relatives and friends to come to work in the Pacific Northwest. This invitation was passed on to Katie by Flossie and Collie.

Katie also recalled hearing President Franklin D. Roosevelt's radio talk encouraging citizens to go work for the war effort in the Pacific Northwest. The combination of the appeal from the President and her mother's invitation was an irresistible magnet for Katie to make Seattle her new home.

While studying for state board examinations, she had read in *The American Journal of Nursing* that, in Seattle, staff nurses were paid $250.00 per month for hospital nursing. This seemed like a lot of money to her at that time, but after arriving in Seattle, she soon recognized that the cost of living was much greater than in Alabama. She also was not worried about getting a job in a hospital in Seattle but was not aware that the first Negro nurse to be hired at Harborview Hospital was Ira Gordon in 1943, less than one year before Katie came to Seattle in September, 1944.

Just months before leaving for Seattle, Katie's father died; so, she returned to Selma for a short time. His death had a great impact on her plans to pursue an undergraduate degree in nursing. She canceled her educational plans and decided that upon reaching Seattle, she would immediately begin working so her sister Josephine could remain at Clark College in Atlanta where she was a sophomore at the time of their father's death.

The long and tiresome train ride to Seattle from Selma gave Katie plenty of time to think about the activities that she would pursue in her new home. Family, church affiliation, and participation in community activities had occupied much of her family's life during their formative years. As student nurses, there was little or no time for anything other than studying and providing direct services to patients. They often worked evenings and nights during their last year in the program, so they really needed to build in time for social activities since there was really very little opportunity for socializing.

Upon arriving at the Seattle train station, Katie was surprised and delighted to observe the absence of signs for Colored on doors, drinking fountains, or restrooms. This made her feel that she had left segregation in Selma and that life in Seattle would be free of such insults.

Almost Immediate Professional Employment

After being in Seattle for only three days, Katie was hired at Harborview Hospital and assigned to the communicable disease ward where she remained for two years. She provided nursing care to Negro and White patients. It was the first time in her brief nursing career that she worked with White patients and she soon learned that she was the fourth Negro nurse to be hired at Harborview Hospital. Others were Ira Gordon, Shelly Burris, and Mary Martyn. However, these nurses and Katie did not meet face-to-face for some time because they worked rotating shifts. She was assigned whatever shifts were left after all of the White nurses were scheduled.

After working at Harborview for several months, Katie concluded that, although racial signs were not posted anywhere, some practices followed in the hospital were very similar to ones that existed at Grady. Negroes occupied most of the jobs as orderlies, aides, maids, and janitors, and her treatment was highly influenced by who served in the role of head nurse, some of whom were very fair and extremely friendly while others were the opposite. At first, she was afraid to speak out about conditions on the ward. Later, when she transferred to another floor that was staffed by several Asian and Jewish nurses, they joined together and requested conferences with the head nurse to discuss their concerns, including working for over five weeks without a Sunday off. She knew that she was the only nurse on that ward to do so. Also, she knew that she worked more evening and night shifts than other nurses.

In 1946, Katie requested and was granted a transfer from the communicable disease ward to pediatrics, where children were assigned according to their disease category. Their room assignments, however, did not discriminate by race, and Negro and White children were allowed to play freely and have contact with one another. This represented a throwback to earlier times, when, even in many parts of the South, young children were allowed to play with different racial/ethnic groups until they reached adolescence. This observation once again reminded Katie that signs were down, but many racial patterns still existed. Katie enjoyed her work on pediatrics, but after several years was ready for a change. Her next assignment was obstetrics and gynecology, where she worked in labor and delivery, a service she had not worked for years. However, she knew that whatever was forgotten would return to her within a relatively short period of time.

Marriage and Motherhood

In 1946, Katie met a sailor, Charles Radliff, whom she married soon afterward. One child, Gloria, was born during their three-year marriage. In 1948, Katie divorced, and she and her sister, Josephine, a widow, were together again. Having purchased their first home, a duplex in Hiawatha Place, they invited their mother to move in with them to make it possible for the sisters to continue their professional careers by her caring for Katie's daughter and Josephine's son. (Incidentally, their land is now part of a park named for Josephine's late husband, Judge Charles M. Stokes, Seattle's first African American State legislator.)

In Seattle during the late 1940s and early 1950s, the church, Phillis Wheatley YWCA, sororities, fraternities, and private social clubs were the principal ways in which people got to know one another. Katie joined the Vogue Social Club, a group that held house parties and dances at other clubs in the Central Area of Seattle. At one of these dances she met King Ashford, whom she dated and in 1953 married. They had their own house on 23rd Avenue South (Seattle), which was a sign of real progress for King and Katie. King worked in a brickyard and later for the Seattle City Light Company, and Katie was a staff nurse in labor and delivery at Harborview.

Professional Ups and Downs

Katie was eventually promoted to head nurse in the labor and delivery unit, although this advancement was short-lived. A White nurse, who was working on her AA degree and was enrolled at a junior college, was soon appointed head nurse to replace her. She was never told why this White nurse was appointed to the head-nurse position, nor did she ever ask questions about this demotion. During an interview in 1993, as she talked about this incident, tears welled in her eyes; she remembered it as one of the most insulting and demeaning developments of her career.

One of the happiest moments of her professional life was the time when two physicians came to Seattle from Grady Hospital to study Harborview's methods and practices for pre- and post-natal education for mothers and fathers. These two doctors recognized her cap and class pin as those worn by graduates of their hospital. Katie served as their consultant along with another nurse. These doctors were very impressed with the excellent content provided by Katie. They passed on their evaluation of Katie's performance to the head nurse and supervisor. Katie considered this action to be the highest and most significant development in her professional career. The head nurse chose her for this responsibility, and she knew she had performed extremely well.

Katie was a charter member of the Mary Mahoney Registered Nurses Club, which was established on July 9, 1949. The 13 charter members were encouraged by Anne Foy Baker to consider organizing a Negro nurses' organization. During these years, many Negro registered nurses thought they could not join the American Nurses Association. Those who did attend local meetings of their state nurses' association were required to sit at the back of the area behind White nurses. In 1948, the ANA officially included Negro nurses in its membership.

Katie was active in MMRNC for nearly a decade (1949-1959), after which she took almost a 30-year recess from participation. Katie is the only charter member in MMRNC to acknowledge that tensions began to be evident between the diploma nurses and college-prepared nurses with degrees. Whether real or imagined, Katie felt personally that the degree nurses were not as friendly to diploma nurses as they were to nurses with degrees. She was also disappointed to observe that new students who received scholarships and financial aid from MMPNO did not come back following graduation to join the organization. Even when Katie returned to the organization in the late 1980s, it was hard for her to accept the fact that new graduate nurses were not joining MMPNO.

Katie's relationship and participation in MMPNO were reestablished during 1989 following a very brief exchange that we had while attending a social function at a local store in downtown Seattle. She must have been ready to return because she did so immediately after we talked. She remained an active member of MMPNO until the time of her death in 1996.

Katie remained at Harborview Hospital for 24 years—from 1944-1968. During her tenure, she realized that she was denied opportunities to advance to head nurse. In terms of leadership and clinical competence, Katie knew she possessed both. Further, she regularly compared her performance with that of White nurses and concluded that she compared favorably with her White counterparts; however, there was very little interest in having Negro nurses serve in leadership roles during this period. Except for that very brief time when she served in that role, she was never approached again for a promotion.

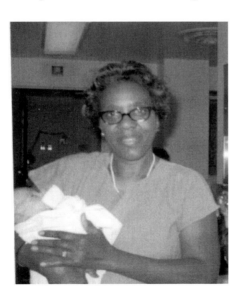

Katie Stratman Ashford in the labor and delivery unit at Group Health Cooperative (GHC) in 1975.

In 1968, at age 49, she learned that Group Health Cooperative (GHC) was hiring nurses for their new obstetrics and gynecology unit. Katie decided to go there to find out for herself if GHC would hire her. The interviewing nurse offered to hire Katie on the spot. Katie told her she needed to give Harborview a two-week notice before resigning. She followed through as planned and in 1968 she began working at GHC in labor and delivery.

Katie felt that GHC was the most satisfying caregiving setting in which she had ever worked. There were obvious differences in the patients who were attracted to GHC. The orientation to service delivery was positive and educational for patients and staff. Consumers set policies and gave attention to the needs of nurses and patients. For the first time in her long professional career, she was assigned permanently to the day shift of 7:00 a.m.-3:00 p.m. She felt the head nurse was fair and supportive of her being there. Her treatment was comparable to that of all other nurses on the unit, but even in this environment she was not promoted to a leadership role in spite of her 24 years of experience.

Participation in continuing nursing education courses is required for any nurse who desires to serve as a licensed professional. During Katie's tenure at Harborview, nurses paid for the continuing education courses. At GHC, this cost was absorbed by the agency. Katie was always interested in learning; so, throughout her professional career she participated in continuing education courses. Learning was a lifelong endeavor for her. Reading articles regularly in nursing journals and in *The New England Journal of Medicine* she felt proud of her knowledge base about developments in medicine. She liked having information and being able to use it for the benefit of her patients and herself.

Fulfillment of a Dream

While she was at GHC, her daughter, Gloria, completed high school and elected to attend Fisk University in Nashville, Tennessee. This development delighted Katie. As a young graduate from Selma University, she had wanted to attend Fisk. This had not been a possibility for her at that time, but now she was able to make this opportunity available to her only daughter. For Katie, this represented the fulfillment of a dream. Gloria completed her studies at Fisk and returned to the Pacific Northwest where she entered graduate school at the University of Washington and received a Master's Degree in Library and Information Science. Gloria's educational accomplishments provided a profound sense of joy and delight for her mother.

At an earlier time in her life, Katie provided some financial assistance to her sister, Josephine, which made it possible for her to complete her undergraduate studies at Clark College in Atlanta. Katie acknowledged that her sister encouraged her to consider pursuing a degree in nursing rather than settling for her diploma, but Katie never felt the time was right to return to school. However, she enjoyed knowing that she helped make it possible for her sister and daughter to obtain college degrees and for both of them to become members of Delta Sigma Theta Sorority. Both Josephine and Gloria became librarians and Katie, vicariously, experienced these accomplishments.

Retirement and Satisfaction

In 1981, after having a 37-year career in nursing, Katie retired from GHC where she spent 13 years in obstetrics and gynecology working in labor and delivery. Katie stated, "I treated each of my patients as if they were members of my family. I received plenty of cards, candy, and flowers as a result of the care that I gave to patients. Doctors and nurses regularly complimented me on the quality of care that I gave." Katie felt the atmosphere at GHC was conducive to promoting professional satisfaction even when professional advancements were denied. The patients made the difference. They felt a level of ownership in this hospital and they wanted it to be the best in the City of Seattle for patients and for nurses and doctors.

Katie Stratman Ashford in 1990. She retired in 1981 after having a 37-year career in nursing.

Katie's husband, King, had retired from Seattle City Light many years before Katie retired. They enjoyed 43 years of married life. Fifteen of those years they spent together in retirement before Katie died on July 2, 1996.

In December of 1993, I interviewed Katie in her new condominium in Seward Park. She was delighted that she and King had moved to this area from their home on 23rd South. I asked her at that time, when she appeared to be so happy with her life, how she would like to be remembered by others. She stated: "I'd like to be remembered as a kind, loving and compassionate person who believed in God. Someone who came up from 'respectable poverty' and tried to make the best of life." Katie knew she had helped to improve the quality of life for her daughter and sister. She also knew that over her entire nursing career she gave the highest quality of service to every client whom she served.

Despite the slights and denials of opportunity, Katie harbored no signs of bitterness. She served others as a confident and caring professional. This seems to be a tribute to the historic generosity and compassion that is part of our African American heritage. Katie Stratman Ashford truly lived as she believed. May she rest in peace.

A Daughter of Pioneers and a Determined Nurse

Maxine Pitter Davis Haynes

Maxine Haynes is the daughter of parents whose ancestors began migrating to the Pacific Northwest in the late nineteenth century. Her mother, Marjorie Allen, told her that two of Marjorie's aunts and uncles began leaving their home state of Pennsylvania, for California in 1889. Approximately two years later they arrived, instead, in Seattle, although her mother remained in Pennsylvania with her parents until her mother died. Following her mother's death, Marjorie moved to Seattle to live with her aunt and uncle where she attended and graduated from Broadway High School.

Born into a Strong Religious and Educational Family

Maxine Pitter at 5 years of age in 1924 sitting on her family's Model A Ford.

Her father, Edward A. Pitter, was born in Jamaica, British West Indies. In 1909 he migrated to the United States, arriving in Seattle in 1914. In 1915, Maxine's parents met and later married, both remaining in Seattle until their deaths. Three girls were born to them, Constance, Maxine, and Marjorie. Maxine, the middle child, was born on February 6, 1919, at Seattle General Hospital. From early childhood until the present time, the Pitter family has been recognized as an important pioneering family in Seattle. Maxine and her sisters have been interviewed for articles, reports, and surveys on African Americans in Seattle's early history and in 1980 they were the subject of a dissertation. The youngest sister, Marjorie, named for her mother, died in 1996. Maxine and Constance are considered to be living resources on Negro history in the Seattle area.

Her father was co-author of the book *Who's Who In Religious, Fraternal, Social, Civic and Commercial Life on the Pacific Coast* (Searchlight Publishing Company, Seattle, 1926-27). He gave significant leadership in data collection and development of the manuscript for publication while at the same time working full-time at his regular job as a deputy sheriff. Later in his career he was appointed Deputy County Clerk of King County. Throughout his life, he continued to record information about the life and times of Negroes in the Puget Sound region.

A full time homemaker, housewife, and creative writer, her mother was also active in the Parent Teachers Association while her children were in public school and worked in their church and in several volunteer associations in the community. She was respected and admired for her activism in the community at a time when Negro women were not encouraged or expected to be involved in civic life. Marjorie Allen is best known for the play she wrote and produced, *The Awakening*, which requires a cast of 250. It was first produced at the Seattle's Civic Auditorium (which became the Opera House in 1962 during the World's Fair in Seattle).

During Maxine's childhood and teenage years, there were few Colored families in Seattle and few opportunities for children to work outside of their own homes. She and her sisters helped to maintain the house and yard and were given an allowance for that work. The sisters were also encouraged to help other families in their church and in the community, for example, in writing letters, filling out applications, or understanding written communications they had

A Daughter of Pioneers and a Determined Nurse

received. They were encouraged to carry out these activities without receiving pay.

While Maxine was growing up, there were four churches in the community that most Negroes attended, First AME, Mt. Zion Baptist, AME Zion, and a Presbyterian church. A very few Negroes from the Islands attended the Episcopal Church which was integrated. It was quite common back then for people to visit among the different churches depending upon what specific activity was occurring. Some churches celebrated women's and men's days on different Sundays of the month. Most members worshipped at their own church on standard holidays like Christmas, Easter, and New Year's. Within the community, religious worship was a social and spiritual occasion.

Religion and academic work were the areas of life most emphasized in Maxine's home. With roots firmly anchored in the First AME Church (between Pike and Pine on 14th Street in Seattle and where her grandfather, Isaiah Allen, was one of three founders), her approach to academics was influenced by her father's suggestion that, in using the newly purchased *World Book Encyclopedia*, she should read the subject before and the one after the subject she was looking up. In this way she always learned more than just the needed information. Home study was a regular part of her education. She established this pattern in grade school and continued doing so until she finished college. Her parents' theme was "You defeat yourself when you fail to get an education."

In 1924, Maxine met Mrs. Theresa Dixon, who was hired by her parents to provide nursing care to her maternal grandfather, Isaiah Allen, until 1925, when he died. This was the first Negro registered nurse she had ever seen. In those days, Colored nurses could not find employment in hospitals in Seattle, so private duty nursing was the primary form of work available. This nurse, whose image is still vivid in Maxine's memory, especially the white uniform and blue cape, spoke softly to Maxine when they first met. It was the combination of Mrs. Dixon's appearance and her manner of behaving and speaking that reinforced Maxine's interest in becoming a registered nurse.

African American Registered Nurses in Seattle

Experiences with Racial Taunting

Social activities in the community were centered at the Phillis Wheatley Young Women's Christian Association and the Sojourner Truth Home. Both were residential and community centers, with a range of activities such as teas, receptions, weddings, and formal dances. The Girl Reserves, a social group for girls and young women, sororities, and other civic organizations held their meetings at these locations. In the early 1930s and 1940s there were no hotels in Seattle where Colored women could stay. The YWCA and the Sojourner Truth Home were residential locations where Colored people could find lodging and a safe environment where they were welcome.

From the early 1920s through the 1960s the social life of most Colored families was separate and distinct from their neighbors', even though they lived in the same neighborhood, sometimes side-by-side. Maxine's family lived near Jewish, Asian American, Filipino, and White families; yet, their religious and community activities were totally different. Neighbors were always polite and friendly towards one another, but for the most part they had superficial exchanges.

When the Pitter children entered public school, they attended Longfellow Elementary, which is now Meany Middle School. Later Maxine and Marjorie attended T.T.Minor and still later they entered and graduated from Garfield High School. It was at school that Maxine became aware of the relevance of color and racial/ethnic affiliation to her personal life. Her older and younger sisters were fair-skinned like their mother, while Maxine was dark-skinned like her father. In their home this difference was of no importance, but in school, for Maxine, it was a big factor. She experienced teasing and being taunted by school children. "I told my parents about the way some children treated me, and I was always encouraged to ignore their behavior. I was regularly told not to fight. My sisters did not experience these incidents and I think it was because they were fair-skinned."

One day a little boy called her *"coon"* and *"nigger"* several times. Finally, she had had enough. She hit the boy and was sent to the office, where the principal scolded her for unladylike behavior. The boy was never sent to the office for his part in this incident.

In another incident, for reasons unknown to her, a girl hit her. Maxine defended herself, returning what she got from this girl. The next day the girl brought her mother to school and her mother hit Maxine, whereupon her parents called the police and reported the incident. Eventually, these families ended up in court, the judge ruling in Maxine's favor but imposing no penalty.

During elementary school she learned about segregation. When she saw White girls in their Girl Scout uniforms, she decided that she wanted to be a Girl Scout. Her mother inquired about membership and was told, "We don't admit Colored girls." When her mother called the Campfire Girls' office, she received the same answer. In recalling these incidents, she emphasizes the deep sense of discrimination and marginalization that existed among racial groups in Seattle at that time. "The White girls had their meetings at our school. We looked at them having fun while we were prevented from joining in with them."

Once it became clear that she would not be allowed to become a scout or a Campfire Girl, she joined the YWCA's Girl Reserves, an organization that stressed principles of self-respect, kindness, honesty, and duty to family and community. In this organization she met many Negro girls from different parts of Seattle, two of whom became her lifelong friends, Mildred (Millie) McIver and Elizabeth Dean. Since these three girls wanted to pursue careers in nursing, they formed a bond that kept them in touch with one another throughout their school years.

When Maxine entered Garfield High School, the overt hostility towards her occurred less frequently. She directed her efforts towards academic course work by taking demanding college-track subjects. "Our parents always talked about when we went to college, not whether we'd go or not. Also, I enjoyed learning new information."

Throughout elementary and high school, all of Maxine's teachers were White, and for the most part, they were very nice to her. "I felt that I received the grades that I deserved in all except about three courses. These three teachers' behavior towards me was very biased. I recognized it and so did they. There was little reason to complain because back then teachers had the very last word and most Negro parents did not challenge them," she says. Indeed, she continues, "When I think back on these early days of my life, I now realize that there was significant segregation going on, but we just did not challenge this system until the mid-1960s."

African American Registered Nurses in Seattle

Entry into the University of Washington

In June 1936, Maxine graduated from Garfield High School and that September entered the University of Washington. Having known long before entering college that she wanted to become a registered nurse, she followed her parents' encouragement to take courses that would help her accomplish her dream. They never tried to influence her choice of a career but just "wanted me to get an education." After entering the U.W., she continued to live at home where Mrs. Dixon consistently encouraged her "to study hard and soon you will be going to nursing school."

During the mid-1930s when she attended the University, she estimates that there were fewer than 20 or 25 Negro students on campus. "We all knew each other and we saw one another at the YWCA and the Sojourner Truth Home. I had joined Delta Sigma Theta Sorority, which held its meetings at the YWCA. Even as students Negroes were alienated from other members of the University community. Almost none of our sorority or fraternity functions were on campus. We were not included in other student activities. Often professors treated us in a neutral or negative manner."

Rejection First But Eventual Acceptance Into Nursing Training

Millie McIver and Elizabeth Dean, who had applied for admission to the School of Nursing about 18 months earlier than Maxine, were told by Dean Elizabeth Soule, "We are not taking Colored girls; we can't put a Colored girl and a White girl in the same room." When Millie told Maxine about their experience, she still felt that there was a chance that she would be admitted when she applied. Nevertheless, two years later, in 1939, when Maxine sought admission to the U.W. School of Nursing, Dean Soule gave her the same answer she had given Millie and Elizabeth: "We are not taking Colored girls."

After this rejection, she took some time to reflect on what life had been like for her at the University up until this incident occurred. She had worked hard to perform well in her classes. Some of the instructors had assigned fair grades; some had not. She had dropped out of a swimming class because "no one seemed to like having Colored girls swimming in the same pool with White students. Even

A Daughter of Pioneers and a Determined Nurse

the instructor ignored us." But in other courses, student interaction was better. "I was very proud of my performance in a physiology and anatomy class. I worked with several students to dissect a human body. We worked well together and I learned a lot. In an anthropology class we took field trips together and those were excellent learning experiences."

During her four years on campus she worked at various jobs, such as typing for a German Professor in Suzzallo Library and for Professor O'Brian, who hired Colored students to research Negro representation in mainstream magazines like *Life, Look,* and *Time.* On weekends Maxine cleaned the homes of several faculty members. Even after being denied admission to the School of Nursing, she continued to save her money for use in becoming a registered nurse.

There were enough positive experiences to keep her interested in remaining in school. "I also decided that I really wanted to be a nurse. In fact, I was determined to become one. Dean Soule's words of rejection motivated me to act." Maxine wrote to the American Nurses Association to request information about schools where Negro women could pursue careers in nursing. ANA sent a list of schools where she could possibly be admitted, among them Lincoln School for Nurses in the Bronx, NY. Since her mother had a brother who lived in New York, she decided to apply. Meanwhile, she completed a major in sociology and received a degree in 1941. Professor O'Brian of the Sociology Department had encouraged her to complete this degree while she worked to earn money to pay out-of-state tuition and other costs. While attending graduation exercises, Maxine realized that she had not reached her professional goal.

Maxine's Uncle Samuel Allen and his wife, her mother's brother and sister-in-law, lived on Long Island, NY. Her uncle worked for the National Labor Relations Board and could be of great psychological, social, and economic support if she were accepted at Lincoln. Within weeks of the time she sent in her application, she had been accepted into Lincoln School of Nursing and in the fall of 1941 left Seattle for New York.

The long train trip from Seattle to New York was an education in itself, the first time she had ever traveled alone. Her parents had given strict instructions about how to manage her money, cautioning her about interactions with strangers and the need to listen to announcements over the loudspeaker. She believed that she would manage very well and she did. However, no one prepared her for the sight she saw in the Chicago train station—more Negroes than she had ever seen before. She replayed that scene in her mind until she reached New York. Late in the evening, Maxine reached Lincoln School and was greeted by the housemother and two upper-class students. Tired from the long trip, she went to bed early, especially appreciating her private dormitory room, a privilege accorded every student. "We were told that we were expected to follow a study schedule that best fits one's personal needs." Before falling off to sleep, she thought she had seen more different people and sights than she had ever seen before in her life.

The school offered a three-year diploma program for Negro students only. Although the dean and three other faculty members were White, the other instructors were Negro. She thought that all of the instructors treated the students well. Maxine was the only student in her class who entered with a degree in sociology, but because she had completed so much college course work, she was given work opportunities not available to other students.

After completing basic nursing courses, she was assigned to clinical work at the Henry Street Visiting Nurse Service. There, she had a regular caseload similar to a social worker's, with a focus on providing health care to individuals and families. For this work she was paid a stipend of $20. "In hindsight and even while I was having this learning experience, I think Henry Street stands out as the most positive and growth-promoting nursing experience I ever had. I was treated as a professional by the other staff at the clinics." Her time of study in the nursing program passed very fast, and, in 1944, she received a diploma in nursing.

From the time she left home in 1941 until 1943, she did not return to Seattle. World War II had started in December 1941, restricting travel; furthermore, she had very limited funds for travel. These obstacles were sufficient to make being away from home acceptable to her, although by 1943 she had saved enough money to visit with her family in Seattle. In a rather short visit, she spent most of her time visiting with family members, church and sorority friends, and old neighbors. She saw many servicemen because the war was still on, including Negro soldiers who were represented in all branches of military service. Seeing large numbers of soldiers wherever she

A Daughter of Pioneers and a Determined Nurse

went, she later observed, "This was one of the most dramatic changes that I recognized on my return visit home."

Nursing Certification and Full-time Employment

Following graduation in 1944, Maxine took and passed state board examinations with flying colors. After learning that she had passed, she requested and was allowed to join the American Nurses Association, remaining a member throughout the time she was employed. (In the 1940s, New York State Nurses Association did accept Colored nurses as members.)

Maxine in 1944 following graduation from Lincoln School of Nursing in New York.

By the time she had graduated, her sister, Constance, had moved to New York to live. While they lived together, Maxine applied for and received a job at Bellevue Psychiatric Hospital, assigned to the violent-women's ward. Bellevue was a large hospital with several thousand patients. At that time, psychotropic medications (tranquilizers) were not used as the principal method of treatment; individual psychotherapy was done mostly by psychiatrists. Patients remained in the hospital for long periods of time, typically treated with electric shock therapy, hydrotherapy, and insulin therapy. For the most part, nurses gave medications, interacted and played games with some patients, and managed the ward.

This psychiatric experience stands out in her mind because it was her first interracial professional experience with Negro and White members of the nursing staff, mostly White physicians and Negro and White patients assigned to room together. The overall atmosphere of the ward did not emphasize racial differences; therefore, she had excellent opportunities to use her medical/surgical nursing knowledge. For patients who needed treatment for chronic diseases of high blood pressure, diabetes, upper respiratory illnesses, and wounds of the feet and hands, she was given the opportunity to carry out treatments and pass medication to over 30 patients each day. After working there for six months, Maxine had demonstrated to herself and to others who wanted to know that she had excellent nursing knowledge and skills. Having been in New York for nearly five years, she was more than ready to return to the Pacific Northwest.

Return to Seattle and Challenging Work

In 1945 she returned to Seattle and on the very Sunday she arrived, she met Edward Cornelius Davis, Jr., her future husband. He had come to the Pitter family's home from church with his mother, who was a good friend of the Pitter family and who played the organ at AME Zion Church. (It was customary then for people to stop in and visit with friends for varying lengths of time after church.)

After being in Seattle for only a few days, she decided to begin looking for employment, well aware that most Negro nurses worked at Harborview Hospital. She decided, however, to see if she could gain employment in a different hospital. Since Providence Hospital was within walking distance of her home, she started there. Catholic nuns were in charge of Providence. Her interview with the Mother Superior was long and quite detailed, more like an interrogation in which she was asked, "Why do you want to work at this hospital? Have you ever worked with White patients, nurses, and White families? How do you think your degree in sociology has prepared you to function in nursing?" When she had answered these questions, the Mother Superior said, "I will contact you later." In those days the phrase *contact you later* was interpreted by most Negroes to mean they would probably not be hired.

While walking back home, she observed more Negroes here than she recalled having seen before. She then realized that many of these people had migrated to Seattle to work in defense plants, the shipyard in Bremerton, and other places where defense work was available. The areas where she walked looked very different to her, bringing the realization that racial segregation was more apparent than it had previously been.

After reaching her home, she described how her interview with the Mother Superior had gone, contrasting the questions asked by the Mother Superior with those asked by the Director of Nursing at

A Daughter of Pioneers and a Determined Nurse

Bellevue Psychiatric Hospital. The latter had looked at her application and stated, "I see you have a degree in sociology and that you have also worked at the Henry Street Nursing Clinic. Did you work with many psychiatric patients in these places?" She had also asked whether or not Maxine knew if other classmates of hers were looking for employment or were already working there. Explaining that there were openings on the women's violent ward for evenings and nights, she told her the salary and asked when she wanted to start working. The next day Maxine started working at Bellevue.

The day following her Providence interview, a call informed her that she could have a job on the obstetrics floor. Could she start on the following Monday? After an affirmative answer, she was instructed to report to work at 7:00 a.m. It was difficult to believe her good fortune, so thrilled was she about getting the job. It didn't occur to her that she was about to begin the most challenging work experience of her entire career.

She reported to work dressed in her starched uniform and cap, having taken time to be sure that she was spotlessly clean. She felt so proud to be walking down the street in her nurse's cape that the distance between her home and the hospital seemed to be shorter than before. Having arrived 20 minutes before the day shift reported and going to the Obstetrics ward, she met a nun, who instructed her to go to the screened porch and remain there until other nurses arrived. Eventually, she was asked to join the other nurses for the morning report and was told where to put her cape and purse. She never received an orientation to the service or to the hospital.

Throughout the workday, she watched what other nurses did. After being told who her patients were in report, no one spoke to her, but she managed all her patients and completed her assignment on time. At 3:30 p.m. she left for home. Each day for the next few months was very similar to the first. None of the other nurses spoke to her; indeed, she was invisible to them. The most notable exception was the behavior of her supervisor, Mrs. Edith Heinemann, who, in the presence of other nurses, complimented her on her caregiving and charting. Even though other nurses heard what Edith said, no one else commented until more than three months later. One by one, other nurses on the floor began to speak to her, and, before the end of her fourth month, all of the nurses on her shift were speaking to her. Later, she learned that the nurses were so unhappy about her being hired that they decided they would not speak to her. While these nurses were ignoring her, she was having excellent success with her patients and their families. "I never had one patient at Providence refuse to receive care from me," she reports.

Away from work, her social and community activities were very satisfying for her. She and Edward Cornelius Davis, Jr. started dating soon after meeting, and, in June of 1946, they were married. Before their marriage, the nurses at Providence gave her a bridal shower and some who were off on the day of the wedding also attended the ceremony. When she became pregnant with their son (Edward Davis III, born June 3, 1948), these same nurses gave her a baby shower.

Joining Mary Mahoney Nurses Club

In 1949 Anne Foy Baker called to ask if she would be interested in joining other nurses who planned to come to her home for a meeting. Accepting, Maxine attended the July meeting of Mary Mahoney Registered Nurses Club. "Remember that, even though I was born here, I had gone away to school. I did not know any of the other nurses except Juanita Davis, a very good friend of my sister, Marjorie. Juanita was denied admission to the University of Washington School of Nursing and went to Homer G. Phillips in St. Louis to obtain her nursing education. Her family was also one of the pioneering families in this area. At that meeting we saw each other for the first time in many years. All of the other nurses were individuals whom I met for the first time that day. Mary Mahoney Registered Nurses Club served a real need. It brought us together in a group. At first, we really focused on socialization and professional problems that we all faced. Our children got to know one another and we had a very good time together. We no longer emphasize this aspect of MMRNC." She remained an active member of MMRNC until she moved to California.

A Move to California, New Jobs, and More Education

Before that move, she was promoted to head nurse on obstetrics and also served as an instructor for the American Red Cross from 1950-51. In 1953 she resigned from both positions to relocate to California because her husband, a professional percussionist and vocalist, wanted

A Daughter of Pioneers and a Determined Nurse

to move to Los Angeles where he thought there would be more opportunities for him to perform than in Seattle. They felt certain that she could find employment there, too; so, with considerable anticipation, they relocated to California. Shortly after their arrival, she did find employment at LA County General Hospital where she was hired as a staff nurse on the obstetrics ward. Within 18 months, she was accepted at UCLA, where she completed her baccalaureate degree in nursing and certification in public health nursing. In 1954 she became a staff nurse for the Los Angeles Visiting Nurses' Association, continued her education at UCLA, and, in 1959, received a M.S. degree in Public Health Nursing.

Next, she was appointed supervisor of staff nurses at the Los Angeles Visiting Nurses' Association and, in 1959, became Education Director. Then, in 1960, she was appointed Assistant Professor of Community Health Nursing at Mount St. Mary's College in Los Angeles. In 1967, at a time when her husband was experiencing increasing success in his musical career, he died suddenly of a basilar artery thrombosis and brain-stem infarction. Within three months' time her mother also died. Prior to the deaths of her husband and mother, she had applied to enter the doctoral program at UCLA in Public Health but was never able to begin this program of study.

Another Return to Seattle, Remarriage, and Prestigious Appointments

In 1969, having returned to Seattle, Maxine married Lionel B. Haynes, whom she had met in church in 1935. He was in the dry cleaning and tailoring business and owner of East Madison Valet Cleaners. Also, shortly after her return, she was employed in the Model Cities Program as a health educator, working at Odessa Brown Clinic. After less than one year, she was asked to join the faculty at the University of Washington in the Division of Continuing Education, School of Nursing. For five years, she worked in this role as an assistant professor, teaching community health nursing and serving as a counselor at the School of Nursing. Fortunately for her, many of the instructors and administrators who were at U.W. when she was denied admission to the School of Nursing had retired. Even though there were still vestiges of racism evident in the school, current staff appeared to have a real desire to establish and maintain a multi-ethnic and racially diverse student body and staff.

In 1976 Maxine joined the faculty at Seattle Pacific University as Associate Professor of Community Health Nursing. Here, she enjoyed a high level of professional and personal happiness until 1981, when her second husband died. She continued full-time employment as she worked through this loss, remaining at SPU until 1986, when she retired. She is most proud of the fact that she designed and implemented a program in Trans-Cultural Nursing, one that enabled undergraduate students to travel to Costa Rica during the summer to live and work with families in their communities. These students broadened their understanding of community practice and their awareness of unique health practices of a specific cultural group.

In reflecting upon her professional career, Maxine believes that her family prepared her very well for the challenges she faced throughout her professional life. She courageously overcame roadblocks and barriers placed in her path as she sought to become a nurse, showing steady progression from rejection to strong personal and professional achievements. The stress at home on religious education and academic success gave her a foundation of strength in both her personal and professional life. Also, Mrs. Theresa Dixon, the nurse who cared for her grandfather, remains a significant image in her memory.

She is especially pleased that she ventured to Providence Hospital to seek employment rather than go to Harborview where other Negro nurses had already pushed back the color barrier for nurses to gain employment. By persevering at Providence, she tested her faith in herself and her faith in God and found strength to continue to work in a place where initially only one nurse treated her with respect and promoted her sense of self-esteem and self-confidence. She is still proud that she endured the isolation and lack of support from other RNs without ever reporting their behavior towards her to anyone. "Eventually, these White nurses came to see that I had the knowledge and skills to meet whatever treatment they directed at me. I met their challenges and ultimately won their respect and later their friendship," she said recently.

Mary Mahoney Registered Nurses Club served as an important resource. As a founding member, she recalls, "In the early life of this organization, members stressed social and professional development. All of the nurses and their children knew one another very well, celebrating birthdays and other holidays together. In addition, we shared the challenges, failures, and successes in our work environments." She continues to be an active member in Mary Mahoney, saying, "I intend to continue to be involved in this organization. We are needed as much today as we were 50 years ago, when the organization was first established. Currently, many nursing schools throughout the county are trying to recruit African American and other ethnic/racial students of color into their programs. Many are having difficulty finding interested and well-prepared students. Our organization must take a more active role in this recruitment effort. I really want to be involved in this recruitment activity."

Maxine Pitter Haynes in 1984. She retired in 1986.

Her biggest regret is that she never went on to complete her doctoral studies in public health. However, she is very happy that she did what she could wherever she lived or worked to give the best care that she could provide to patients and their families. These efforts won her the 1981 outstanding service award from the Organization of Continuing Education American Nurses (OCEAN) and in 1988 the King County Nurses Association (KCNA) Presidential Award.

In summarizing her present life, she says, "I have many family responsibilities that I still have to carry out on behalf of my sisters. Even in retirement I remain very busy. As a matter of fact, I never have enough time in a given day to get everything on my 'to do' list done. When I look at myself and at many of my friends, I realize that I am very fortunate to enjoy good health, independent living, and the support of many friends and relatives. In the late 1930s, when I worked against all odds to become a nurse, I really thought that it would always be possible for me to get a job. Also, it occurred to me that I could integrate religious principles in ways to really serve God and my fellow persons and to satisfy myself too. In spite of it all, I've had a good life and a very satisfying career."

Nursing: The Journey from Pediatric Patient Through a Professional Career

Mary Scott Marshal Davis Hooks

In 1925, at age six, Mary was first exposed to professional nurses and nursing care. As a patient in Good Samaritan Hospital recovering from tonsillectomy surgery, minor complications made it necessary for her to remain in the hospital a few days longer than patients usually stayed. Since her mother was with her, she felt safe and secure in this environment.

From this early experience, Mary learned to love watching nurses care for other children and receiving nursing care herself. The different caps that nurses wore and their white uniforms fascinated her and made her hope that one day she too would become a nurse. She held onto this vision and 20 plus years later became a registered nurse.

A Busy, Supportive Family

Born in Selma, Alabama, on June 12, 1919, she was the fourth child and first of two daughters of Mary Hill Scott and William Scott, Sr. The five children in the Scott family were, in order of birth, William, Alfonso, Edgar, Mary, and Cecelia, and all were sufficiently close in age that they were home together for a considerable period of time.

Home life in the Scott household was a beehive of activities. Their father owned a taxicab business, a seven-days-a-week operation, and the boys worked very closely with him. The boys were expected to wash, wax, and polish the two cabs regularly, as well as to learn how to do mechanical repairs on the cabs. When the boys were old enough to drive, they alternated driving the second cab for their father. The girls were never encouraged to help with anything related to the taxicab business except to be frequent passengers as their father gave them rides to school and to various community activities. They worked mostly with their mother.

Neither their mother nor the two daughters ever worked outside the home; however, they were kept busy keeping the household in excellent shape. These tasks developed skills of cooking and home management that have served Mary well throughout her life. Everyone in the family attended church when circumstances allowed, but Mary, her mother, and sister were the most actively involved in the church. As a teenager, Mary taught Sunday school and sang in the choir.

Mary Scott on her 16th birthday.

She attended Clark School from elementary through the 10th grade and completed 11th and 12th grades in Selma University High School and Junior College. Her classmate from kindergarten through graduation from high school in 1938 was Katie Stratman, who was later to become Katie Stratman Ashford, a life-long friend. They lived across the street from each other and were close in their personal and professional lives until Katie's death in 1996.

School activities which always involved Mary and her sister included the glee club, student government, and social events such as football and basketball games and school dances at Selma University. She does not recall ever talking with her teachers or a school counselor about her career plans. She isn't really sure whether they even had academic counselors at her school. She does recall her classmate, Addie Mae Edwards, telling her that she planned to go to Brewster Hospital Nursing School in Jacksonville, Florida. Although she had never heard of it, Mary told her parents that she wanted to attend this nursing school. They agreed and later provided the necessary financial support.

African American Registered Nurses in Seattle

First Encounters with Racial Discrimination

In 1938 when she graduated from high school, she was not ready to leave and decided to remain at home for a while. It was during this period that Mary came face-to-face with the negative effects of segregation and discrimination that existed in Selma during the late 1930s and throughout her residence in that area.

Since she loved nice clothes and always had stylish things to wear, she decided it might be fun to work as a department store clerk. She went to two of the nicest department stores in Selma to apply for a job, but she never received an application from either store. She was told they did not hire Negroes. She considered doing secretarial work but, again, was unable to get an application at any of the places where she tried to apply. She soon became aware of how much her parents had shielded her from the harsh realities of racism. These experiences of rejection and denial of opportunity helped Mary understand why she saw so many Negroes working as janitors, maids, elevator operators, and baby sitters.

Becoming a Registered Nurse

Informed by these negative experiences, she entered Brewster Hospital School of Nursing in 1939. By then, she was delighted to be away from home, in a setting with many other women who looked like her, and she was thrilled that she was really pursuing her dream of becoming a registered nurse. Brewster was a Methodist school, serving Negro students with Negro clinical instructors, but all the administrators were White. She thought the instruction was excellent until she and her classmates went on affiliation at Grady Hospital in Atlanta for some of their nursing training. Although it was fun to be in a different learning environment and she willingly received some instruction from White nurses for the first time, she and her other classmates disliked the nurses' residence, where they encountered rats and roaches. These pests were also in the Negro side of the hospital. When Mary and her other classmates returned to Brewster following their Grady affiliation, they reported these conditions to the school administration. Perhaps as a result, Mary's class was the last one to affiliate with Grady Hospital, although Mary remains

Nursing: The Journey

grateful to the instructors at Grady for providing her and other students with a very high quality education. It was the unequal treatment of Negroes in the living and treatment settings that tarnished their learning experience.

While in nursing school, Addie Mae Edwards, Mary's hometown friend, died of tuberculosis just six months before completing the nursing program. Even today this loss by death evokes a strong emotional response in her. Addie's death made most of the students feel very vulnerable. Mary smiled and threw her head back when she recalled how it was common for students to feel that they had the very disease symptoms they were studying, but their long-time schoolmate's death sent a jolt throughout the nursing school. Mary and Katie Stratman spent much time together as they tried to cope with the shock of Addie's death.

Despite the shock, Mary completed nursing school in 1942 and decided, with four other nurses from Brewster, to seek a job in Miami, Florida. After their positive learning experience at Brewster, she and her classmates wanted the experience of working and living on their own, having their own apartment and the opportunity to perform as professional nurses. Each one saw this move as a form of liberation. Finished with school and no longer dependent upon their families for financial support, by remaining together they could feel safe in moving to a new city and beginning their professional careers together.

More Experiences of Inequality

They were all hired at Dade County Hospital in Miami and, finding an apartment, they quickly established a routine they enjoyed. Soon, these Brewster nurses realized that conditions in Miami were similar to those in Atlanta. Negro and White patients received care on separate sides of the hospital, where treatment settings were unequal with the Negro section more rundown than the White. In spite of these physical deficiencies, these nurses knew they could equal or exceed the quality of care provided to patients by other nurses, and they set about giving excellent care.

They also worked with other hospital personnel to substantially improve the overall quality of care provided to Negro patients. Hospital orderlies followed their requests to improve services to patients. Janitors and maids improved their job performance and the physical appearance of the wards greatly improved. By working as a team, they were so successful that they attracted the attention of supervisors, administrators, and family members. One day when these five nurses reported to work, they discovered that each of them had been transferred to the other side of the hospital to care for White patients. No administrator ever spoke to any one of them about this change. Each was assigned to a different ward where they encountered new and unexpected professional insults. They would not be allowed to pour and prepare medicines for their patients. Instead, the White nurses would perform that task, and the Negro nurse would pass these medicines to the patients. To a person, each of these nurses refused to accept this practice, having been taught never to pass medications they did not themselves prepare. The very next day, this rule was changed.

Other work experiences also changed dramatically. Conflicts over responsibilities occurred frequently, requiring negotiation nearly every day. Since neither the Negro nor the White nurses were prepared to work together, problems of basic communication, trust, and respect needed to be settled, thus making work less satisfying for Mary than it had previously been.

Furthermore, at that time Negro nurses were paid less than White nurses with equivalent education and experiences. Mary and her colleagues resented the fact that they were providing high quality care to patients and receiving less pay for their efforts. As dissatisfaction built, by the end of the year Mary took her vacation and returned to Selma and never returned to Dade County Hospital. The remaining four nurses also eventually left.

A Transcontinental Move and Immediate Reemployment

While in Selma, Mary learned that her friend, Katie Stratman, had moved to Seattle; so, she contacted Katie and her parents to ask if she could live with them. Since they were as close as family members, they immediately invited her to join them.

Arriving by train in 1944 and making a quick and smooth transition to life in the Northwest, she wasted no time in applying for a job. On her second day in Seattle, she applied for work at

Harborview Hospital where she was hired on the spot, and on the third day of being in the city she began working. For 30 years Mary practiced in different wards throughout Harborview Hospital.

The fifth Negro nurse hired at Harborview, she was preceded by Ira Gordon, Shelly Burris, Mary Martyn, and Katie Stratman Ashford. Eventually they all met at the hospital; however, it took some time for them to become acquainted because of their different ward and shift assignments.

Mary began in the medical ward. She recalls how White nurses came down to her ward just to see what she looked like with none disguising the reason for her visit. They came in, looked at her and left, not with hostility but with curiosity and surprise. This attitude did not make her uncomfortable because most of the nurses were friendly and nice. She realized that she, like the other Negro nurses, was assigned the sickest patients and worked more split shifts than her White counterparts. At that time, she was afraid to complain about these different working conditions because she felt lucky to be employed.

Once Mary began caring for patients, she realized once again how well prepared she was to deliver high quality care to patients. The knowledge and skills she had acquired in her training program served her well both at Dade County Hospital and at Harborview.

Marriages, Deaths, and Professional Advancement

Mary adjusted well to Seattle. On her days off she rode her bicycle and enjoyed the beautiful scenery of the city. One day while riding her bike, Mary met Frank Marshall. They dated for a short time before marrying. After marriage, Mary moved out of the Stratman-Livingston home into her apartment and later, in 1950, they purchased their own home. Mary and Frank had a happy relationship for nearly a decade before divorcing in 1956.

Along with Katie, Ira Gordon, and Mary Martyn, she was among the 13 charter members in 1949 of the Mary Mahoney Registered Nurses Club, in which she remained active for the first 10 years of her professional career. Like Katie, she became inactive for a time but returned to active status in the late 1980s when Katie returned and has remained an active member. (Mary and Katie were together at a downtown department store when I asked each of them to return to the organization and help us continue to provide scholarship support to deserving students.) She now serves as corresponding secretary of MMPNO.

In 1951, after her mother's death, Mary's father moved from Selma to Seattle to live with her in the house she had purchased a decade earlier (and in which she still resides). Delighted to have her father with her, she shared the pleasure of his company with her sister, Cecelia, and her eight children, all of whom lived in Seattle. She also had the pleasure of undertaking a second marriage to Ezekiel Davis, who was in the Air Force. Their marriage lasted happily for three years until his death from cancer. Her father died in 1970.

During these family realignments, her nursing career continued. In 1957, Mary requested and was granted a transfer from medicine to orthopedics. She worked on this new ward for several years and was later promoted to head nurse, the second Negro nurse to be promoted to head nurse at Harborview Hospital. Since she knew she was an excellent nurse, she was delighted to know that her supervisor also perceived her to be qualified for this role and had worked to help her receive a promotion. Thrilled to receive it, she loved serving as a leader, a particularly enjoyable time for her.

By her choice, however, she served as head nurse on the orthopedic ward for only one year, after which she requested and received a transfer to the outpatient clinic. There she worked in otolaryngology, ophthalmology, endocrinology, and obstetrics/gynecology, eventually being named clinic coordinator in outpatient services and remaining in this role until retirement in 1974. She said, "The Outpatient Clinic at Harborview fitted my life style. I liked working days and having

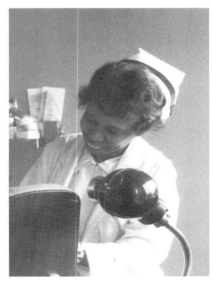

Mary in 1968 as Outpatient Clinic Coordinator at Harborview Hospital, Seattle, WA.

Nursing: The Journey

weekends off. I also liked the patients, the doctors, and nurses with whom I worked. Harborview was really an exciting place to work."

From the mid-1960s until retirement, her perception was of more equitable treatment in all areas, including pay, hours of work, days off, and opportunities for participation in continuing education, than what she had experienced at the beginning of her employment at Harborview.

Promotion in 1968 to clinic coordinator, the equivalent of head nurse in an inpatient setting, pleased her because patients, many of their family members and other staff were very accepting of her care, as expressed by flowers, cards, and candy. Throughout her time at Harborview, only one White patient absolutely refused to accept care from her, an awkwardness she handled by honoring his request and assigning a White nurse to his care. In those days she felt it was easier to give patients what they wanted rather than challenge them. Indeed, some of her White nurse colleagues who demonstrated similar racial attitudes towards Mary were individuals whom she tried also to avoid. She takes satisfaction in still maintaining contact with a few of the White nurses from Harborview, exchanging Christmas cards each year and telephone calls from time to time.

Her third marriage occurred in 1981 to Ezra Hooks, a retired Boeing employee. They reside happily in the same home she purchased in 1950. God has been good to her, she declares.

Reflections in Retirement

In retrospect, her professional life has left her with a sense of pride in progress toward harmonious racial relations, although she also hopes to be alive when African American and other nurses of color receive the same opportunities for education and professional advancement that White nurses have always enjoyed. As she looks back on her early years of work with the four classmates who went to Miami, she recalls how easy it was to make a difference by getting the orderlies, aides, maids, and janitors to cooperate with them to improve the quality of services provided to Negro patients. She recalls, "We were young, energetic and eager to show our stuff. The other employees enjoyed having us there. What was difficult was being reassigned without ever being asked if we wanted to move." This represented to Mary a form of desegregation without conversation, with neither the Negro nor White nurses prepared for this abrupt change. Most significant of all, the change placed Negro nurses in a subservient position to White nurses.

Her promotion to head nurse at Harborview was significant, she thinks, not only because her skills qualified her but also because this seemingly color-blind recognition came at a time when some hospitals in the area were only beginning to hire Negroes in staff-nurse positions.

Having been retired for 25 years, just five years less than the entire time she worked, Mary remains healthy and has filled her life with meaningful activities. An active member in the community, she is a member of Mt. Zion Baptist Church, where she serves on the health unit and is very active in Women's Ministry. In both of these activities, members of MMPNO serve in leadership roles. She enjoys working with these individuals in church and in MMPNO and intends to remain active as long as her health allows. She declares, with conviction, "God continues to bless me each day I remain on this earth. Mine is a good life."

Mary Davis Hooks in 2000. She had been retired for 25 years.

Upon reflection, Mary feels grateful for the experience of illness she had in 1925 at age six, the one that introduced her to professional nurses and professional nursing care. Without it, she might have chosen another path, one that might have deprived her of the enjoyment of providing nursing care to others and the rewards from those services. "It has been a win-win situation for me and for the patients I served. In spite of all the opportunities available to women today, I'd still choose to be a nurse."

Inspired by a Pioneering Spirit to Become a Nurse

Juanita Alexander Davis

Pioneering Grandparents with Determination

Juanita Alexander Davis, a native of Seattle, Washington, is understandably proud of her family heritage. In the early 1880s her maternal grandfather worked on the Northern Pacific Railroad that had a run from his hometown in Minneapolis to Portland,

Juanita's grandparents, Charles and Eva Harvey, in 1915, with their first grandchild.

with connections to Seattle. Exposure to the Pacific Northwest convinced him that he really wanted to someday make Seattle his home. He used his ingenuity, systematic planning, and frugality to make this wish a reality.

Her grandparents, Charles H. Harvey and his new bride, Eva Ellis Harvey, started their life together in 1887, living in a rented room in the Belltown area of Seattle. They passed on to their children and grandchildren their spirit of adventure, self-confidence, and determination to succeed. This spirit motivated her to pursue a career in nursing even while she experienced rejection and segregation.

Juanita's grandparents made a very successful adjustment to Seattle, in a time when very few other Negroes lived in Seattle. They went about daily life as most of their Caucasian neighbors did since their physical features alone would not have been an accurate indicator of their ethnic/racial affiliation. After her grandfather stopped working for the railroad, he built a home on 29th Avenue near Thomas in the Madison Valley area. Soon afterward, he became a carpenter and later established his own construction company, Charles H. Harvey and Son.

Juanita spent lots of time with her grandparents, seeing her grandfather in his basement making shoes, which all of the children in her family wore. Work was his life, with the result that holidays, birthdays, and other special occasions were times when family members often received gifts he had created.

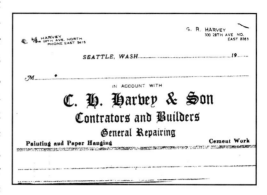

Business stationary of the Charles H. Harvey & Son construction company from the early 1900s.

He was also one of three founders of the First African Methodist Episcopal Church of Seattle, whose names are on the cornerstone, but Juanita knows that her grandmother gave significant help to bring this church into being. Her grandfather built the original part of the First AME Church, which is still located on 14th Avenue between Pine and Pike Streets in Seattle, and both grandparents were lifetime members. Of the eight children who were born to this couple, Juanita's mother, Irene Harvey, was the seventh. She, like most of her sisters and brothers, remained in Seattle throughout her life.

Supportive Parents and Siblings

Irene Harvey met and married Ernest Alexander, a career Navy man. During his 39-year career, he rose to the rank of Chief Petty Officer in the submarine division of the Navy. Four children were born to Irene and Ernest Alexander, Dorothy Alexander Vickers, Juanita Alexander Davis, Donald Alexander, and Jacqueline Alexander Lawson. Donald is deceased, and Dorothy makes her home now in

Inspired by a Pioneering Spirit to Become a Nurse

California after having lived for many years in Portland, Oregon. Juanita and Jacqueline live in Seattle. The three sisters continue to maintain the very close and supportive relationship they established in childhood.

Until the start of World War II, Juanita's mother was primarily a housewife and homemaker. During the war she worked in the tool-supply area at Sand Point Naval Station (Seattle), where her husband, Ernest, was stationed. Home life in the Alexander family was "as my father experienced life in the navy—orderly, clean, and very supportive." When their father was stationed at Bremerton Navy Yard (outside Seattle), the family lived in Bremerton part of the time and the rest with Juanita's grandparents in Seattle. Whether their father was at home or at sea, their mother ran the home in a very systematic manner. "For the most part we did what we were expected to do," she said, recalling that each of the children had assigned housekeeping and home management responsibilities and understood what their parents and grandparents valued and expected of them.

The Alexander family lived in Madison Valley, an integrated neighborhood where there were very few Negroes but many Asian, Jewish, and Caucasian families in their area. Their family got along well with all of their neighbors. The nearby schools, Harrison Elementary, Madrona Junior High, and Garfield High, were ethnically similar to the neighborhood, although all the teachers were Caucasian. In high school, Juanita had many friends, two of whom were Jewish girls. They palled around together at school and, occasionally, called each other on the telephone. They did not visit at each other's homes, nor did they engage in any activities outside of school hours. The Girls Advisory Group was one of the school activities in which Juanita was most active. Members were expected to serve as role models for other students. If they observed other girls breaking school rules, they were to report these students to their advisor. Academically, Juanita claims that she "was an average student and I felt my teachers evaluated me fairly when they assigned me grades." At Garfield High School there may have been academic counselors to assist students in making career choices; however, Juanita did not seek or receive their counsel. Instead, she relied on her parents and grandparents as well as family friends to provide guidance in this area.

As it had with the grandparents, religion played a significant role in the lives of parents and children, all of whom were members of the First AME Church. Her mother was a member of the Usher Board and the children attended Sunday school and participated in Christian Endeavor, a young adult religious education group.

Juanita and her sisters were also members of Girl Reserves, a social club located at the Phillis Wheatley YWCA, whose members were then mostly Negro women. There, they experienced some of their most significant social activities.

None of the Alexander children were required to work while they attended public school. Their parents made it very clear that their most important job was to get an education; however, before completing junior high school, Juanita's father began encouraging her to consider nursing as a career and he continued to do so until she entered nursing school.

Transition to University Study

After graduation from Garfield High School in 1938, Juanita wanted and was able to take some time off before going to college. From the time she was a little girl, playing with dolls, she knew she wanted to be a registered nurse and apparently never considered another profession or occupation. Knowing, too, that she wanted to earn her own money and have some time to decide what she really wanted to do with her life, she announced her decision to take some time off before pursuing her college education. Her parents concurred.

After taking a job as a baby sitter for a family in Broadmoor (a wealthy, walled community in Seattle) she enjoyed caring for these children, although that feeling was short-lived. The parents soon asked her to do more than care for the children. When she was asked to clean the toilet, she thought things had gone too far, as work expectations had increased and pay had remained the same. Within ten months Juanita began applying for admission to college.

Acceptance at the University of Washington came quickly and without difficulty. With hard study she completed all course requirements for admission into the nursing program. College was a full-time job for her. She thinks her instructors evaluated her work fairly and that college was satisfying and problem-free in most respects.

Inspired by a Pioneering Spirit to Become a Nurse

Initial Rejection for Nursing Training

Prerequisites completed, she made an admissions appointment at the School of Nursing. When she arrived for the appointment, a staff person said, "You will need to see the dean." Thinking this in no way unusual because she had never applied to any special departments at this school before, she soon understood why the staff person responded as she did. Before even saying hello to her, Dean Soule said to Juanita, "There are no Negro RNs working in Seattle and I don't think we can start now. I recommend that you find another occupation." That remark hit her right between the eyes, her first rejection and first recognition of racism and segregation at the University. She managed to say, "It's time to start" before their meeting ended. She also realized just how protective her parents had been.

When she told her mother about her meeting with the dean, her mother wanted to go talk with the woman, although her father's reaction was, "There are plenty of hospitals where you can go and become a nurse." Since his travels had taken him to many cities in the East and West, without too much thought he named four schools that he wanted Juanita to contact for an admission application: Lincoln Hospital (New York), a hospital in Omaha, Nebraska, Homer G. Phillips in St. Louis and Los Angeles General Hospital. She wrote to all four schools and received responses from two.

Exploration and Acceptance

In order to help her make a choice, her father suggested visits to the two schools. Since he had always wanted to purchase a car directly from the factory in Detroit, he took her, her brother and an auto-mechanic friend on this dual-purpose trip. It was during this trip that Juanita realized just how much her father really wanted her to become a nurse. He systematically made comparisons between the schools to help Juanita make the best choice for herself. Her reaction, however, was largely based on appearance and feelings. Lincoln Hospital was unappealing to her, but Homer G. Phillips was new and very appealing. Its building and grounds were beautiful and "looked like a college building. I knew I would be happy there."

When they returned from the trip, she received letters from LA General and Lincoln Hospitals. She learned that it was necessary to be a resident of California in order to attend LA General. Deciding to comply with that requirement, she moved to LA to live for six months with her mother's brother and his wife. After arriving in LA, she found that her aunt was a practical nurse who wanted to become a registered nurse and that she had already made arrangements to attend a nursing conference scheduled to occur in just a few weeks. At this conference and through a friend of a friend of her aunt, Juanita met Estelle Massey Riddle, Superintendent of Nursing at Homer G. Phillips. She explained that she had applied to Homer G. but had not received a response. Questioning her about her school performance and grades, Mrs. Riddle soon told her she was sure Juanita could attend the school—a thrilling moment for Juanita. She could enter right away rather than having to meet residency requirements as she was being required to do for LA General.

Shortly thereafter, she returned to Seattle to make plans for the move to St. Louis. Her parents were as thrilled as she and they bid her goodbye in September 1941, apparently not knowing or telling her she was about to enter a totally Negro community. All of the doctors, nurses, staff, students, and patients were Negro. When she went out on the streets, she noticed that businesses were also segregated. While there were no signs restricting public facilities for Negroes or Whites only, she observed the way people acted and realized that this was almost total racial segregation, the first time she had ever been in a racially separate community.

Among the students, Juanita also recognized that light-skinned students tended to be friends with other light-skinned students and dark-skinned students clustered together. This phenomenon of separation by skin color among Blacks was also new to her. In the YWCA Girl Reserves, the Negro girls were of every hue, from very dark to nearly white-skinned. These color differences had seemed unimportant in her girlhood. In St. Louis not only did these differences seem important, but so did the manner of speech. Other students teased her about the way she talked and for coming from "cowboy country", west of Chicago. (She asked her parents to send maps of Washington State to help these geographically naive young people understand a little about where she was from.)

Inspired by a Pioneering Spirit to Become a Nurse

At least 55 students were admitted with her to Homer G., most from the South and East. She learned later that she was, indeed, the first student to attend Homer G. from as far west as Seattle. They entered a three-year diploma program, consisting of theoretical and clinical studies, including all the traditional services except tuberculosis. For that, students had to go to a sanitarium in the county. During the last six months of this program, students were allowed to decide the clinical service in which they wanted to develop greater skills.

Shortly after Juanita's arrival at Homer G., World War II started, which led to all of the students' being made members of the Cadet Corps. In addition to signing papers and wearing uniforms, students were able to get financial assistance through the government. In exchange, these students, if needed, were well prepared to step in if established registered nurses were drafted for military service.

Juanita Alexander in 1941 following her capping ceremony at Homer G. Philips School of Nursing in St. Louis, MO.

Since she was so far away from home, she couldn't return often to Seattle for holidays and vacations; she did return once during the three years. At other times, students who lived in Detroit and Indianapolis invited her to visit at their homes. On one of these visits to Indianapolis, she developed pneumonia and really learned who her friends were. They organized themselves, brought her class assignments, and provided nursing care which enabled her to make up lost clinical time after her recovery.

Juanita knew that she had selected the right profession and had no difficulty completing the theoretical or clinical content with the help of instructors who were interested and eager for all students to succeed. Furthermore, whether she worked in the hospital or the clinic, she saw just about every kind of disease described in textbooks. During the last six months of the emergency-room-service program, she realized that she was having more fun than she had ever had. Racial segregation and color separation still existed, but she focused her attention on doing her best work in all the courses and she completed the nursing program in 1944. Her mother came to St. Louis to attend her graduation, but leaving Homer G. caused some sadness. For many years, she stayed in touch with several of her classmates.

Employment as a Nurse

Before leaving St. Louis, Juanita studied for and passed the state board examination and soon thereafter followed her father's advice about visiting a newly opened hospital in Phoenix, Arizona. Scheduling an appointment with the Director of Nursing at St. Monica's Hospital, she interviewed with the director and was offered a job which she immediately accepted.

In 1945 she started her first professional job, assigned to the afternoon shift (3 to 11) on the general medicine floor, and she rented a room in a Negro family's house. Shortly before she was oriented, she was assigned to give intravenous fluids and injectable medicine to patients all over the hospital. It was this assignment that brought her into contact with John Lawrence Davis, a pharmacist technician who worked for his brother, a pharmacist in town contracted to service the hospital with drugs and various medical supplies.

John worked very long hours at the hospital which facilitated his seeing Juanita. They started dating shortly after they met and he learned that she had rented a room in the home of his brother and sister-in-law. John had his own apartment and he was so busy at the hospital pharmacy, he did not have much time to visit his relatives. Juanita and John were married on February 5, 1945.

Juanita loved her experiences at the hospital. She worked on the special unit for patients with upper respiratory infections, most with asthma or severe bronchitis, and continued to give IVs and injections throughout the hospital. Before long, she also assisted a doctor in opening a venereal disease unit for military men who needed short-term in-patient treatment. Eventually, though, the heat in Phoenix got the better of her. She and John were also having trouble finding time to spend with one another. This combination of circumstances led them to leave Phoenix for Seattle. Her father, thinking that civil service might lead to secure employment, sent papers for John to take a civil service examination.

Return to Seattle

After less than a week back in Seattle, Juanita applied for a job at the King County Public Health Department. During her interview, she was offered a job as a staff nurse in the Health Department's Venereal Disease Clinic. (Nurses in the Public Health Clinic provided services to patients who came to the clinic for treatment. They did not go into patients' homes.) She accepted this position and became the first Negro RN to work in the Health Department, later becoming charge nurse of the Civil Service Medical Service, a position she felt competent to hold. When the Civil Service Medical Department was closed for lack of funds, Juanita worked in other clinics such as child welfare, venereal disease, and family planning.

Never completing his pharmacy training, Juanita's husband passed the civil service examination and began working at Pier 91 as stock person for the military supply depot. Nevertheless, he maintained a fund of knowledge about medicines and used this information to understand the drugs he was required to take for a later illness.

Juanita returned to the First AME Church where she met Mary Martyn, who was a professional nurse at Harborview Hospital. Soon, she joined Mary and eleven other nurses to become a charter member of the Mary Mahoney Registered Nurses Club. From the time that the club was founded in 1949 to 1955, she was very active, serving in 1955 as president. That same year, she and John had their first and only son, Arthur Eugene Davis. When she could, she started working part-time at the Health Department.

Life went very well for the Davis family until 1960, when John had a massive stroke and was left partially paralyzed and unable to return to full-time work. After the stroke, he helped take care of Arthur so that Juanita could return to full-time employment. When she became eligible for promotion to supervisor, she learned that she would be promoted but without a salary increase. She wrote to Wes Uhlman, then Mayor of Seattle, who, in turn, pointed out the city's shortage of funds. Juanita decided it was time to quit. Having lost her husband in 1971, she knew she had done a superior job of caring for him during his illness and wanted to have time to enjoy her son; therefore, in 1977 she retired.

Retirement and Reflections on a Nursing Career

Looking back over her professional life, Juanita feels that she has been well served by nursing. She worked in only two settings during her professional career, but she had a breadth of experiences in each location. An incident that stands out relates to being the Negro nurse in the venereal disease clinic in Seattle. She observed that Negro patients, in contrast to Caucasians, preferred to receive services from Caucasian nurses. Mustering confidence to ask a client why he tried to avoid receiving care from her, she discovered that this patient was ashamed to have a venereal disease. He was fearful that he would see Juanita in the community, whereas he knew how unlikely was a later encounter with any of the Caucasian nurses.

One of her most memorable cases was a patient with a severe allergic reaction to penicillin. She gave the antidote to penicillin and saw before her very eyes the effects of this medication in reversing the allergic reaction.

Juanita Alexander Davis in 2000. She had been retired for over 22 years. In 1945 Juanita was the first Negro nurse hired to work in the Seattle Public Health Department Clinic.

Now retired, she is a member of two senior citizen centers and is very active with the Black Heritage Society, of which her sister, Jacqueline, is president. She remains a member of the First AME

Inspired by a Pioneering Spirit to Become a Nurse

Church. For many years Juanita has financially supported the MMPNO Scholarship Luncheon. She is not otherwise active in MMPNO.

Arthur Eugene Davis, her son, is very attentive to her, as she acknowledged when she said, "He occupies a very, very special place in my life." She knows that family has always been the center of her being. Her relationships with her sisters, her son, family members, and the many friends that she has maintained from childhood all serve to remind Juanita that her grandparents started a family heritage that stretches back over three generations. Daily she feels the spirit of these grandparents as well as the spirit of her parents.

Turning Obstacles into Opportunities

Gertrude Robinson Dawson

Caregiving at an Early Age

Gertrude was an early Christmas present to her parents, Mary and Robert Robinson, vegetable and chicken farmers in Union Springs, Alabama. Born on December 22, 1919, she was the tenth child, 12 years younger than the ninth Robinson child. Her early memories of family life were shaped by the daily activities of the farm with the ground being plowed and prepared for planting, vegetables peeking out of the soil and growing, the birth of animals, their nourishment and growth. All of these activities gave her an understanding of the opportunities and the obstacles entailed in life, growth, and death.

At an early age Gertrude learned about caregiving. She saw her parents care for sick and ailing animals. Soon, she was allowed to do some of the things that she saw her parents do. She was attracted to the baby chicks with their soft down feathers and developed an intense liking for the sick ones, many of whom were not expected to live. Under her skilled care many of these chicks returned to health. She derived great pleasure from doing this and received frequent praise and admiration from her family members for being so effective in their care. On occasion she even took survivors in her jacket pocket and showed them to neighbors when she accompanied her father on his rounds to sell vegetables, chickens, and eggs to his customers, one of whom was Mr. Maytag (of Maytag washing-machine fame). He nicknamed Gertrude the "chicken doctor" to acknowledge her caregiving successes. Gertrude now considers these experiences as significant in her choice of nursing as a professional career, although in her small town she did see many professional Colored women who were teachers and nurses.

Overcoming Obstacles

In the process of becoming a professional nurse Gertrude had to overcome many obstacles in pursuit of her dream. Just trying to obtain an elementary education and, later, a high school diploma required inordinate effort by any Colored child in small-town Alabama. Public schools were segregated at the elementary level and non-existent for Colored children at the high-school level. As they watched the yellow school bus carrying only White children regularly pass them by, some children who attended elementary school walked more than two miles to reach the schoolhouse. These were common conditions in the South during the 1920s and 1930s.

Fortunately for Gertrude, her parents, sisters, and brothers all wanted her to have the very best available education. They worked together by pooling money and other material resources to help Gertrude achieve this goal. Various members of the family regularly demonstrated, in words and deeds, how much they wanted her to receive a better education than theirs. She recalls that she also understood her responsibility to perform in order to meet everyone's expectations.

Among the first educational obstacles was the difficulty of just making it to school every day. The elementary school was over a mile from home and the path was often, alternatively, very dusty or very muddy. When the path was muddy, Gertrude was given a ride on the horse by her older brother to the paved section of the road. At other times, she walked fast to try to make it to school before the Whites-only bus passed her. She never succeeded in that attempt, but it made getting to school a bit of fun.

After completing elementary school, Gertrude's parents sent her to live with her older sister, Virginia Plato, in Waugh, Alabama, where there was a high school for Colored children. Though she missed being with her family on the farm, she was very busy with housework, cooking, and shopping for her sister. In exchange, she received room and board and an opportunity to advance her education. Before she completed high school, their father became ill and died. Adjusting to this loss was difficult for Gertrude and her sister, but she remembered how much her dad wanted her to graduate from high school; so, she worked even harder than before to do so.

Struggle for Further Education

In 1941, Gertrude graduated with honors from high school. As a result, she was awarded a small scholarship from Tuskegee Institute (now Tuskegee University). That opportunity turned into an obstacle, however, because her family could not afford to pay the difference between the scholarship and the remaining costs. Disappointed, she forfeited this award, never applying for admission to Tuskegee. However, Gertrude's sister, who worked at Morrison's Cafeteria in Montgomery, was able to pay tuition for her at Montgomery Training School for Nurses. Gertrude entered this three-year diploma program. After being there only six months, the nursing director died; the school was closed and all enrolled students were sent to other schools of nursing in the area with the senior nurses going to Tuskegee Institute and Gertrude's class to Brewster Hospital in Jacksonville, Florida. At this hospital most of the instructors and support staff were White; the nursing students and patients whom they cared for were Negroes.

Before she moved there, her tuition-paying sister died, which was a shattering event and period in her life. The losses associated with death and the changes they wrought were a serious threat to her dreams; however, she persevered and was able to transfer to Brewster Hospital with 27 other classmates, who supported one another.

At Brewster, these students encountered a different obstacle in the person of a very influential and unsupportive instructor, whom they nicknamed "Miss Evil." This woman seemed to delight in belittling students, making them appear dumb. Many students were either asked to leave or left on their own initiative because of "Miss Evil." Since her abusive behavior was well known, these students wondered why other faculty and administrators allowed her to get away with it and to remain on the staff. They never got an answer. By their senior year, only eight of the entering 27 students remained in this program. This attrition prompted Gertrude and the remaining

Turning Obstacles into Opportunities

Gertrude Robinson at the time of graduation from Brewster Hospital, Jacksonville, FL in 1944.

seven students to agree to stick together until graduation, secretly deciding that, if one student were asked to leave, all eight would go. Their plan worked and in 1944 they all graduated. She is certain that the plan worked because of their solidarity, mutual trust and support, and desire to succeed.

Beginning a Nursing Career

Gertrude remained at Brewster Hospital, working as a staff nurse at a salary of $90 per month with free room and board. By using off-duty hours to study for the state board examinations, she passed, thereby making herself ready to leave Florida. She thought that most of her obstacles were behind her. She soon realized this was not the case.

Among ads in the *American Journal of Nursing,* Gertrude saw one for nurses at Harborview Hospital in Seattle. In comparison to all other ads in that journal, she realized that nurses were being paid the highest salary in Seattle. She called the nursing supervisor and was hired over the phone. After obtaining information about living in the nurses' residence, she decided to move to Seattle.

Before leaving Florida, Gertrude decided to visit her mother and other family members in Union Springs. While there, she and her mother went to the train station to buy her ticket to Seattle. She encountered another small obstacle, a ticket agent who stated that he had never heard of Seattle. Indeed, it would be necessary for Gertrude to wait for another day to purchase her ticket because the agent needed to call Montgomery to determine how to make a ticket for her to travel to Seattle.

When Gertrude and her mother returned the next day, the agent told them that Seattle was almost in Alaska and that Gertrude would likely catch pneumonia if she traveled that far from home. "But she needs to go to the place where she already has a job," her mother protested. They bought the ticket and the next morning Gertrude left Union Springs for Seattle. As a footnote to this incident, the book *Up South* edited by Malaika Adero (1992) describes the role that train personnel like Gertrude's ticket agent played in efforts to prevent Negroes from leaving the South. They were charged with devising obstacles. Neither Gertrude nor her mother were aware that the Great Migration was taking place in the United States. All they knew was that Gertrude had a job in Seattle and that all people in America were supposed to be free to go wherever they could afford to go.

Upon boarding the train, Gertrude encountered segregation signs which indicated Whites in the forward coaches and Colored people in the back. After four days of less-than-comfortable travel, Gertrude reached Seattle, catching a cold en route and arriving weary and apprehensive.

Once off the train and her belongings gathered, she signaled a cab and asked to be taken to Harborview Hospital. The White cab driver said, "Harborview Hospital don't hire no Negro nurses. Maybe you mean the nursing home in Georgetown." He drove to the nursing home and went to the door to inquire about whether they expected a Negro nurse. Sheepishly, he returned to the cab and took her to Harborview Hall, the nurses' residence. The matron greeted them, saying, "We expected you long ago." Gertrude explained the cab driver's error and asked the matron how much to pay him. "I'd say $2 is fair enough." With that as backing, Gertrude said to the driver, "The rest is on you," and went into the building.

Before she could begin work, the ticket agent's prophecy came true as her cold turned into pneumonia. She was also anemic. Too sick to work, she spent several days being cared for by a doctor and nurses at Harborview Hospital, several of whom donated blood. These expressions of kindness by relative strangers helped Gertrude return to physical health and also reassured her that she had attained membership in a professional group in which she would be treated with respect and support.

In 1945, Gertrude began her employment at Harborview Hospital, working the 3:00-to-11:00 p.m. shift on several services.

Turning Obstacles into Opportunities

While employed there, she encountered patients who did not want to be cared for by a Negro nurse. On one occasion, when a White, automobile-accident victim realized that Gertrude was to be his nurse, he told the doctor on duty that he did not want to receive care from her. The doctor replied, "Gertrude and I are here to serve you. If you don't want our care, you are free to leave." The patient decided to leave. Gertrude felt supported by the doctor, as well as by other doctors and nurses, although some staff were neutral or negative towards her. No staff person ever engaged in behaviors that were directly designed to be harmful to her. These reactions helped her draw upon her own inner strength to recognize that she was not alone, even though she was far away from her family and friends. They also forced her to recall earlier life experiences that had involved obstacles. Now, she realized more fully that she could function effectively and efficiently in this environment, where there were both obstacles to overcome and opportunities to enjoy.

Seeking Expanded Opportunities and Meeting Obstacles

After being at Harborview several months, Gertrude met Katie Ashford and Mary Hooks, two Negro nurses, who, along with Gertrude, would become founding members of Mary Mahoney Registered Nurses Club. She also met other Negroes who served in professional and non-professional roles, seeking and sharing information with them about job and educational opportunities throughout the region. She looked continually for advancement opportunities.

As she got around the city on days off, to her surprise she almost never saw Negroes. According to the National Urban League, Seattle was supposed to have been home to at least 3,700 Negroes, but, she seldom saw anyone who looked like her. Soon, however, she met the man who would eventually become her husband, Simeon C. Dawson, who was stationed in Seattle with the U.S. Navy. After a brief courtship, they were married in November 1945. Gertrude moved out of Harborview Hall and into the Central Area of Seattle, while continuing to work at Harborview Hospital and becoming very active in civic and professional organizations. She also bore three children: Carol, Patricia, and Carl Michael.

In 1949 Gertrude received a telephone call and invitation from Anne Foy Baker to attend a meeting at Anne's house on July 9, 1949. Her acceptance led to her being among the 13 Negro nurses who founded Mary Mahoney Professional Nurses Club and met monthly to share information and to support one another. Gertrude found in this organization a level of support, caring, and trust which was reminiscent of her family in Alabama that eventually helped her to develop enough confidence to leave Harborview Hospital. After nine years of experience there and significant opportunities to work in responsible roles, she had not had promotions commensurate with these responsibilities. Gertrude knew that the education and training that she received at Brewster had prepared her to successfully compete with her White counterparts. She also knew that she had demonstrated to herself and other fair-minded professionals that she was competent and effective in her practice. In spite of this she suspected it was highly unlikely that she would rise above the level of charge nurse at Harborview; furthermore, she needed some time off to enjoy her two girls and young son.

Revitalized, in 1956 Gertrude became the first African American nurse to be hired at Group Health Cooperative (GHC), where the guiding philosophy was and remains the provision of the highest quality of care at the lowest costs by the most experienced providers. But even in this supposedly bias-free setting, factors other than professional competence influenced access to opportunities for African Americans. Gertrude worked on several different units in the hospital and became known as an excellent nurse as well as chief nurse-negotiator for salaries and benefits in 1965. In this role, she negotiated the highest monthly salary increase ($45) that nurses in the State of Washington had ever received. Prior salary increases for nurses had typically been $5 to $10 per month.

Following this performance, Gertrude became head nurse in the outpatient clinic, the first significant promotion in her 22-year experience as a professional nurse. Along the way she knew she had been passed over for leadership opportunities. She felt at last that her persistence and her excellent service had paid off.

In 1970 she became manager of the Capitol Hill Family Medical Center and nursing supervisor, the first woman and nurse of any race to hold the manager's position. With extensive responsibilities,

Turning Obstacles into Opportunities

she derived significant satisfaction from fulfilling them. During her tenure, Senator Edward Kennedy, who was chair of the Senate Health Subcommittee, visited the clinic and personally commended Gertrude for managing a model health clinic. After serving in these roles for three years, Gertrude created the opportunity to serve in another leadership position.

In 1973, she earned appointment as Outreach Supervisor and Program

Gertrude Dawson pictured with Senator Edward Kennedy. Gertrude was the first professional nurse to be appointed Nurse Manager at Group Health Hospital. She was serving in this capacity when Senator Kennedy visited this clinic in 1971.

Coordinator for a pilot program for low-income families who had been hard hit by recent Boeing layoffs. The job required that she work with a lay board, several of whose members resented her salary and denied her the use of a GHC car to do outreach work in their community. Using her considerable diplomatic and negotiation skills, she eventually won the hearts and minds of many of the 500 families to whom she provided services. Regrettably, federal funds for this pilot program were discontinued after three years. She sought a comparable position at GHC Central hospital. Again she experienced barriers to opportunities. After considerable effort, she filed and eventually won a grievance of discrimination against GHC, which resulted in an award of benefits and back pay and her appointment as training supervisor for the night shift. With only three years left before retirement, she accepted this appointment. After nearly 39 years of professional practice, Gertrude returned to provide direct care to very appreciative patients and to promote knowledge and skill development among the night staff. Gertrude rose above this conflict with GHC administrators and delivered outstanding service to other staff nurses and patients with whom she worked until her very last day at GHC. Gertrude reflects, "I look back on my years at GHC with a sense of accomplishment. I did what I could to make a difference."

Other Roles

In 1970 Gertrude founded the Metropolitan Sickle Cell Task Force, an organization that provided screening and counseling to families and children affected by this disease. That organization established a scholarship in Gertrude's honor; because of it children in these families are eligible to receive financial support for their education. This scholarship program is still in existence.

Gertrude retired in 1984. Yet, she continues her active involvement in civic and religious organizations. At Mount Zion Baptist Church where she served for over 50 years, she established the health unit, and she continues to assist other nurses throughout Puget Sound to do the same in their churches. After serving on the Board of the Central Area Senior Citizen's Center, she remains an active supporter of the Center. Gertrude continues to provide consultation to a director of a day care center in Seattle. Through effective management of her time, Gertrude enjoys being with her four grandchildren, Edwinta, David, Avrey, and Rosalie, and her four great-grandchildren, JoVaughn, DaVonte, Jolonie and Eric.

Gertrude Dawson in 2000. She retired in 1984.

For more than 50 years Gertrude has remained an active member of MMPNO. During her tenure, she has served in every leadership role in this organization and currently serves as financial secretary. Her life continues to be one of giving through service to others. Indeed, her efforts, energy and determination reflect a capacity to turn obstacles into opportunities. In the process, she experiences considerable personal and professional success. According to Gertrude, "I will continue to give as long as my health allows me to do so."

Her life is a testament to her effort and determination to turn obstacles into opportunities. In the process she has experienced considerable personal and professional success. In retirement Gertrude remains very active, giving help to others and enjoying good health.

A Quiet Spirit in a Comforting Caregiver

Mary Turner Stephens Lanier
(1921-1988)

Since childhood, Mary Turner was referred to as a "quiet spirit" by her maternal grandfather (a Methodist minister) and by her parents, Ellen Jury Turner and Elbert Turner. As she matured from childhood to adulthood, her demeanor and character continued to reflect this early and accurate description. Even up until the time of her death in 1988, she still seemed quiet and hopeful, despite her battle with cancer.

Born to a Family with Strong Values

The Turners had six children. Elbert and William (now deceased) were the oldest. Mary was the eldest daughter. The three younger

Mary Turner as a child with her "church family". She is the 4th from the right in the front row. According to Mary, her church family met the spiritual, social and health needs of members of the congregation.

A Quiet Spirit in a Comforting Caregiver

daughters in descending birth order were Lillian, Veora, and Erbie (Lillian and Erbie are deceased). All of the children were close enough in ages to live at home together during their childhood and into their early teens. Mary often referred to the family values and the ways their parents raised them where religion, work, and education were primary values stressed in their home. Besides the parents' regular church attendance, all the children participated in church, Sunday school, and youth activities. Sunday was also the day when the family spent the most time together, visiting with one another and with other families in the community after church.

Their father was a cotton and corn farmer who taught his children to farm and how to be helpful in completing chores, such as housecleaning, cooking, and ironing. Work in their family had no gender distinctions since both boys and girls learned how to do the same farm and home tasks.

Colfax, Louisiana, their hometown, had both a public elementary and high school for Negro children. Mary attended Grant Parish Training school from the first to the sixth grades, and for seventh

Mary Turner as an adolescent, third from the right, with her family. This picture was taken during her high school years.

through eleventh grades she went to Mary Graham High School. She graduated from high school in 1939.

Choice of the Nursing Profession

No one is quite sure why Mary selected nursing as her profession. Nor are they able to definitely explain why she decided to attend Brewster Hospital School of Nursing in Jacksonville, Florida. What is known is that Mary was 16 when her mother died. Before her death, Ellen Jury Turner experienced severe headaches that often required her to be in bed for a few days. Mary was similarly affected and her oldest daughter also experiences these debilitating headaches. She may have thought that in the profession of nursing she would learn and better understand what may have happened to her mother and how this increased knowledge could help her as well.

Her reason for choosing Brewster may have been influenced strongly by its financial policy. Once students were accepted into

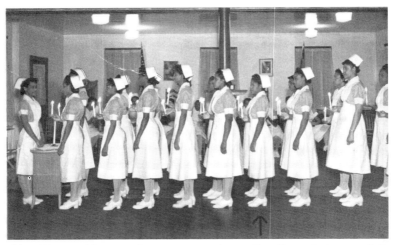

Mary Turner at her capping ceremony six months after entering nursing school at Brewster Hospital. She is the 6th from the left in the row nearest the camera.

the school's program, they were not required to pay for their education. While attending classes, students also worked in the hospital caring for patients. The services that student nurses rendered to the patients represented a *quid pro quo* between the administrators of the hospital and the enrolled students.

A Quiet Spirit in a Comforting Caregiver

MIGRATION TO SEATTLE

Entering the Brewster Hospital Nursing Program in 1942, Mary was a classmate of Rachel Suggs Pitts and one year behind Gertrude Robinson Dawson (both MMPNO members). Exactly how she fared during these years is unknown, but she graduated in 1945, passed state board examinations, and then worked at Brewster for a few months. Following graduation she married Aaron Stephens, who at that time was in the U.S. Army. In 1946, Mary migrated to Seattle with her classmate, Rachel Suggs Pitts. They were hired at Harborview Hospital before leaving Florida. Following his discharge from the U.S. Army, her husband, Aaron, joined Mary in Seattle where he obtained a job as an orderly at Harborview. After their daughter, Marilyn Stephens (Cooks), was born, they were together for a short period, but in 1949 they divorced.

Later in 1949, Mary was asked to join other Negro nurses in the area to form the Mary Mahoney Registered Nurses Club. She became a founding member along with four other nurses who had been in training at Brewster Hospital. About this same time, she was going through her divorce and found that membership in this organization served important professional, personal, and social functions for her. Furthermore, her daughter became a friend of other members' children, so that, when she needed help with childcare, her classmates and schoolmates provided assistance. MMRNC was a network of personal and professional support for Mary and for other members as well.

Mary Lanier in 1986 following her retirement from Providence Hospital, Seattle, WA. She worked there for 36 years.

After working at Harborview for four years, Mary transferred to Providence Hospital (also in Seattle), where she elected to work the graveyard shift, 11:00 p.m. to 7:00 a.m. She chose to be a float nurse, working on different floors or services throughout the hospital. She preferred nights because she could be home to see her daughter off to school and could be home when the school day ended. During the hours in between, she slept. She had other compelling reasons to work the graveyard shift as she told her children and MMRNC members. With fewer people on staff at night and few family members who visited then, racial incidents seldom occurred, enabling her to give nursing care in a climate of support. Marilyn as an adult provided an emotionally strong portrayal of her experiences while her mother participated in MMRNC. "As children of all of these nurses, we knew each other and socialized as a family. We celebrated special holidays, birthdays, high school graduations and departures for college. We also participated in parades and other social activities too. Having 12 other nurses as friends and family was a very meaningful experience for me and the other children," she says.

In 1951 Mary married Howard Lanier, a boilermaker who worked for King County. Three daughters were born to Mary and Howard. In order of their births they were Lillie Lanier (Flavors), Karen D. Lanier, and Pamela Lanier (Calloway). These three daughters, along with Mary's daughter, Marilyn, from her first marriage, still have homes in Seattle.

Mary remained a member of Mary Mahoney throughout her professional life. She worked as a staff nurse at Providence for 36 years, retiring in 1986 after completing a 40-year career as a professional nurse. While nursing fulltime for most of her adult life, she made time to enjoy her four daughters, five grandchildren, and 11 great grandchildren. She was especially proud of Janita Cooks, Arthur Cooks, Jr., Ferron Earl Flavors, Leslie Flavors, and LaNaya Flavors Hall.

Retirement and Respect

At her retirement reception, several nurses and other administrators of Providence Hospital spoke about her as the "quiet comforter and caregiver." But she, too, received the values of dedicated service and comfort, which she regularly provided to others, from her children, grandchildren, church members, and members of MMRNC (and MMPNO). Mary is remembered by her family and friends whose lives were touched by her quiet spirit and comforting care.

A Colored Girl Who Became a Professional Nurse

Rachel Suggs Jones Pitts

Imagine being born at a time and in a place where professional health care services were not available. Consider as well the lack of public elementary and high schools for Colored children; yet, at the same time and place, both health care services and public schools were available to White people. Rachel Pitts was born and spent nearly six years of her life in such an environment.

The Experience of Subordination to Whites

Lakeland, Georgia, her place of birth, was a community where "Colored folks" took care of one another. Racial segregation was so deeply entrenched into the culture that daily life for most Colored children and adults was separate and very distant from the lives of White people. The one exception was in work situations. Most of the adults in Rachel's community worked in the homes of White people or in settings where their work required subordination to White people. When some of these same adults attended church, visited with their neighbors, or went to the barbershop or beauty parlor, they interacted with and received services from Colored folks. Only among themselves did they experience treatment and feelings of being equal.

The fourth of five children born to Emma Johnson Suggs and Travis Suggs, Rachel's birth date is June 13, 1921. Her three older siblings in order of their births were JP (Joseph Paul), Pauline, and Ruby. Willie Mae is her younger sister. All are close enough in age that they were all at home together during their formative years. She vividly recalls what home and community life were like for her family.

Long before Rachel had words to convey her observations, she knew who the midwife was who delivered babies in different people's homes. She also knew who her father's Masonic Lodge (a fraternal organization for men) brothers were and she saw them visiting several different neighbors in the community. Most of all, she knew who her Sunday school teachers were and understood that some of these teachers taught them reading, writing, and arithmetic on days other than Sunday. At times it was difficult to distinguish regular school from Sunday school, especially when some of the same songs and Scriptures were read in weekday school classes. Later in life, she realized that these early experiences influenced her decision to become a professional nurse.

Emma Suggs was a domestic who took in washing and ironing for White families. She worked at home so that she could manage the children at the same time. When they were old enough, the children also helped their mother by doing some of the work. They washed on a washboard, not using an automatic washing machine, which was a process that required hard physical labor to scrub clothes and household items until they were clean. The main responsibility was their mother's, of course, including the task of ironing the clothes with heavy irons that were heated in front of the fireplace and on a wood-burning stove. The children helped pack in the wood to keep the fire burning and the irons hot.

Travis Suggs was a "pine chipper", a laborer who traveled into the woods each day to cut slits in the pine trees and place a tray in the slit to collect resin. This by-product was used to manufacture turpentine, paint, and perfume, among other products, although her father was not involved in the manufacturing process.

A Firm Religious Grounding

The hard physical work of both parents allowed the family to have adequate money to meet basic expenses for food, housing, and clothes. Their house was a small, wood-frame structure located in a dilapidated neighborhood. Children shared beds and bedrooms; therefore, they grew up being physically, and also emotionally, close, both within the family and in the community. During the week, everyone was busy helping to get the work done. On Sundays, church and Sunday school consumed much of the day.

A Colored Girl Who Became a Professional Nurse

Their father was Baptist, their mother Methodist. As Rachel later recalled, "My father had a 'born-again' experience in the Baptist Church. After that, Mother and all of us children attended the Baptist Church." The children's early attendance at Sunday school was followed, when they were old enough, by participation in the Baptist Young People's Union. Rachel also sang in the choir.

Many of the families in the area were members of the Baptist Church, gathering often on church grounds for potlucks, picnics, and other social events. The one-room school for Colored kids was also on the Baptist church grounds, but it was sponsored as well by other churches in the community. It included grades one through eight, with only one or two teachers and many students. She remembers "Scripture reading and many of the same songs sung in Sunday school were also sung at regular school." Rachel began attending school early because she knew the alphabet and could do the work expected of her.

Without television, once the workday ended, the children in the neighborhood played together. "We played things like hop scotch, blind man's bluff, and bat-and-ball games. As little girls, we played with grass dolls that we made ourselves because there was no money to buy such items. In the summer evenings, when the workday ended, many adults sat on their stoops or porches and watched the children play or played with us. My mother used to play baseball with us. Some of the other mothers played other games with us also."

DEATH OF A FATHER AND A MOVE TO A NEW HOME

When she was five and a half years old, her father became ill and unable to work. Traveling to Valdosta, Georgia, to see a doctor, her father learned that he had a blood tumor and that he had a short time to live. She remembers overhearing "adult family members talking about my dad's condition and I knew that he would not be with us very long. My father died within six months after he was diagnosed with this disease." Now, as a professional nurse, she believes that he "had leukemia but that was not the word that the doctor used who examined him."

As a member of the Masonic Lodge, her father had arranged to have the Masonic orphanage care for all five children, but when representatives from the Masonic Lodge came to take the children to the orphanage, "Mother could not part with us" and declined the invitation. Shortly thereafter, the Suggs family moved first to Naylor, Georgia, where her mother's best friend lived, and then to Jacksonville, Florida, where the maternal grandmother, Ella, lived. "Before our family arrived, my grandmother rented a house for us next door to her. We saw my grandmother anytime that we wanted to." This was a special treat for Rachel because her grandmother taught her how to cook, sew, knit, tat, and crochet. She has used these skills for her own pleasure and passed them on to her children and some of her grandchildren.

In Jacksonville, her mother continued working as a domestic but in living conditions that were much better in Florida than they had been in Georgia. Soon her mother established herself well enough that it was possible for the children to begin working in the homes of the families for whom their mother did washing and ironing. The children were also able to enter public school for the first time. "It was fun to be in school with lots of other children. In public school we still had chapel, scripture reading, and bible memory work. We also had school plays at Christmas and Easter time. Religion was part of school life."

Beginnings of Self-Sufficiency

At age 11, Rachel began working as a babysitter for one of the families for whom her mother worked. The family paid Rachel 35 cents a week for her labor. An assigned task was to clean the bathroom and kitchen, which included washing the floors. With no mop in sight, she did the job on her hands and knees. This effort made a favorable impression even on a neighbor, Mrs. Pinkney, across the street, who asked Rachel to work for her, too. Mrs. Pinkney, a registered nurse with a sick husband, needed someone to help her care for him. So, when Rachel was about 14 years old, she began providing care to Mr. Pinkney with his wife's help, continuing this work for about a year and a half. When Mr. Pinkney died, she dropped out of school for three months to help restore the house to the state it was in before his death. Years later, summarizing the effect of these work experiences, she said, "All of the children who worked outside of our home contributed to general household expenses. We were also

A Colored Girl Who Became a Professional Nurse

expected to buy our own shoes and clothes. Even today, it is easy to remember how hard I worked scrubbing floors on my hands and knees in order to earn the money that I had." She believes she became an excellent adult money manager because she was taught as a child to manage her money.

Her graduation from high school occurred on schedule in 1939 because she had made up the time lost while working full-time for the Pinkneys by going to summer school in another city. At the graduation exercise she realized that she had been so busy working that she had not participated in school sports or other extracurricular activities. However, these activities were of no interest to her, especially when she was busy taking the mathematics, foreign language, and science courses that prepared her to go to nursing school.

Entry into a Nurse-Training Program

She could not take that next step, however, without earning money. The opportunity that presented itself was the NYA (National Youth Auxiliary), one of the public works programs started during President Franklin Delano Roosevelt's term in office. (Most men entered the Civilian Conservation Corps, women the NYA.) From 1939 to 1941 she worked in hospitals, schools, and other businesses and saved enough money to enter nursing school at Brewster Hospital School of Nursing in Jacksonville. Entering in 1941, she was in a class of 12 or 13 Colored

Rachel Suggs at her high school graduation in 1939.

women with Caucasian instructors. This three-year diploma program included affiliation with Freedmen's Hospital (located on the Howard University campus) in Washington, D.C.

For the most part, she enjoyed being in nursing school, although the course work was hard and clinical practice extremely demanding. By the end of six months several of her classmates had either dropped out voluntarily or been dismissed. Some of their instructors were very nice; others were the opposite. At times, several students wondered if the unsupportive and mean-spirited instructors were trying to break their spirit and force them to leave the program. Fortunately, most of the remaining students successfully completed the program.

During the nursing-school program, three symbols marked significant milestones. These were receiving caps at six months, adding a narrow, black band to the cap after one year, a second a year later, and finally replacing the narrow bands with one wider black one just before graduation. They identified students' status in the program and they were also intended to be a motivation for reaching their goal of graduation.

Completing a clinical affiliation also represented another measure of professional success. At Freedmen's Hospital, Brewster students worked in pediatrics, psychiatry, and communicable diseases. Negro and White nurses and doctors provided instruction. Rachel and her fellow student nurses served only Negro patients, and they did have an opportunity to compare their nursing skills with those of students from Howard and other schools whose affiliations were at Freedmen's. The program was so demanding that few students had time to see the historic sites in Washington, D.C., but Rachel recalls that "during the time that we spent in D.C., I believe that it was as segregated as Florida."

A Secret Marriage and a Job in Seattle

In 1943, during her final year in the program, Rachel's high school boyfriend, Matthew Jones, asked her to marry him. She accepted and they were secretly married, although marriage was against school rules. They had not planned to get married when they did, but he was in the Navy, expecting to be sent overseas into combat any day.

A Colored Girl Who Became a Professional Nurse

The uncertainty of his situation led to their marriage on the last day of his leave. She wrongly believed their marriage could remain a secret. When she received a letter from a former classmate, addressed to Mrs. Rachel Suggs Jones, she was immediately called into the director's office and asked to explain herself. She told the truth about her marriage. The director's response pleased her; she was allowed to remain in school with six months of work to complete before graduation. Not only that, but when the director learned that her husband had gone to Texas immediately after they were married and that they had spent no time together, she gave Rachel two weeks off to go to Corpus Christi to visit her husband. After the visit, she contacted her letter-writing classmate to let her know of the outcome. Everyone knew that she was married; yet, she would still be able to become a registered nurse.

After performing well in the nursing program, in 1944 Rachel graduated and was asked to stay on and work as a graduate nurse. She did so and passed state board examinations in October 1944. In October 1945 her son, Anthony, was born, exactly nine months after she had visited her husband in Texas.

From 1945 until August 1946 she remained at Brewster Hospital while her husband was in the Far East war zone. Since he had embarked from Seattle, she wanted to relocate there so that they might have more time together whenever he returned to the States. She discussed this idea with the supervisor of nursing at Brewster, who was a friend of the nursing supervisor at Seattle's Harborview Hospital. The result was her being hired to work at Harborview.

When Rachel arrived in Seattle, she found that she had already been assigned to Harborview's communicable disease unit and that she could rent a room in Harborview Hall (the nurses' residence where other Negro nurses lived when they first arrived in Seattle). Katie Ashford, who had attended Grady Hospital School of Nursing and moved to Seattle some years before Rachel arrived, also worked on the communicable disease unit. They supported each other and got along well with other nurses on their unit. By the time Rachel was hired, most patients had become accustomed to seeing and receiving nursing services from Negro nurses.

Despite these positive signs, she quickly saw a few negative ones. According to her present memory, "In the 1940s, in Seattle, there was housing and employment segregation. Most Negroes lived in the Central Area of the city. Back then it was possible to spend the entire day downtown without ever seeing another Negro. In some of the department stores downtown, salespersons would give Negroes looks to let it be known that Negroes were not welcome."

Like other Negro nurses before her, Rachel was given her share of split shifts, nights, and evenings. However, she did not complain, partly because she lived alone since her son, Anthony, was in the care of her mother in Jacksonville and her husband was away at sea. Her salary had increased from $90 (after room and board) at Brewster Hospital to $230 (after room and board) at Harborview. Work and church consumed most of her time between August and November, when her mother brought Anthony to live with her in Seattle.

In 1947, when her husband returned and was discharged from the Navy, housing for Negroes was still very scarce. With the help of classmates, she was able to find a room to rent in the same Central Area building where two of her classmates, Gertrude Dawson and Mary Lanier, lived with their husbands.

Some months later, she worked in general medicine, serving as charge nurse on days when the head nurse was off duty. Although Rachel was never paid additional money for serving in this leadership role, the real pay for her was in having the respect from the head nurse signified by being selected for these increased responsibilities. It was also gratifying to successfully meet the expectations of patients, their family members, and other nurses on the unit. "It was a great experience and I took it very seriously."

A Founding Member of Mary Mahoney Registered Nurses Club

Rachel in 1949 at the founding of MMRNC.

In 1949, Anne Foy Baker invited Rachel to attend a meeting in her home to start a nurses' club. She eagerly accepted, partly because she already knew five of the 13 nurses who would assemble in Anne's home. From July 9, 1949, when the Mary Mahoney Registered Nurses Club was established, she attended meetings regularly. At each meeting, time was available to talk about conditions at work. In listening to these conversations and since Rachel's treatment at work was more positive than negative, she began to feel that she enjoyed a high level of professional and personal satisfaction in her life. She eagerly shared this information with the other nurses.

Struggles with Tuberculosis and an Unfaithful Husband

After his discharge from the Navy, her husband found work as a merchant seaman and later worked at the United States Post Office. With two incomes they could purchase their own home on Alder Street in Seattle; however, all was not well. Between 1948 and December 1949, Rachel felt frequent chest discomfort and had regular chest x-rays which showed a suspicious shadow in one area on her lung that had been there for some time. On December 23, 1949, after a routine chest x-ray, she was diagnosed with tuberculosis. She was not allowed to return to work. Having come for the x-ray while she was on her break, the doctor would not allow her to return to the floor to pick-up her personal belongings and make a smooth transfer of nursing responsibilities to another nurse. Fortunately, Mary Davis was on duty so that she could turn over the narcotics keys to Mary and discuss a transition of nursing duties. She remained as a patient at Harborview hospital until a bed was available at Firland Sanitarium (Seattle). During her one-year stay there she received the standard treatment of streptomycin, bed rest, and a therapeutic diet.

Her former nursing school roommate, Gertrude Robinson Dawson, kept her son until someone in Rachel's family could care for him. Eventually, her niece, who was just 18 years old, moved to Seattle to manage the home and to care for Anthony. Her husband continued to work full-time at the post office, but she learned on one of her visits home that he had developed an intimate relationship with her niece. This time, when she returned to Firland, she remembers, "I was the saddest person in the whole world. I cried many buckets of tears. I just never thought that my husband would get involved with my niece the way he did." (Rachel agreed to include this incident in her story because she realizes that similar incidents have happened to other people. She wants others to know how she coped, pulled her life back together, and went on to become the person that she is today. As with other disappointments in life, she found the strength to cope from her deep religious beliefs.) "At that time it was a real stigma among my family, friends, and culture to experience marital infidelity. There was no one for me to talk to. Everybody knew, but it was a hush-hush thing. I don't remember that there were any social workers at Firlands to provide counseling. I just had to work this problem out by myself." Furthermore, she was reluctant to discuss the problem with her minister. "It was one of the loneliest times of my life. But with the help of God, I pulled through."

Shortly after being discharged from Firlands, she and Matthew divorced. Since she was eligible for rehabilitation support from the Department of Labor and Industries, a caseworker encouraged her to seek a baccalaureate degree in nursing. Taking the suggestion, she applied and was admitted in 1952 to the baccalaureate program in the School of Nursing at the University of Washington. Her mother returned to Seattle from Jacksonville to help care for Rachel's son, Anthony, and remained until Rachel felt confident enough to balance the demands of being a student while continuing to work at Harborview.

Remarriage, Motherhood, and a Transforming Experience

In 1953 her life took another apparently positive turn when she met and married Lon Pitts. One year later their first daughter, Lalonai, was born. That event did not dissuade her from continuing either work or nursing school; consequently, in 1956 she both received her B.S. degree and was hired as a public health nurse by the Seattle Department of Public Health.

Between 1956 and 1958, on loan from the Health Department, she worked with Dr. Fox at the University of Washington, head of a virus-watch study. "Dr. Fox was one of the nicest professionals that I ever worked with. Even after the project ended and I returned to the Health Department, I consulted with him on a variety of topics." In 1958 her second daughter, Cynthia, was born.

A Colored Girl Who Became a Professional Nurse

A spiritual experience transformed her life in 1960. Today, she identifies herself as a born-again, spirit-filled Christian of the Pentecostal Church. The integration of this strong spiritual base with her devotion to caregiving has, she thinks, strengthened her effectiveness as a nurse. Although she does not push her spirituality on her patients, she brings to her practice of nursing a sense of serenity and peace that those who know and love the Lord immediately detect. "Religion is as much a part of me as being a female is," she proclaims.

In 1963 Rachel and Lon divorced. As she had done before, she relied on her faith in God to help her cope with this loss, continuing fulltime work at the Health Department in the roles as educator, counselor, and facilitator. In addition to working with individuals and families, she did school nursing and was a team member on the Sudden Infant Death Syndrome project, sickle-cell screening service, and genetic-counseling program. She also served as a facilitator on the maternal- and child-health group. In observing changes during her 30 years of service, she remarked, "The introduction of computers into the work setting hastened my exit from work. Sometimes, I observed nurses spending more time at the computer than they spent in the delivery of health care. It was an interesting transition to watch. I'm a 'people person' and I like to give hands-on care to people. I feel that I left at the right time."

Retirement and Continuing Service

Since retiring in 1986, she has continued to provide healthcare services to members of her family, members of MMPNO, members of her church, and others in the community. She makes time to enjoy her six grand-

Rachel Suggs Jones Pitts in 2000. She has been retired since 1986.

children. Her son, Anthony, has two girls, Jeanne and Mattchelle. Lalonai also has two children, Kristopher and Aderial. Cindy has two girls, Ginia and Leslie. "All of my grandchildren are very close to me and we spend as much time together as we possibly can. Holidays and birthdays are times when we gather as a family to celebrate life."

Her active membership in MMPNO has continued since 1949 and she remained active in Washington State Nurses and King County Nurses Associations until 1987. As part of her personal ministry, she attends professional meetings, where she makes presentations on loss, grief, spirituality, and other health-related topics. She has made presentations in various parts of the United States and in Europe.

"I continue to give health care services to members of my family, members of my church and others in the community who request help. For my services I gladly accept gratuities, but I would not refuse help to anyone on the basis of money. I was born to be a nurse and I will always give care as long as I can."

She recently celebrated her 79th birthday, saying, "I have lived through times when I was called Colored, Negro, Black, and now African American. No matter what name was used, I knew I was a nurse. In my own mind the most accurate description is 'Rachel, the nurse.'"

A Caring and Compassionate Nurse

Ernestine Rutledge Williams

During Ernestine's formative years in the town where she was born, family life centered on her father owning a grocery store. The three Rutledge boys, Leonard, Charles Jr., and Talmadge, worked with their father in the store, serving customers and delivering groceries by bicycle all over the community. Though none of the girls, Marjorie, Lydia and Ernestine, was ever asked to make home deliveries, they occasionally waited on customers during busy times. This store in Clearwater, Florida, has remained in the family for many years and is now run by a grandson.

Born April 23, 1922, Ernestine, the fourth of the six children, recalls many happy times in her growing-up years. "My mother was a housewife and church worker. She was a beautiful seamstress. For my eighth grade graduation, she made the white organdy dresses for all of the girls in my class. Mother also made robes for the church choir. She sang in the choir, was a member of the Stewardess Board, and helped organize church conventions. We girls also managed the house with our mother."

"Before I was in high school, my father built us a four-bedroom home. We still call this the 'Big House.' Many years later my sister, Lydia, moved back to live in our family home after her husband died. Dad was really proud of that home and our family had many happy times there."

"Our family was a member of Mount Zion Methodist/Episcopal Church and church was a very important part of our lives. My father was a deacon. His father was district superintendent of the Methodist Church and an uncle was a presiding elder of the Methodist Church. All of us children were involved in church and Sunday school and young people's Christian activities. As teens each of us took turns being superintendent of the Sunday school for one year. It was a wonderful experience to serve in that way. We did work in groups of four or five to prepare the church for the first Sunday services. We were paid to do that work. And that is the only employment that we girls had."

Outstanding School Performance

In addition to being active in church activities, she was involved in school activities. "I attended Curtis Elementary School, which was named in honor of a former principal of the school. After graduation from eighth grade, I attended Pinellas High School, which went from the ninth through the 12th grades. Only Negro children attended these elementary and high schools, and we had all Negro teachers. But those teachers really cared about us. They knew our parents and our brothers and sisters. They also lived in our community."

Relatively tall for her age and grade, Ernestine played forward on the basketball team. She was also a member of the debate team and she sang in the school choir. After school she was active in Girl Reserves (a Negro girl's equivalent to Girl Scouts), since Negro girls were not allowed to become members of Girl Scouts.

"Mrs. Vivian Henry was my French and social studies teacher and she was director of the choir. She took a personal interest in my development. She helped me select the courses that I would need to get into nursing school. I followed her advice and performed well in all of my subjects, graduating as valedictorian of my class. I really had to study hard. I stayed busy with schoolwork, church activities, and home responsibilities.

"As a child I lived across the street from a woman who was a public health nurse. At that time nurses wore blue uniforms with a white collar. This woman went out early in the morning and returned late in the evening. I told my mother that I wanted to be a nurse like our neighbor. Mother told this nurse that I wanted to be like her. On several occasions when I was older she took me in her car to visit patients. After that I never wondered what I would do. I wanted to be a nurse."

A Caring and Compassionate Nurse

More Outstanding Achievement in Nursing Training

Graduating in 1939 from high school at the top of her class, Ernestine knew about the Brewster Hospital program in Jacksonville, Florida, because she had a cousin who was a supervisor at that hospital. "My cousin Hettie Thompson Mills was the first Negro supervisor at Brewster. She married Dr. Roosevelt F. Mills. While we were students, they invited us to their home and gave us good food to eat." She was admitted to the Brewster Hospital School of Nursing in 1940. Large classes entered in fall and winter. It appeared that administrators expected that some students would drop out of school before completing this program. Since some of the teachers had reputations as "tough and mean," successful students had to learn survival strategies in order to get through the program.

Ernestine remembers the program as long on work and marked by symbols of transition. "The work was really hard but we learned a lot. Along the way we had real markers to indicate our progress. When we first arrived, we wore blue uniforms, black stockings, and black shoes. During this period we were referred to as 'probes' because we were exploring new territory. Senior students asked us to do different things for them. We washed their stockings or ran to the store to get sodas for them. We put up with that treatment because we knew that if we stuck to the program we'd have our turn to do this to other students."

After being in the nursing program for six months, students received plain, white caps in an impressive, candlelight ceremony. "Once we received our caps we wore striped uniforms with white aprons. We also got to wear white stockings and white shoes. As sophomores, students wore one narrow black band on their caps; juniors wore two black bands. Just before graduation we replaced the two bands with one wide black band. Doctors used these symbols to determine what help nurses could be expected to give when they cared for patients." One indicator of Ernestine's success in this stage of training was her election as class president.

That class was the first to complete an affiliation at Freedmen's Hospital on the campus of Howard University in Washington, D.C. "Before leaving for Freedmen's, the nursing supervisor, Mrs. Jones, told me that I should write or call her every two weeks to let her know how we were doing. Once I reached Freedmen's, I was supposed to meet the superintendent of nurses there, Mrs. Reva Speaks, to introduce the other nurses and myself. We followed these instructions to the letter.

"We traveled by train and everyone had berths to sleep in. We were really treated very well. I believe that someone had alerted the porters that we were nursing students. We got to eat in the dining car and when we tried to give them tips, they said 'Oh, no, you don't have to do that.' For some students, this was their first time sleeping in a berth and eating in the dining car of the train. It was a real treat for all of us.

"Once we arrived at Freedmen's Hospital, the nurses there were really impressed with our uniforms. We wore white stockings and white shoes. They still wore black shoes and stockings. We got along well together and things went smoothly for our class.

"Most of our instructors were White and our patients were Negro. We saw some of everything that we learned about in our textbooks. It was especially great to see people get well, and we'd roll them out in wheelchairs to go home. Of course, everyone did not make it, but, for those who did, it felt great to be a nurse.

"The most renowned physician was Dr. Charles Drew, a pioneering specialist in blood research. We learned directly from him how to administer blood transfusions to patients. In the laboratory he watched each one of us carry out this procedure until we had it perfectly correct. We really left knowing our stuff in that area.

"While there, we completed studies in medical/surgical nursing, communicable diseases, psychiatry, and pediatrics. Even though we were really busy, we had time to see well-known artists who visited Howard University's campus. We also got to see historic sites in D.C. I wrote to the superintendent of nurses every two weeks as I was expected to do. All of my classmates helped me get the letter together. We made steady progress and all of us successfully completed our affiliation. We returned to Brewster and shortly thereafter, in 1943 we graduated."

Ernestine keeps the certificate that indicates her having passed the state-board examination in 1943, still in the envelope it came in 57 years ago and in the same place for many years. She got it out to show it to me on the day of our interview. "When I received this certificate, I used a post card to write to my mother. On it, I said, 'I passed RN.' This was truly one of the happiest days of my life."

Entry Into the Professional Work World

"A classmate of mine was from Miami. I wanted to remain in the state. She talked about where she was going to practice and I decided to go with her. My first job was at Dade County Hospital, where I remained from 1943 to 1945.

"Our education occurred during a time of war. Once we finished school and passed our boards, we needed to register, saying that we would go to war if we were needed. Our teachers wanted us to be prepared to give efficient and appropriate care on the front lines if we were called to do so. I remember Dr. Drew telling us that in battle we would not have a lot of time to read directions. He expected us to learn and perform without having to read directions in order to know what to do. This was especially important in the administration of blood in crisis situations. Of course, we were always to take time to be sure the right blood was being given to the right person.

"Gertrude Robinson Dawson is responsible for my moving to Seattle. She wrote and told me about how much money she was making at Harborview. She also told me about the nurses' residence; so, I decided to move here. My dad told me to come home for a visit before going so far away and I did."

Ernestine began working nights at King County (now Harborview) Hospital on the medical floor. "Most of the patients were indigent. Whenever there were patients who did not want me to provide care to them, I had the supervisor talk to them. The supervisors usually just told them I was assigned to give this person care. In terms of my own feelings, I just considered the source and still gave the patient the best care I could give. At that period in our history, many Whites felt and acted on their feelings of being superior to Negroes."

Marriage, Children, and Increasing Professional Success

"After being in Seattle for a period of time, I learned about the Washington Social and Educational Club on 23rd and Madison Streets.

Well-known musicians came to that club and I spent a lot of leisure time there. The war was on and lots of soldiers came to the club. The sister of the owner of the club, Beatrice Sims, introduced me to Bertram (Buddy) Christopher Williams, who later became my husband. We were married in Bea's home on July 2, 1947." Bea felt a responsibility toward nurses, inviting those who could not be accommodated at Harborview Hall, where Ernestine lived, to live in her home. "She used to refer to us as her girls and she really looked after all of us." She also often invited Ernestine to dinner at her home on condition that Buddy accompany her.

After their marriage, both continued to work, with him on the day shift at Boeing Aircraft Company as a supervisor of materials, and with her at night in four Seattle hospitals throughout her career. They also became parents of three children: Barbara Jean (born January 23, 1948), Loretta (born October 23, 1954 and now deceased), and Bertram Jr. (born December 22, 1956). During these childbearing years, she responded to Anne Foy Baker's invitation to attend the 1949 founding meeting of Mary Mahoney Registered Nurses Club. She remained active in this organization until about 1960.

In 1950 Ernestine began working at St. Cabrini Hospital as a relief night supervisor. "This was a wonderful job and I loved doing it. During this same time, I worked part-time at Providence Hospital as a staff nurse on the medical/surgical floors. As a young nurse I really got some of my best experiences at Harborview. I remember one night when a fellow with a gunshot wound was brought to the hospital. He was hemorrhaging, and the interns were having trouble getting the blood transfusion set up. After being quiet and watchful for a minute or so, I said I knew how to

Ernestine Rutledge Williams in 1949 at the founding of MMRNC.

A Caring and Compassionate Nurse

do this. In a very few minutes I had gotten the IV going. After everything was going well, I told the interns that Dr. Charles Drew, a Negro physician who was a specialist in this area and the person who discovered how blood could be stored and later used for transfusions, taught me how to start IVs. Some weeks later these same interns came back and said they wanted to apologize because at first they did not believe me. I told them, 'That's on you, not me.'" She remains proud of her performance in that life-threatening situation. Ernestine recalled the reference made during her student days to the fact that under crisis situations she should be able to function in an efficient and accurate manner. She knew she had done so in this situation.

In 1960 she moved to Group Health Cooperative. "It is there that I was welcomed with open arms. In the supervisor's letter to me she stated that she wished that she had more nurses from Brewster Hospital. The nurses before me had established such a wonderful reputation that they made a place for me. At GHC the supervisor, Mrs. Mary Kay Gillespie, was fair and she really treated all of us very well. I remember one time shortly after I started working there that one White patient did not want me to start his IV fluids. He said to Dr. Robert Bourdeau, who was trying to draw blood on the other side, that he didn't want me to work on him. Dr. Bourdeau said, 'She already has your IV going. She's one of the best nurses that we have.' When he said that, I really tried even harder than before to always do a very good job."

Retirement and Pride in Lifetime Achievement

Ernestine stayed at GHC for 25 years, retiring in May 1985, for a career total of over 32 years, with specialties in medical/surgical and orthopedic nursing. "I never regretted my choice of a profession. Even when my brothers used to tease me and try to scare me about being a nurse, I paid no attention to

Ernestine Williams in 1985 at her retirement party.

them. Mother would always say to them, 'She can be whatever she wants to be.' I still cannot remember the name of the nurse who lived across the street from me when I was growing up. But she really influenced my decision to become a nurse."

Her husband retired from his position as a Boeing engineer where he rose to become a corporate manager of Equal Opportunity and Urban Affairs. They now enjoy retirement and their three grandchildren, Danielle Ruth Banon and Alexis and Michael Williams.

"I made my contribution to nursing by working on a daily basis, for many years, often in life-threatening situations. Even when patients did not want to receive care from me, I overlooked their prejudice and treated them the way that I hope to be treated, if ever I require health care in a hospital or other type of caregiving facility." Ernestine knows that her decision to move to Seattle from Miami was the right one. "I had the opportunity to uphold the 'Brewster nursing tradition' of performing at a very high level of professionalism in every hospital in which I worked. I also helped to forge a path for other Negro nurses who followed after me."

Throughout Ernestine's many years in nursing, she and other Negro nurses realized from professional experiences and from sharing information with one another, that the way they performed would have an effect on whether future Negro nurses would be given employment opportunities in the same hospitals or clinics. The very presence of one Negro was often translated by some decision-makers to be representative of our entire group or race.

Ernestine Williams in 1998, thirteen years after her retirement.

Upon reflection, Ernestine concluded: "At a personal level, I met Buddy who served his country while in the Army. He is a former Buffalo soldier who received two battle stars and an infantry badge for distinguished service. Together we worked as a team to raise our children and to participate in our grandchildren's development. We will continue to be active in our social and community activities and in church life. In these situations I can continue to be a caring and compassionate person."

Ira Gordon

Following considerable effort to find a family member or friend who knew this nurse, no one was found. If any reader can supply information about this nurse, it will be gratefully received and included in future editions of this book.

What is known is that in 1943 Ira Gordon became the first Negro nurse hired at Harborview Hospital. It is further known that she remained at Harborview for over 30 years until her retirement.

Ira Gordon in 1949 at the founding of MMRNC.

Mary Martyn

Following considerable effort to find a family member or friend who knew this nurse, no one was found. If any reader can supply information about this nurse, it will be gratefully received and included in future editions of this book.

What is known is that in 1941 Mary Martyn applied for a job at Harborview Hospital. She is known as the first Negro nurse to seek and be denied employment at Harborview. Prior to her death, she shared this information with Katie Stratman Ashford and Mary Marshall Davis Hooks.

Mary Martyn in 1949 at the founding of MMRNC.

Part II
Members of Mary Mahoney Professional Nurses Organization (MMPNO) for At Least One Quarter of a Century

Part 2 members: Standing, left to right: Gwendolyn Browne, Wilma Gayden, Rosa Young, Frances Demisse, Vivian Lee, Verna Hill. Sitting, left to right: Mary Lee Bell, Thelma Pegues, Lois Price Spratlen, Frances Terry, Muriel Softli. Not shown: Shirley Gilford, Elizabeth Thomas. (Photo Courtesy of Jannine Young)

A Long Road and a Late Entry into Nursing

Leola Sarah Fobbs Lewis
(1908-1998)

Gwendolyn Irene Lewis, Leola's daughter, provided the recorded interview on which this narrative is based. In addition, she has been available by phone to fill in details that were needed to adequately describe her mother's path to professional nursing. Quotations are her version of her mother's words.

On May 24, 1998, just one month away from her 90th birthday, Leola Lewis died, having completed two careers during her lifetime. Along the way she touched many individuals and was also touched by many others. She pursued a life of dedication to the ideals of education and professional service.

Leola followed a circuitous route to become a professional nurse. Graduating from high school in 1926, she left her birthplace of Jackson, Mississippi, and relocated in Coconut Grove, Florida. Holding various jobs and meeting the man she would eventually marry took her to different cities that included Baltimore, Maryland, and Seattle, Washington. At the age of 40, she entered nursing school at Montana State University in Bozeman, Montana. It was her late entry into nursing and the broad range of experiences in living and working that provided a solid foundation upon which she built her professional career in nursing. Her story illustrates how a person with unshakable determination encountered barriers and roadblocks and then developed creative responses to overcome those obstacles.

Leola Sarah was born to Laura and Robert Fobbs in Jackson, Mississippi, on June 24, 1908, one of five children, two boys and three girls. In order of their births they were Allen, Christopher Columbus, Alice, Leola, and Ethel. These children were close enough in age that all five were in the home for several years and attended Catholic schools in Jackson. Leola's mother was a seamstress and teacher, her father a drayman (truck driver) and legal advocate. Although he accompanied community residents to court when they got in trouble with the law, Robert Fobbs was not an attorney. Since law school was out of the question, he, like many others at this time who were interested in law, learned it through self-study. A very articulate man, he helped many people who needed legal-advocacy services but could not afford the fees of an attorney.

Education—An Important Home Value

Leola's mother, Laura, aspired to teaching, but teaching jobs for Negroes in the Mississippi of the early 1900s were in short supply. She found, however, that she could earn a decent income as a seamstress, an occupation that allowed her to be at home with her children and one that she continued even after the children left home. Education was an important value in the Fobbs' home, one that was concretely demonstrated by Laura's working long hours six days each week to enable all five children to attend Catholic schools. Each child shared their parents' emphasis on getting an education; each attended college. Allen Fobbs, Leola's oldest brother, was a professor at Alcorn College (Lorman, Mississippi); Christopher Columbus and Alice became public school teachers; Ethel was a social worker, and Leola became a registered nurse.

When Leola left home following high-school graduation to seek employment, she assumed that more opportunities for employment would be available to her in Florida than in her hometown. Furthermore, distant relatives there had agreed to help her find work. It took some time before Leola found a job working in a medical supply company, where the pay was very low but the work was steady. Sticking with this company for 19 years, including its relocation from Florida to Baltimore, enabled her to save money for her further education.

The move to Baltimore made her aware of the Johns Hopkins School of Nursing. It was so near yet so far! She had not saved enough money to support her attendance there, but its existence evidently strengthened her determination to attend college as soon as it was financially feasible.

A Long Road and a Late Entry into Nursing

Shortly after moving to Maryland, Leola met Howard Lewis, a taxi driver. He, too, wanted to improve his work situation and told Leola that he expected to hear from the Northern Pacific Railroad Company about his prospects for a job as cook on the train route between Baltimore and Seattle. Successful in his application, he began traveling regularly to Seattle. He told Leola about the beauty of the Pacific Northwest and stressed that there were at least two colleges in the area with schools of nursing. Realizing that if she moved to Seattle, she would still need to work before she could apply for nursing school, she read newspaper ads from the Boeing Company for Rosie-the-Riveter-type positions. In 1945, just as World War II was ending, Leola relocated to Seattle and secured a riveter position, making more money than she had ever previously earned. While working for Boeing, she began applying to schools of nursing in Seattle. Though there is no record of what happened to these applications, it seems likely that Leola either did not receive a response or was refused admission to the schools to which she applied. (The first Negro nurse was admitted to the University of Washington School of Nursing in 1946). However, by 1948, her savings were sufficient to enable her to enter college.

Admission to Nurses' Training

Before Leola resigned from her job at Boeing, her sister Alice married Reverend Richard Washington, an African Methodist Episcopal (AME) minister assigned to churches at Billings and Great Falls, Montana. On one of several visits there she learned that Montana State University at Bozeman had a nursing school. She requested, by mail, an admission application and completed it with one important exception—not identifying herself as Negro. At that time, applicants at most institutions were required to send a picture, but MSU had no such requirement. Leola's insight and her decision to leave unanswered the question about her racial identity proved to be crucial. Soon after applying, she was informed that she was admitted into the nursing program at MSU, but she said later, "You know, if that race thing had been filled in, I believe I wouldn't have been admitted."

Since administrators at the MSU School of Nursing did not know in advance that she was Negro, her arrival caused considerable commotion. One of the other instructors had a pronounced emotional reaction, which led her to blurt out, "We have never had a nigger at Montana State; no nigger is going to attend this school and no nigger is ever going to graduate from Montana State." Leola responded to this person's outburst by saying, "The NAACP sent me here to go to school, and I'm staying." Apparently, Leola's not wholly truthful but justifiable and expedient response was sufficiently convincing. The staff proceeded to process her admission.

For many, many years Leola told of her admission to MSU and the responses from staff and students to her presence there, responses ranging from hostility to curiosity ("Montana State students had not seen that many of us. At first they were real curious.") to friendliness. She credited Dean Sherrick, a White woman, with providing the necessary leadership to staff, to students, and to her, personally, helping everyone to face the challenge of Leola's being the only Negro in the School of Nursing. Dean Sherrick assumed an activist's role in working to retain Leola in the nursing program, advising her to remain calm when she encountered overt expressions of racism in the classroom or in the clinic setting. She encouraged Leola to call upon her instructors and classmates as sources of support, although, in the beginning, they were of limited value to her. After being in the program for some time, Leola realized that she had gained the respect of several of her classmates and some of her instructors. As she reflected on this experience of many years ago, she said, "One girl used the term *nigger* when she was talking to some of us. Then she apologized. Another classmate said, 'Leola is one of us.'" This awareness boosted her ego, helping her to try even harder than before to succeed.

There were other circumstances that helped Leola to remain in school. They included the presence of her sister and brother-in-law in Montana, her marriage to Howard, and the increased self-confidence she gained as a mature student in the nursing program. Alice and her husband, Robert, visited Leola whenever they could. Leola also visited them in their home, especially during the early weeks of her adjustment to the program. The spiritual guidance they provided continued to be a source of real strength and support for her throughout her life. Leola recalls the frequent telephone conversations with her sister and brother-in-law, which enabled them to pray together for Leola's continuation of her journey toward becoming a professional nurse. Even after finishing nursing school, the three of them often continued the telephone prayers that they began while Leola was at MSU.

Marriage and Continued Study

Leola and Howard Lewis were married on November 28, 1948, just after she began nursing school. The demands of his work and her academic responsibilities prevented them from seeing each other on a daily basis. However, they exchanged letters often and visited when time and money allowed. She credits this emotional bond and support from him as a major reason for her remaining in the nursing program until graduation, although she does not discount the continuous support from family members and Dean Sherrick, who remained one of her role models throughout her life.

Her emotional maturity also served her well. Older than some of her instructors and most other students in the program, she was able to endure the rejection and isolation which she initially and periodically thereafter experienced from instructors and fellow students. She insisted later that a dream had been very important to her survival, one that made attainment of a goal through constant application of energy and determination extremely vivid to her. That dream left her with the conviction that one should let nothing stand in one's way of achieving a goal.

Gradually, the attitudes of colleagues and instructors changed for the better, a fortuitous development that she could also take in stride. One student who stands out in Leola's memory came to her prior to graduation to apologize for the way she had reacted to Leola's presence throughout the past three years. She admitted that she had really thought that Leola didn't deserve to be in the nursing program. But Leola had proven her wrong. She hugged Leola and acknowledged that she was wrong in behaving as she had for so long.

By the time Leola entered the public health rotation, she felt very well prepared to provide high quality health care to patients in rural Montana settings. After her hospital-based experiences that required two years of great effort and tension, she needed a reprieve; however, she still needed to confront patients' doubts about her race. She was often asked by rural patients, "What are you?" She realized that these individuals were unsure of her ethnic-racial identity, especially because Leola was fair-skinned. She responded by being direct and friendly. Her standard response was, "I am Negro and I am here to provide nursing care to you." Most patients accepted her care without further questions.

Children by Adoption

After completing and passing the state board examination, Leola realized that both age and the residual effects of a bus accident prevented her from having children. Over the next several years, she and Howard adopted three children, Leola Howard, Robert Erskine and Gwendolyn Irene. All of the Lewis children had the opportunity to attend college, although only two did. Leola Howard went to Ohio State University but did not complete her degree. She did, however, become an administrator in the personnel division of Dow Chemical Company. Gwendolyn Irene completed degrees at MSU in petroleum and general engineering. One of the ironies of Gwendolyn's experience at MSU is that in 1982 she, too, left the race question unanswered on her application. When she arrived on campus, an instructor again made the statement which was later retracted, that her admission was a mistake. Robert Erskine Lewis is the owner/operator of a trucking company in Seattle. These adults, and Gwendolyn in particular, retell with delight the story of their mother's experience in nursing school.

Leola Fobbs Lewis as a young professional nurse in the early 1950s.

A Long Road and a Late Entry into Nursing

Nursing in a Hospital Setting and in Private-duty

After completing her nursing program and returning to Seattle, finding work was a real challenge for Leola. Eventually, in the mid-1950s she was hired at Group Health Central Hospital. She discovered very limited opportunities for advancement there. Despite these limitations, Leola rose to the rank of charge nurse; however, the demands of work life were sufficiently great and the rewards so small that Leola decided to work part-time as a private-duty nurse which she continued until 1970. This allowed her to spend more time with her children and husband.

Satisfactions of Later Life, Clouded by Alzheimer's Disease

When she retired from nursing in 1970, she traveled with her family throughout the United States, Canada, and Mexico. She said that the later years of her life were full of happiness and satisfaction, especially because of the ways her children structured their professional and personal lives. They were a source of joy for her as long as she was aware of their activities. Following the death of her husband in 1989, she began exhibiting signs of Alzheimer's disease, receiving care in a long-term GHC facility—Kelsey Creed, in Bellevue, Washington.

An early member of Mary Mahoney Registered Nurses Club, she remained an active member well past her retirement from nursing. She was also a life member of NAACP, the organization she credited with contributing more to her success as a professional nurse than any single person ever had. Indeed, her claim that she was sent to that school by the NAACP served her well. She remained at

Leola Fobbs Lewis in 1959 at a meeting of the Mary Mahoney Registered Nurses Club.

MSU because no one bothered to investigate her claim. In truth the claim was baseless, except from divine inspiration, which was all she needed. She substantiated that inspiration by remarkable perseverance, prayer, and performance, qualities that sustained Leola on the long road to nursing and a very satisfying personal and professional life.

Love, Learning, and Living Life as My Mother Taught Me

Thelma Jacobs Pegues

Early Learning

Thelma says of life in her hometown, Hattiesburg, Mississippi, "My education began long before I ever stepped into a public school." She recalls houses in her neighborhood that stood like matchboxes on stilts that supported and protected them from flooding whenever the nearby creek rose to floor level. Her grandmother lived just up the road, on a farm where she raised chickens and bees. From an early age her mother spent hours with her and her brother reading to them and teaching them how to cook very simple dishes like eggs, oat cereal, and pancakes. Learning was the centerpiece of their activities. Singing was the method her mother used to make learning fun. She and her brother played counting games often enough with their mother that Thelma learned to count to 100. They learned the alphabet by singing, too. She often practiced reading while her mother brushed and later braided her hair. Tears come to her eyes when she speaks about these enjoyable times of learning with her mother.

Born in her parents' home in Hattiesburg, Mississippi, on May 13, 1921, Thelma was the first child and only daughter born to Leuvenia Putman Jacobs and Eugene Jacobs. Her brother, Eugene Jacobs Jr., is 13 months her junior. The only two children in their family, they have always been very attached to each other.

Her mother was an elementary school teacher who had completed the two-year teacher-education program at Tougaloo Normal School in Mississippi. Her father was called to the ministry when Thelma was very young. In those days many Baptist ministers did not complete formal studies in a seminary; instead, they studied the Bible on their own and went about preaching wherever they found work. After his calling, he left the family and traveled to Kansas City, Missouri, where he pastored a small church, although he kept in regular touch with the family by letter and later sent for them to join him in Kansas City. His absence did not have significant negative effects because of the close relationship the children had with their mother and grandparents.

Thelma Jacobs in childhood.

All of their neighbors were Negroes which was normal for that time when segregation laws required separate drinking fountains, restrooms, and entrances in some public buildings. Thus, until she was six years old, she had no contact with White people.

After teaching elementary school during the day, her mother turned her attention to Thelma, telling her, "You are dark-skinned. Your hair is short and it will not grow. But you are very smart, and I want your beauty to shine through your brightness. Your brother is fair-skinned, and he will make it in this world by his charm and good looks." Thelma now says that her mother was visionary; her predictions have come to pass.

Eugene never finished college but went into the armed services and learned a trade. When he was honorably discharged, he got a job with the federal government and later worked for the Seattle Housing Authority as a foreman for the painting department. Now retired after a successful career, he and his family enjoy a comfortable life, living near Thelma and seeing her often.

Rewarding School Experiences

Building on the study habits instilled by her mother, Thelma has always been a good student. Before leaving Mississippi for Kansas

Love, Learning, and Living Life

City, Missouri, she could read. She knew many of her multiplication tables and could write in cursive. Once her family arrived in Kansas City, she entered public school, spending only a few days in the first grade. As soon as her teacher discovered that she could read, she was moved to the second grade and completed grades one through five in Kansas City.

Shortly after they arrived in Kansas City, the children's mother looked for a teaching position. At that time, married women were not allowed to work as teachers in Missouri; however, she was able to find a teaching position in Kansas City, Kansas, just across the river from Missouri.

After the family was somewhat settled in their new home state, Thelma's father moved to Phoenix, Arizona, where he was called to pastor a much larger church. Thelma's mother decided that she and the two children would remain in Missouri, although, during several summers, they traveled to Phoenix to be with their father. Her mother, however, preferred to live in Kansas and teach school rather than serve in the role of a preacher's wife.

After being in Missouri for several years, her mother became very ill. Thelma was never informed of her mother's diagnosis, but her mother's illness made it necessary for the children to live in a Catholic orphanage. While there, the nuns discovered that Thelma was an excellent student. Having learned many of the Psalms and other parts of the Bible, she was often asked to recite Bible passages for the Mother Superior when she visited the orphanage. Her performance won her praise from the nuns and other students and a reward of five cents, which was enough for her and her brother to purchase a peanut-butter ribbon-candy stick and divide it between them. They walked back from the corner store to the orphanage together, happily eating their candy. Another of her prizes for outstanding Bible study was the opportunity to have music lessons, taught by one of the nuns. How she enjoyed this added attention! Though they missed being with their mother, they realized that they received very good care in the orphanage.

When Thelma was 10 years old, their mother's death initiated a devastating and disruptive period in the children's lives. They had to move to Arizona to live with their father. Never before had they lived with their father for long periods. Growing even closer to each other and with the help of members of her father's church and other family members in the area, they made a successful adjustment to their new home and remained in Phoenix until Thelma's sophomore year of high school. Still with good study habits and the self-confidence cultivated in the orphanage, she was recognized and rewarded in Phoenix for her outstanding academic performance.

Honor Student, Entrepreneur, and Wife

During her sophomore year, Thelma went to live with her mother's brother and his family in Chicago, where she completed high school at Wendell Phillips High and graduated as class salutatorian. That honor resulted in a Delta Sigma Theta Sorority scholarship to Dillard University (New Orleans). Before leaving for college and knowing that she would need money for books, room and board, and other necessities, she completed a course in cosmetology. She established a beauty shop in the attic of her dormitory with permission from the university administration, as well as maintaining the B-or-better average required for her tuition scholarship.

During her first three years at Dillard as an honor student, she met J.D. Pegues, who eventually became her husband. She then had competing loyalties among work, study, and being in love. Her marriage in 1942 occurred just one year before graduation and was kept a secret until her graduation because, at that time, married students could not live in the dormitory.

During Thelma's senior year at Dillard, J.D. Pegues, whose nickname was "Piggy," moved from Chicago to Seattle. World War II was going on, so he worked in a defense job at the shipyard in Bremerton. After the war, he found a job at Boeing in Seattle. Following graduation in 1943, Thelma joined Piggy in the Pacific Northwest. She had never been to that part of the country before and the long train trip gave her an opportunity to see its beauty.

Once together in Seattle, they had a very difficult time finding a place to live because of segregation. For a while, they lived in one room of a hotel in the Central Area, where most Negroes were forced to live. After completion of the housing project in the Duwamish Bend section of Georgetown in Seattle's south end, they found a one-bedroom apartment there.

Love, Learning, and Living Life

Rejection and Disappointment

After getting settled in the apartment, Thelma sought employment. She had submitted the appropriate papers to a clearinghouse in Muncie, Indiana, and learned that the BA (in pre-med) degree from Dillard entitled her to be a certified medical technologist. She thought these qualifications would enable her to get a job in a hospital laboratory or in a private laboratory. After a valiant try, she was rejected every place where she applied with the upfront explanation, "We never hire Negroes." She had anticipated having some trouble finding a job but never dreamed that *no one* would hire her. Those first weeks in Seattle were frustrating and disappointing for Thelma.

Fortunately, "Piggy" had learned a trade and was working full time at Boeing. They had no children; so, life was not too hard for them. Nevertheless, she abandoned her dream of becoming a doctor, deciding instead to enroll in graduate school in microbiology. She had no problems in gaining admission to the graduate school at the University of Washington; however, she then learned that she was essentially invisible. Other students and the professors "never paid any attention to me." When she sought an appointment with professors to clarify new concepts, she was made to wait for weeks before anyone would meet with her. After six weeks, with no appointments with professors, Thelma knew that she was going to fail and she did, for the first time in her life. Before leaving the University, Thelma met with an advisor and recounted her experiences to her. While this was no help to her, she later learned that teaching assistants were assigned to assist future students, an institutional change that occurred, she now thinks, partly at her expense.

Beginnings of Success

She also remains convinced that she could have tolerated the rejection or inattention from other students, but the combination of lack of help from professors and rejection from students were too much to endure. She retreated to her home where "Piggy" remained her staunch supporter, helping her gain the emotional strength to begin thinking about getting a part-time job. She also drew strength from her faith in God, the members of Mt. Zion Baptist Church, and from volunteer work that she did in the community. Still, Thelma knew she really wanted to use her knowledge and skills working in a professional role, as she had been prepared to do. Concluding that this was not to be, she sought employment at Harborview Hospital and took a job in central supply. Harborview, a county hospital, was one place where Negroes could find work, but she never attempted to get a job there as a laboratory technologist. Instead, she applied for and was hired as a nurse's aide.

Thrilled to be working part-time, as she desired, she did not dwell on the fact that she had a college degree and should have been hired as a laboratory technologist. Instead, she threw her energy into learning as much as she could about every aspect of her nurse's-aide job. Soon, she knew all of the names of instruments and what they were used for in surgery, how to assemble surgical packs and other supplies needed for various procedures, and the labeling and storage system for autoclave sterilization. She loved the recognition from doctors and nurses who came to recognize her skills and talents as a nurse's aide familiar with equipment on the tray as well as their uses on the hospital ward. Soon, she was promoted to the level of a practical nurse and remained in this role until she resigned.

Eventually, Thelma met three Negro nurses employed at Harborview Hospital, Gertrude Dawson, Celestine Thomas, and Sadie Berrysmith, all charter members of MMRNC. Gertrude Dawson, recognizing Thelma's full potential, was the first person to tell her that she should become a registered nurse. Soon after that encouragement, Thelma and "Piggy" heard their minister encouraging men to "send your wives to school. They live longer than we do and they need to be able to care for themselves and their family if we die first." During that same week, in 1950, she heard radio announcements about a shortage of nurses. The ads encouraged students over 35 years old to become practical nurses and those under 35 to become registered nurses.

Thelma told "Piggy" that she really wanted to become a registered nurse since she was 29 and felt certain that she could successfully complete all work to attain that goal. He agreed, so she applied for admission to undergraduate program in the nursing school at the

Love, Learning, and Living Life

University of Washington and was admitted, the fifth African-American student to enter that program. But soon after beginning the first of 17 academic quarters, she learned that she was pregnant. Happy about this development, she called the dean and planned to drop out. The dean, however, encouraged her to remain in school until the quarter ended, which she did. She remained out of school for one and a half years until her daughter, Linda, was old enough for day care.

Completion of a Nursing Degree

Thelma Jacobs Pegues in 1955 at the Harborview Division of the University of Washington School of Nursing.

Returning to the University in 1953, she completed her undergraduate degree at the end of two years. Although she found the instructors attentive and supportive of her career aspirations, she received very few A's, even though she knew she had performed as well as or better than some of her White classmates who received consistently higher grades. This observation bears out what other African American nursing students who preceded her in the nursing program also think; they were not evaluated fairly for their academic and clinical performances.

Only one major racial incident occurred while she was completing her clinical rotation at Harborview Hospital. One morning when Thelma entered the clinical setting with her White classmates, she realized that she had been assigned four patients and the other students were assigned only two. She went to the head nurse and asked why. The instructor replied, "You know why." Thelma said, "No, I don't." After several of these do-don't exchanges, the head nurse said, "Because you are Negro and you've worked as a nurse's aide". Thelma left the clinical unit and went to get Florence Gray, the clinical dean, who was in an office across the street from the hospital. As a result Dean Gray came to the unit and spoke with the head nurse, who changed her assignment to be consistent with those of her classmates.

Aside from this incident, which was not the fault of her classmates, she found the other students to be friendly and supportive. They shared notes if any one missed class and studied together whenever convenient. Over the past 44 years since graduation, Thelma has remained in contact with several of them; indeed, the entire group of former classmates who live in the Puget Sound area attempt to get together socially at least every 12 to 18 months.

A Nursing Career and Family

After completing state board examinations, Thelma joined Mary Mahoney Registered Nurses Club, which was a high point in her career. These nurses were role models for her while she pursued her studies at the university. She is proud of the fact that for more than 44 years she has been an active member of MMPNO. She also joined Washington State Nurses Association and later she was selected for membership in Sigma Theta Tau, the national honorary society in nursing.

Throughout the period 1955 to 1969, when three (Cheryl, Harvey, and Rodger) of her four children were born, she gave priority to raising her family. Once able to make an appropriate babysitting arrangement, she worked evenings or weekends on various services at Harborview Hospital and was appointed instructor of in-service education at Harborview, the first African American nurse to serve in this role. Her rise from nurse's aide to instructor especially delighted her.

Another Outstanding Achievement

As a consequence of her successful performance, her supervisor encouraged her to enter graduate school. Following this suggestion, she applied at the University of Washington and was quickly admitted. Not only that but, to her surprise, Thelma learned that she could be paid by the U.S. government to learn. Like many other nurses, she was granted this support. She ran home to tell Piggy that not only would she be in graduate school, but she would also receive a stipend for tuition, books, and living expenses. She wished many a day that she could "talk to my mother to tell her, 'You were right! I am now being paid to learn.'"

Most of the time being in graduate school was a delight, but there was one small crisis. One night she boohooed and cried because she could not get all the reading done. Graduate study was a hard job. Piggy got up out of bed and reminded her, "You're being paid to learn. You shouldn't use time on the job crying." Years later, they laughed about this incident, but it wasn't funny at the time.

In August 1969, Thelma completed graduate school with a 3.89 grade point average (on a 4.0 scale) and a Master's in Nursing. The following June, she marched in the graduation ceremony wearing the beautiful Master's of Nursing cap and gown that signified her achievement. This was vindication enough for having been flunked out of the microbiology program earlier.

She anticipated that she would return to Harborview as the in-service supervisor, but to her surprise and disappointment, her job had gone to another nurse. Feeling this blow to her ego, she sought out her graduate advisor and received a great deal of help from her in finding a job. After many interviews, Thelma joined the St. Francis Cabrini Hospital (Seattle) staff as in-service supervisor. Both the help she had received from the graduate advisor and the job thrilled her. For the first time in her professional life, she received the salary that she requested, which was $10,500 per year with one month paid vacation. She flourished in this position, once again working in the presence of nuns and feeling secure in this setting. In her teaching role, she became well known to doctors and nurses in the hospital and in the community. She remained in this role for only one year because a group of African-American physicians asked her to apply for a teaching position advertised by Seattle Central Community College. She followed through at their urging and was appointed clinical instructor.

Working at SCCC in a program for non-traditional students who were mature, often low-income individuals, she flourished, and drew upon earlier experiences at Harborview and in other settings to develop relevant and successful learning modules for students. She also enjoyed developing curriculum content for theory courses. Among the first class of 30 students to complete the program, 29 passed state-board examination. She recalls, "Several of these students told me they had never before received instructions from an African American. I know I made a significant contribution in that program."

Also in 1969, the Western Interstate Commission for Higher Education launched an initiative to increase ethnic-racial content in nursing programs. She represented SCCC in this project, along with many other nurses from different nursing schools in the area, working with the project director, Marie Branch, to assist in the development of curriculum content. An article bearing her name, "Physical and Psychological Assessment of the Black Patient," appeared in *Washington State Journal of Nursing*, Special Supplement, 1979 (pp. 4-8). Many of the written documents that were developed during this project do not bear her name, but she and other nurses in the Puget Sound area were active contributors to the success of this project.

Career Reflections and Retirement Activities

When "Piggy" was diagnosed with cancer, she took a leave of absence from SCCC to care for him. Following a long illness, he passed away in 1981, and Thelma returned to SCCC, continuing to develop new curricula. She retired in 1986.

During her 17-year tenure at SCCC, she had only one negative racially based experience— "the darkest, most negative experience of my professional nursing career," as she tearfully termed it, and one that she cannot talk about. Instead, she prefers to emphasize the positive: "I have been an excellent nurse, and nursing has been good for and to me. Throughout my professional career in nursing, I have worked with students and helped them learn the content needed to be successful in nursing. I have tutored nursing students in MMPNO and others who asked for help. I intend to continue in this helping role as long as I can be of service to students. I am no longer active in Washington State Nurses Association or in Sigma Theta Tau, but I read any materials that are sent to me by those organizations. I love nursing and never once regretted that I did not become a doctor. Nursing served me very well.

Love, Learning, and Living Life

"Now that I am retired I remain very active and I am extremely satisfied with my life. One of the activities that helped me adjust to widowhood was being a volunteer for the American Association of Retired Persons. I served as the Assistant State Director for four years, as state trainer for four years, and as national trainer for one year. As national trainer, I traveled all over the United States, putting on training sessions. I have had experiences where, upon my walking into a room, the attendees started clapping. These volunteers for AARP knew that I came well prepared with appropriate overheads and handouts. My voice is loud and they did not need to strain to hear me. I have had similar experiences at the state level. I never agree to do anything that I don't enjoy doing. So I learn what I need to know to engage those who come to hear me. My experiences in AARP truly helped me adjust to being a widow. Now I attend AARP meetings in the Central Area in the chapter that I founded. It's gratifying to see how this chapter has grown." Thelma added that she also gets to see other residents of the community whom she would not otherwise see if she did not attend AARP.

She further summarizes her retirement experiences thus: "I am very active in MMNPO and I intend to remain active until I can no longer do so. In 1997-98, I took on the task of developing the necessary papers for MMPNO to become a 501(c)3 non-profit organization. I had never done anything like this before. But I read and learned everything that I needed to know to successfully carry out this responsibility.

"In 1999, I served as the chairperson of educational workshops for my sorority, Delta Sigma Theta. In January, 1999, I was asked to chair Seattle Delta Sigma Theta Alumnae Chapter's forward thrust mental health program on clinical depression for the community. Our national headquarters requested that chapters provide one or more programs relevant to the needs of our community. At the regional meeting, our chapter, Seattle Alumnae, won first prize for the poster we developed to represent, in pictures and text, aspects of the clinical depression workshop. This was such a gratifying activity to do, especially working with very talented and coordinated committee members, that we have already begun work on the next workshop, which will take place later this year.

"Since joining Mt. Zion Church in 1944, I have been active in religious education. I served as superintendent of Sunday school for over a decade. More recently I have been president of the Women's Ministry. In sum, my mother was absolutely right. I have used my love of learning to contribute to the development of others and myself in my personal, professional, organizational, and community life. Recently, I purchased a computer and I am taking classes because I, too, want to be computer literate. It will take me a long time to become computer savvy. But this is purely for my own enjoyment, just as playing the piano is.

"Currently, I enjoy excellent health. At age 79, I am able to remain in my own home, and I am independent in all of my daily activities. As long as I maintain my mental and physical health, I intend to continue learning new things. And whatever it is that I learn, I will always be willing to share my information and knowledge with others.

Thelma Jacobs Pegues in December of 2000. She has been retired since 1986.

"As I think back on my early years in Seattle, they were very difficult ones for me, but it was difficult for most Negroes at that time. There was a shortage of housing even when there were jobs to be had. Segregation was everywhere, and people did not try to disguise their feelings towards us. Even the School of Nursing, a state institution, did not admit its first African American student until 1946. I'm glad that I kept trying until I got the education I sought."

Life in Seattle is much better now than it was 57 years ago, when Thelma first arrived, but, even now, there are still barriers to overcome. As the 21st century begins, racial bias still affects the lives of African Americans and other ethnic persons of color. Thelma's life offers hope for success and fulfillment for those who learn to pursue their dreams in the face of significant obstacles.

A Nurse and a Community Activist

Willa Theresa White Lee
(1922-1999)

Willa Theresa White was born on September 9, 1922 in Henning, Tennessee, the first and only daughter of Willa Young and Charles Allen White. Preferring to be known as Theresa both then and throughout her life, she spent her first 17 years in that town, located approximately 60 miles north of Memphis, Tennessee. Later, she enjoyed telling people that she grew up in the same town and neighborhood where Alex Haley, the author of *Roots* (1976), lived and is buried. (In 1991, when Haley served as the keynote speaker for the Metropolitan Seattle Urban League's fund-raising dinner, he recognized Theresa in the audience and acknowledged their being childhood playmates and longtime friends. This public recognition delighted her.)

Growing up in a Pleasant Home

Her father worked installing gambling machines on boats and luxury ships, an occupation that required him to spend a considerable amount of time away from home. Theresa's mother was a music teacher who charged 25 cents a lesson. The family lived in what she recalled as "a nice, large home," a place where many members of the community often congregated to attend social

(Willa) Theresa White as a young girl about three years old.

functions. Since her mother was Catholic and her father Episcopalian, members of both churches were among these guests.

This kind of congeniality was also reflected in a decision about her church attendance. With her father frequently away, she attended the Catholic Church with her mother, although the family would later become members of an Episcopal Church.

When it came time to think about school attendance, her grandfather felt that Theresa seemed very bright and ready to learn. He tried to enroll her in a public school, but because she was not yet old enough, she was enrolled instead in a Catholic school where she continued until high school graduation in 1939.

College Attendance and Early Marriage

Immediately thereafter, Theresa entered Henderson Business School in Memphis, conforming to her parents' desire that she acquire skills needed to find work and care for herself. She successfully completed the business courses and soon left home for Southern Illinois University, in Carbondale, only a three-hour drive from Henning and where she completed the first year of college. Relatives in Carbondale allowed her to live with them while she attended college. Before the second year began, she dropped out of school to work for what was planned as a short period. Instead of returning to school, she met Meredith Louis Lee when he and another U.S. Army buddy were visiting in Illinois. Their courtship began quickly and culminated on July 19, 1943, when they were married in Seattle. It was a move across the country dictated by Meredith's being stationed at Camp Jordan in Seattle.

Theresa arrived in Seattle at a time when few Negroes lived there and legal segregation existed in housing and employment. Even the Armed Services were segregated, with Camp Jordan where Negro soldiers were housed and Fort Lawton for Whites. (In 1948 President Harry S. Truman signed Executive Order 9918, mandating desegregation of the armed services, although legal segregation continued throughout the United States in housing and employment until the Civil Rights Act was passed in 1964.) They found a place to live in the Central Area of Seattle.

A Nurse and a Community Activist

In early childhood Theresa had known she wanted to become a nurse, although her mother wanted her to become a doctor. Her father was the one who encouraged her to go to business school, mindful that employment in civil service settings would more likely be governed by greater equity, fairness, and work opportunities than were prevalent in the private sector. She complied with her father's wishes, all the while maintaining her plan to become a nurse.

Hospitalization and the Dream of a Nursing Career

In 1943 Theresa delivered her first child who lived only a few days. Complications associated with the birth required that she have lengthy care. Since Meredith was in the Army, and unable to care for her and no family member lived nearby, she remained in the hospital (Harborview in Seattle) for nearly a full year. Even after her discharge from the hospital, she continued to receive daily care through the outpatient clinic. During this hospitalization she closely observed nurses at work, other patients, their family members, and doctors, observations that reinforced her interest and determination to become a registered nurse.

While a patient at Harborview, she also met Ira Gordon, the first Negro nurse to be hired there, as well as Katie Ashford and Mary Davis Hooks, all later to become founding members of the Mary Mahoney Registered Nurses Club. She continued to see these nurses when she returned to receive care in the outpatient clinic.

When Theresa became healthy enough to work, she was hired as a nurse's aide by Mrs. White, a nurse administrator at Harborview, and worked in this role until Edison Technical School (in Seattle) established its Licensed Practical Nurses Program. With Mrs. White's assistance in gaining admission, she completed the program, passed the examination, and became a licensed practical nurse at Harborview.

After his honorable discharge in 1946, Meredith, who had worked as a barber while in the service, opened and operated his own barbershop. According to Cevesus, their daughter (born in 1949), "My father's first barbershop was in Chinatown. This was in the 1940s when train travel brought porters and other African Americans into that area of the city, located next to the downtown train station.

It was much later that my dad's barbershop and beauty parlor were located on Madison Street in the Central Area of Seattle."

With Meredith out of the service and running a business, Theresa was ready to pursue her professional education as a nurse. She was in good health and had derived satisfaction from working as a LPN, but she still had her dream. Hearing that the first Negro nurse had been admitted to the University of Washington's School of Nursing, she knew that she, too, had the interest and the ability to complete that program of study. She asked and answered the question: Why not try it?

Beginnings of Community Activism

Before she had time to apply to the University of Washington, she and Meredith became the parents of Jacqueline Cevesus Lee on November 1, 1949, an event that required her to devote her energies to being a mother and homemaker. Then, on January 20, 1952, Meredith Louis Lee Jr. arrived. That additional responsibility increased her concern for the kind of community her children would grow up in; so, she turned her attention to the specific conditions that would affect them. She became a community activist and a fulltime mother.

In the early 1950s, she was instrumental in establishing the Capitol Hill Community Council, which concerned itself with issues of housing, schools, and community services. With her major interest of services for children, she identified Jefferson Woods as one person who regularly responded to her requests for help in achieving some needed change in the community. Woods later said, "Theresa and I worked on various projects until the time of her death. She knew that she could count on me to say yes to most of her requests." Fabiola Woods, who also knew and worked with Theresa, said, "We were as close as sisters. For a period of time Theresa and I attended the same Catholic Church. Eventually Theresa joined St. Mark's Episcopal Church and we remained friends until her death, even though we did not go to church together." (Theresa's entire family were members of St. Mark's Episcopal Church, where she worked in women's groups. Her daughter, Cevesus, is still active in this church.)

A Nurse and a Community Activist

While her children were growing up and attending school, she also worked in the Parent Teachers Association, served as den mother while her children were active in scouting, and worked in YMCA activities. She regularly invited other residents of the community to join her in these activities.

Completion of Professional Nurse's Training

(Willa) Theresa at graduation from the University of Washington School of Nursing in 1962 with her BSN.

Finally, she was admitted to the U.W. School of Nursing and completed her undergraduate degree in 1962. Once hired as a public health nurse in Southeast Seattle in the Children and Youth Program, she joined MMRNC. Immediately, she felt at home because she knew many of the members from her days as a patient at Harborview Hospital. She also joined Washington State Nurses and King County Nurses Associations.

Bringing to her practice a repertoire of understanding and a commitment to provide the highest quality of care to others, she also viewed nursing service as a resource for exchange among her patients. She gave nursing care and she asked patients to give back to themselves and to their communities by participating in scouting, Black Achievers, and other YMCA programs and by excelling in their academic endeavors at school. She asked parents, foster caregivers, and other adults to participate in community organizations, especially PTA. She knew from firsthand experience just how important it was for parents to participate in their children's school life. She used nursing as a vehicle for moving beyond ministering to the physical and psychological needs of patients to strengthening shared cultural and spiritual relationships. This perspective allowed her to touch and be touched by many others, thus integrating her activist orientation in a complementary way for providing nursing care to the individual, small groups, and the community at large.

Cevesus recalls that, while she was growing up, the family engaged in many activities together: "Our dad was very interested in photography. We always had a car; so, we took many trips on logging roads and to view waterways. Dad loved taking pictures in those areas. My dad was very creative. He built an air-conditioning system for our car long before this was a standard feature in cars. We traveled each year to the South where I saw places where my mother had lived and visited as a girl. When we traveled as a family, we never stayed in hotels. We always slept in our car because hotels were segregated, and few, if any, allowed Negroes to stay in them. We packed a lot of food because we could not get service in restaurants. We had hogshead cheese, chicken, and sodas.

"Our entire family joined St. Mark's Episcopal Church when I was a child. At the time that we joined, there were very few other Negro families who attended services. Mother remained active until her recent illnesses prevented her from attending. I remain an active member of this church.

"Our home was really the place where people congregated to party. My father had a license to buy liquor during the war when it was scarce. People came to play bid whist and bridge. In those days there were few public places where Negroes could go to have fun; so, home parties were very popular. My father and mother met lots of people through their work and community activities," she recalls. Cevesus and her brother also met many of their parents' friends at these social events.

"Throughout our entire lives our parents were very supportive of my brother and me. Once I graduated from high school and entered college, I told my mother that I was lesbian. She never changed in her attitude towards me. She did tell me that once she told some of her friends about my sexual orientation. At least one woman told her that she should put me out of the house. I was already in college and out of my parent's home, but mother supported me in my lifestyle until her death. I'm telling you this because many members of our community have a long way to go before they accept me and other gay people as my mother accepted me."

A Nurse and a Community Activist

In 1976 Meredith Sr. died. For a while, Theresa, age 54, focused her energies inward. As part of the adjustment to this loss, she decided to travel to China, thinking she would remain for only a few weeks. After arriving there, she obtained the necessary papers and remained for nearly a year. She traveled throughout Asia and taught English for several months in one of the provinces of China. These travel experiences expanded her perception of community, inspiring her to view it in world terms. She returned to Seattle determined to develop opportunities for children to become contributing citizens of the world community.

Volunteer Work with YMCA

Beginning in the early 1970s and continuing through 1996, Theresa was an active member of the Central District Board of the Seattle YMCA. As part of this work in the 1980s, she helped to establish the Black Achievers' Program, whose focus is the promotion of excellence in academic performance. Students who meet the criteria are awarded scholarship support to attend college. As a public health nurse, she worked with children, youth, and their parents, identifying children whom she felt exhibited potential to become excellent citizens in school and community activities as well as high achievers in academic performance. Several of these children received scholarship assistance from the Black Achievers' Program. It was through this and related community work that she brought together her interests as a professional nurse and community activist.

In 1995 the Black Achievers' Program named a scholarship in honor of Theresa Lee, and in 1996 she was named a lifetime member of the Meredith Matthews Board of the YMCA

(Willa) Theresa White Lee in 1994. (pictured in the center between Sadie Berrysmith Wallace on the left and Mary Lee Bell on the right)

(the Central Area branch). A plaque installed there honors her outstanding contributions to students and community residents through her work in the Black Achievers' Program.

A Lasting Contribution to Mary Mahoney Professional Nurses Organization

In MMRNC (later MMPNO) Theresa was one of the first nurses to become a member of the Endowment Committee, whose responsibility is to fund scholarships for student nurses. She showed her dedication to this endeavor by continuing to serve on this committee after she had a serious illness. In order to benefit from her wisdom and expertise in fundraising, the committee held meetings at her home until the time of her death.

Theresa died on June 13, 1999, having used her time on this earth to make a significant difference in the lives of the children whom she met and cared for, as well as contributing to the lives of many parents. She understood the value and use of organizations such as the Capitol Hill Council, the YMCA, and MMPNO to cooperate with others who shared her values and dreams of promoting the optimal development of children so that they could perform as responsible citizens of the world.

Cevesus was pleased to give the eulogy at her mother's funeral. "It was a hard thing to do, but I did it. I wanted people to know that mother was a warm and very generous person. She gave her time and money to things that she believed in. As a child I took money to a family in our neighborhood for several years. They had a big family and Mother knew they needed help. She was just this neat person who really cared about others."

In addition to the contributions of time and information to the MMPNO Endowment, Theresa bequeathed $5,000 to MMPNO. It will support the values and goals that she espoused, to provide financial support to young Black students so that they may become excellent professional nurses and contributing citizens to the world.

Theresa's physical presence will be missed, but the generosity of spirit and verve with which she lived life will continue to be with all who knew her.

A Spirit of Hope and Determination

Verna Ward Hill

Verna rose from abject poverty to a professional status that today is considered middle class. Using her survival skills to meet her personal needs and to enable her to serve others, she drew upon deep springs of determination fed by a lifetime of persistent effort. Born on February 25, 1927, in Hope, Arkansas, she has quested ever since, as a student, professional nurse, parent, and Puget Sound resident for over 40 years, to make the name of her birthplace a token for her approach to life which is hope combined with determination to turn her dreams and goals into reality.

A Sharecropper Childhood

Verna was the fifth of 11 children born to Amelia Jamison and Frank Roy Ward. Augusta, Elnora, Walter, and Allie Mae are older siblings; Tyree, Alvin, Calvin, Malvin, Mary, and Louise are younger. Verna realizes there were real advantages to being the middle child. As her older siblings worked on the farm with their parents, she was needed as a babysitter; so, she did not do any farming. "As a babysitter I really learned how to manage children. This skill served me throughout my life in a very beneficial manner."

Because the parents were struggling sharecroppers, Verna recalls her home life as being full of long days of hard, manual labor. Her parents and older siblings were in the fields from sun up to sun down, usually for 12 or more hours, six days a week. Sundays were for church, the biggest diversion for the Ward family, and time off from work. Devoted Southern Baptists, everyone was expected both to attend church and, from age 12 on, to give money at church and Sunday school, as little as a few pennies but always something.

As sharecroppers the family shared half of what they produced with the landowners for rent; the remaining half was sold or used to meet family needs. At times their real poverty was apparent to Verna. As she put it, "We lived in a shotgun house. It was so small that a bullet could travel easily from the front to the back of the house." The house had three rooms, a kitchen, also used for eating, and two bedrooms. Parents and children slept in the same room, with more than one bed in each room and at least three people sleeping in each bed. The person who occupied the middle place slept with his or her head facing the opposite direction of the people on the edges. Sleeping with a brother's or sister's feet in your face was better than being cramped shoulder to shoulder and unable to move. They put up with this all winter, but Verna recalls how she welcomed the arrival of spring and summer when "we could sleep on pallets and stretch out for comfort."

The house had no desk or even space to do homework, nor does she remember how or where they studied as children. What she does vividly recall is how much encouragement they received as children, especially from her mother, to do well in school. Her mother even encouraged the children to compete among themselves to see who could perform best in school. It took a lot of pride in the intangible to sustain the competition because there was virtually no money for prizes or visible rewards for superior performance.

While there was very limited space at home, their parents allowed the children to go to the nearby school yard to play and as teens to a "juke joint" to dance, play cards, and have fun. Verna loved to dance. No matter how hard she had worked during the day, she was seldom too tired to dance. She says, "Even today dancing is something that I love to do."

The parents separated when she was about 12 years old, her father leaving to pursue his dream to become a train porter on the Missouri-Pacific Railroad. Verna's oldest sister was married and had left home. The remaining 10 children (including Verna) used to keep in touch with their father by going to the Hope railroad station to visit him while the train was there. He generally gave each child 10 to 15 cents before they parted, money they usually spent for treats before they reached their home. Also, as a porter he was eligible to get passes for the family to ride the train, a great help when Verna later needed to travel long distances.

A Spirit of Hope and Determination

For one year after the separation, her mother managed the farm with the help of the older children, but after that she began taking in washing and ironing. During World War II, her mother washed for many servicemen, the increased income making it possible for the family to move off the farm and into a bigger house. Her mother was an excellent manager who used half of the money the children earned to help pay household expenses; the other half was for their own use.

School Failures and Successes

Verna does not remember much about her first few years in grade school; however, a defining experience in fourth grade is etched in her memory. It was failure. Her teacher, Mrs. Clover, told Verna and her mother that Verna had not performed well enough to be passed to the fifth grade, so Verna remained in Mrs. Clover's class. With encouragement to perform well, she followed Mrs. Clover's instructions and, by the time the school year ended, was at the top of the class. She is now certain that this conversion of failure into success served her well throughout the remainder of her public school years and beyond.

In seventh grade she caught the attention of the high school principal's wife, Mrs. Lucinda Harris, who gave Verna a job cleaning her home. Delighted to work for this family, she was paid and treated almost like a family member. Then, in 10th grade her home economics teacher, Mrs. Velma Frye, encouraged her to learn how to sew. Using the school sewing machine, she became an accomplished seamstress and, through the help of her teacher, got a job sewing for a "full-figured woman" in town, who could not find nice clothes to fit her in Hope. Acquiring these skills led in 1946 to Verna's receiving the Future Homemakers of America Award and to Mrs. Frye's encouragement to run for president of FHA. She ran but did not win the election. Nonetheless, she had picked up skills that she later used throughout her life in competing for leadership opportunities.

One day before graduating from high school, Verna, who was walking with her head down and her shoulders slouched, met the basketball and football coach, Mr. Loeb, in the school hallway. He said, "Stand up straight because you really are going to be somebody." From then on Verna began walking very straight, conscious of her posture as she had not been before; even today she automatically walks very erect. Mr. Loeb's comments helped Verna define her own self-image. In a society where height is valued, Verna feels that she is perceived to be taller than she really is because of her posture.

With her improved self-image, she ran for student-body officer and became a cheerleader and class officer at Yerger High School. In 1947 Verna graduated, the fourth in her class. According to Verna, "In our high school we did not have a year book. Instead, we each made predictions about our future which, at our graduation exercises, were shared with those in attendance. I said that I will go to college and become a registered nurse. This was what I hoped would happen. At that time, I did not know whether I would ever make it to college, but I talked about getting there anyway." Verna recalls telling herself at age 12 that "one day I will go to college and become a registered nurse." This thought occurred to her because she was performing housekeeping chores for a registered nurse. It was this dream that Verna used for her prediction at graduation. Verna goes on to say, "When I attended school, we were lucky to have textbooks for each of our subjects. We used to be given used books when White students got new ones. We always got their cast-offs."

Upon graduation, Verna received a $100 scholarship to attend college. This was not enough money to cover all of her expenses, so she decided instead to work for a while before entering college. A cousin had invited her to come live with her in Robbins, Illinois, suggesting that Verna could find a job there more easily than in Hope.

Interim Work Experience

Within days of arriving in Illinois, she was hired as a seamstress in a slipcover factory in Chicago. Riding the train to work each day, she entered a workplace where she was surrounded by sewing machines and partially finished slipcovers, stacked in varying size piles. Though the room was big and well lighted, the noise of the machines prevented people from talking very much with one another. They just bent over their machine and worked at a very fast pace. The fabrics she worked with were beautiful, but, beyond that, little else was appealing. Verna had confirmed to her satisfaction that she really was a very accomplished seamstress, able to keep up with the best of her peers,

A Spirit of Hope and Determination

but, once this fact was established, her interest in the job began to wane. This was not the way she wanted to use her talents nor was this the place where she wanted to be. After six months she decided to return home to Hope.

Once she returned home, Verna learned that her sister Allie Mae had attended Philander Smith College. Since her father was living in Little Rock, where the college is located, Verna asked him to help her attend there also. After completing one semester, she realized that, since this was a non-accredited college, she would be limited as to job-placement and should therefore find another college. Fortunately, another sister, Elnora, who was working at the Boeing Company in Seattle, invited her to come and live with her. She accepted the invitation and in 1948 Verna moved to Seattle. Once again, thanks to a train pass provided by her father, she could accept the invitation and travel by train to this new destination.

Her first plan was to work for a few years and save her money so she could eventually enter the fully accredited nursing school at the University of Washington. Verna was shocked to experience the racism from Whites and the coolness for Negroes who were not born in Seattle. Legalized segregation was rampant. "My sisters lived in Yesler Terrace Projects. Most Negroes who migrated to Seattle in those days lived in the projects that were located in different parts of the city. Today, I understand that Whites were being racists and Negroes were demonstrating their snootiness. We newcomers were considered carpetbaggers by the native Negro Seattleites. Most of the Negro families who were native to Seattle would deny this description of the attitudes that they exhibited toward us newcomers. But, believe me," Verna says, "I experienced treatment that I had never experienced before from our own people."

She did find work in a factory making coats and jackets but soon realized that, although this sewing factory was a bit better than the slipcover factory in Chicago, the work was "mind-numbing." She longed to be in college. With her sister's encouragement, she got information about admission to the University of Washington and found other work, this time as a babysitter for a family in Broadmoor, an upscale White section of Seattle. She was promised a raise and other things after one month of work, which was a promise not fulfilled. Acting on a tip from the maid in this house, Verna went to a nearby family's home for an interview, was hired on the spot, and moved in with the Harvitz family. The husband owned a fabric store; his wife desired help in managing their young son. While enjoying good treatment from this family, she learned that it was possible for her to keep this job as babysitter and attend college too. At last! Verna began to experience a sense of hope and anticipation of reaching her goal.

Attainment of a Dream: Graduation from Nursing School

Verna applied for and was admitted to the University of Washington in 1949. But after only one quarter's work, she became ill and was admitted to Harborview Hospital. This illness had some beneficial outcomes. First, she'd never been in a hospital before and therefore didn't know at first hand what went on in hospitals. As a child her mother had tended sick children entirely at home, using herbs and mixtures of her own making to treat any and every kind of illness. As Verna put it, "Matter of fact, as children, we were very rarely sick." Even though the family lived in only three rooms, they remained healthy under these conditions. Not only did she not go to a hospital, she does not recall even going to a doctor in Hope or even seeing a Negro nurse there.

In her first hospital experience at Seattle's Harborview, she stayed long enough that she started helping the nurses, talking to patients and feeding them when needed. For the first time in her life Verna saw and met Negro nurses, including three who were organizing Mary Mahoney Registered Nurses Club, Gertrude Dawson, Rachel Pitts, and Celestine Thomas. One clear memory was of their appearance: "They always had on stiff starched uniforms and perfectly

Verna Ward in 1952 when she was a student nurse at the University of Washington, Harborview Division.

A Spirit of Hope and Determination

cleaned white shoes." Verna also saw Thelma Pegues—who then was a nurse's aide—and possibly encountered Sadie Berrysmith Wallace, both longtime MMRNC members.

After several weeks Verna's health returned, and she returned to the Harvitz family, where she lived until she was readmitted in 1950 to the U.W. Her required pre-nursing work in the College of Arts and Sciences aroused her lasting negative reactions. She recalled, "One professor told me to my face, 'You do not have the IQ to be a registered nurse.'" Never before had anyone belittled her academic ability so blatantly. She'd always had confidence in her ability to learn, but this professor's remark was a stunning blow to her ego. It also helped her understand why there were so few Negro students at the University. She believed that the grades that she'd received really reflected several professors' racial attitudes rather than her ability or performance. This particular professor was bold enough to put in words what others expressed more covertly through the grades they assigned her. Other Negro students with whom she talked generally shared her views about U.W. professors' grading practices. They had all concluded that Negro students were *persona non grata*, at base, not wanted on the U.W. campus.

Verna had hit rock bottom and was just about ready to leave the University, but something told her to stand up and fight for an opportunity to learn. She'd come to Seattle to become a college-educated nurse, and she had to achieve this goal. The springs of strength and determination bubbled up, leading her to go to faculty in the School of Nursing to see if they could help her. "I was truly rescued by those people," she said. Before all hope was gone, "In 1952 I entered the School of Nursing, Harborview Division. I was given $100 to purchase uniforms. It was possible for me to move into Harborview Hall where I had my very own private room." (Most students had private rooms in those days.) Verna's life had taken a turn for the better.

Of the 22 students in Verna's cohort, one was Negro, three Asian American, and all others White. At first, she had little or no contact with these classmates. When she was "invisible" to these students or when she experienced their rejection, she had decided that she would keep her shoulders up, to stand tall, as Mr. Loeb had suggested, and carry on. She decided to demonstrate through her behavior that she could perform and succeed by her own efforts. It did not take long for a few classmates to befriend her, among them some who remain professional friends today.

In contrast to the faculty in the College of Arts and Sciences, Verna's nursing instructors treated her well, although, again, their real attitudes were expressed through their assignment of grades. She inferred that instructors were reluctant to award her a grade higher than *B*, even in clinical practice, where she really excelled.

Among Harborview patients, which was always a diverse group, she encountered overt racism from some. There were White patients who did not want her to give them care. She always ignored this initial reaction because she knew from experience that, once they had received care from her, they would request her services again. Verna credits the nursing instructors with helping to create an atmosphere of acceptance. Not one ever changed her assignment when a patient balked at having Verna provide his or her care. She remains grateful to these instructors for the consistent support they gave her during this period.

Having completed her clinical courses at Harborview, she went back to complete the pre-nursing courses, which was an unusual step for any nursing student. That she was allowed to reverse the order reflected another level of support from the School of Nursing. For reasons never explained but because of this rule exception, Verna graduated in 1954 with a nursing degree.

Early Nursing Career and Marriage

After completing state board examinations, Verna began working as a post-operative nurse in Harborview which was considered at that time the most difficult kind of service. With no intensive-care units, patients went directly from surgery to this post-operative unit where the work was demanding, the hours long, and the pay low. Furthermore, she felt limited in her ability to make independent professional decisions, and she observed that many of the doctors were disrespectful of nurses generally and Negro nurses in particular. When she had acquired excellent professional skills, she thought it time to move on, seeking and finding a new professional challenge in public health after four years of employment in a hospital setting.

A Spirit of Hope and Determination

In 1958, assigned to Seattle's Columbia City Public Health Division where several Negro nurses were already working, she quickly found a level of professional autonomy and challenge that was extremely rewarding. She continued full-time employment in this setting until 1960.

Public health posed ethnic/racial challenges too. Again, some White patients did not want to be cared for by a Negro nurse. For example, one patient's daughter opened the door and stated outright, "My mother does not like Negroes." Verna instructed the child to go back into the room and ask her mother if she still needed the nursing care she had requested. The child returned and acknowledged that, yes, the need was urgent. Verna catheterized the patient and provided the needed services. When asked if this patient ever apologized to her about her daughter's comment, Verna replied, "No! That was the way it was back then. It's reasonable to think that this woman probably felt she was doing me a favor to let me in her house to give her nursing care." Since Verna never expected an apology, neither of them ever mentioned the incident again, even during two years of subsequent, episodic care for the patient and other members of her family.

During this early career experience and, indeed, during most of her nursing training, Verna had a supportive husband, Nelson Hill. She had met him in the late 1940s at a YWCA social function when he was also a student at the University of Washington. In 1948, when she had moved to Seattle, there were very few Negroes present at the places she frequented and even fewer at the U.W. campus. Black was not beautiful at that time. Negroes therefore used the Y's for residential and social purposes; certainly, Verna recalls feeling safe and accepted there.

Four children resulted from the marriage, Sheryl, Nelson II, Stewart, and Tracy. By 1960, Verna decided to withdraw temporarily from public health nursing in order to devote attention to these children. So, for 10 years she and her husband concentrated on raising the expectation level of each child. That they succeeded is evident in the fact that all four attended college. Sheryl entered college at the U.W. when her mother returned in 1976 to pursue graduate studies. She has a B.A. degree in communications. Tracy received his degree from Washington State University. Stewart attended the University of Washington, where, as co-captain of his team, he was a football star and went on to play professional football for a decade in Canada for the BC Lions. Nelson has a trucking and auto detailing business. Each of the children is doing what they want to do. Verna has one grandchild, Courtney, who lives in Woodinville, near Seattle, with her parents. She has excellent relationships with her children and grandchild; they have regular contact with one another.

Having gotten her children off to a good start, in 1970 Verna returned to full-time public health practice. One of her first projects was to start a Teenage Parent Program which enabled pregnant students who desired to do so to remain in school. Previously, pregnant teenage students usually left public school, although some returned after the births. Initially, parents on the generally high-income East Side of Lake Washington felt that this program was not needed in Bellevue, but Verna persevered there even without dedicated funds. Within six months, 23 girls and some "boyfriends" had enrolled. Before Verna left to attend graduate school, this program was fully funded.

The invitation and urging to begin graduate work came from Oliver H. Osborne, a professor at the U.W. Department of Psychosocial Nursing who had a federal grant to prepare students to become specialists in psychosocial/mental health nursing. Verna entered the program in 1976 and completed it in 1979. During that time several significant people in her life died, including her husband, mother, and brother. Not only did she weather these losses, she completed the program with a 3.6 g.p.a., grades she thinks really reflected her true academic ability and performance. During the 22 years since she had last been a student there, the entire atmosphere on campus had improved, according to her assessment. The School of Nursing was even actively recruiting African American and other ethnic students of color into programs.

Later Nursing Career and Awards

Verna returned to public health, practicing from 1979 to 1982 as Maternal Child Health and Crippled Children Services Program Coordinator, and in this capacity managing a $1.5 million budget. As a mid-level manager, she was responsible for the establishment of

A Spirit of Hope and Determination

standards of care and for selecting a multi-disciplinary team of professionals to provide services. One professional group, which she prefers to leave unnamed, posed a very significant challenge to her authority, but she endured and overcame this threat and established a very successful program. Verna received commendations and recognition for an outstanding performance, but, when federal funds were cut, she was reassigned to the East Side as Personal Health Services Supervisor.

In this new role, she used all of her expertise in psychosocial and interpersonal relations to resolve conflicts among staff and to answer complaints from patients about staff. The increasing demands of this role, along with funding cuts and other changes in regulations, motivated her to move on to another phase of her life: retirement in February, 1989.

Her career had led to forms of recognition for distinguished service. During the late 1970s Verna was elected to the board of Washington State Nurses Association, where, as Chair of the Minority Affairs Committee, she fought for the inclusion of more ethnic/racial content in the nursing curriculum, as well as inclusion of such content on state-board examinations. She also advocated for organizational

Verna Hill in 1981 as Coordinator of the County Division Maternal Child Health and Crippled Children's Services. (Photo from *The Carrier*, Vol. 4, Issue 2, March 1981, published by the Seattle King County Department of Public Health.)

changes in policies and practices that would enhance participation in WSNA by other ethnic/racial groups of color. In 1978, the American Nurses Association presented Verna and WSNA an award for her work as chair of the group's Minority Affairs Committee. She was photographed with WSNA President Louise Shores installing the plaque in the WSNA office. During this same period Verna was given an award by Mary Mahoney Registered Nurses Club, which she had

African American Registered Nurses in Seattle

joined in 1954, for her outstanding work at the local and regional levels in professional nurses' organizations on behalf of ethnic/racial equity in the profession.

She had joined MMRNC immediately after passing her state-board examination and remained active except for one year when the demands of family life and work prevented her from participating. Encouraged by the members' open-armed welcome, she declares that each has provided the support and attention that she expected and needed. After being a member for one year, Verna was elected president and during her 44 years as a member has occupied every role except parliamentarian. Her most recent role, begun in 1998 and ending in 2000, is treasurer. In her words, "I have remained active in this organization because I am committed to its goals and purposes. We provide scholarships to aspiring students. And we serve our community. We're growing again and I want to mentor a new generation of nurses." She intends to remain active in adding to this organization's legacy of giving back to the community.

Verna Hill served as Secretary of MMPNO in 1984 when this photo was taken. She has been retired since 1989.

In addition to being active in MMPNO, Verna occupied leadership roles in the Washington State Nurses Association, King County Nurses Association, and the American Nurses Association. She also served on other health and social service boards at the state and local levels.

Other realms of recognition are national and international. In 1980 Verna was appointed by the State of Washington to be a delegate to the Regional National White House Conference on Families. Other delegates then elected her to represent Washington State at the National White House Conference on Families in Washington, D.C. Then, in 1983 Verna was selected to be one of 25 health-care

A Spirit of Hope and Determination

professionals to go to the People's Republic of China to share healthcare information with representatives in that country. It was also during this tour that Verna reflected upon her experiences in Hope that gave her the confidence and determination to compete, succeed, and give to others, or as she says, "in terms of receiving support from folks who cared about me."

As a retired professional nurse, Verna serves the Red Cross as a volunteer for disaster services. In addition, she works in the local office in a variety of roles. Most importantly, Verna is back providing direct services in a setting where she is expected to use her professional knowledge to preserve life and to promote health and wellness among residents of many different communities in the nation.

A Prediction Fulfilled

The prediction that Verna made at her high-school graduation was realized—against the odds of racism and personal remarks that threatened her confidence in her own academic ability. She has worked and succeeded in environments where individuals were hostile toward her very presence. Yet she feels that she has made a difference through her work to the lives of many others. She has traveled the rocky road that Steele (1997) depicts, achieving despite being discriminated against in virtually every situation, from growing up in poverty and attending under-funded public schools to being limited in many work environments. Along the way, she demonstrated her ability to focus on professional development while she was raising a family of successful children. She incorporated in her professional performance opportunities to uplift the race as mentioned by Brooks and Nisberg (1972). In so doing she has extended service across ethnic/racial and professional lines to achieve her personal goals. In addition, she has combined her roles of wife, mother, and nurse as she envisioned her future during her early years in Hope.

A Nurse Anesthetist

FRANCES WORKCUFF FRAIZER DEMISSE

Frances Workcuff is proud of her family's heritage. Since she was old enough to remember, she has known that her grandfather, Charles Porter Grove, was a runaway slave who migrated from the South to Helena, Montana, where he found freedom. Her grandfather was very industrious and accumulated enough money to buy land in Montana, where he suspected that copper and gold were buried. He was sufficiently successful that he could recruit Negro men and their families to come work for him in his Montana mines. Frances still has newspaper clippings announcing her grandfather's demise: he was found frozen to death outside one of his mines. She feels that she has inherited some of her grandfather's spirit, drive, and commitment to succeed in achieving personal and professional goals. Her grandfather accomplished a great deal during his lifetime and passed that entrepreneurial spirit to his children and many descendants.

Early Years

Born in Butte, Montana, on September 5, 1929, she is one of the three daughters of Mabel Grove and Clyde Workcuff. Her two oldest sisters are Viola and Hettie. Frances' father was a professional baseball player, playing for the Giants in the Negro League, although she knows very little about him because he died less than two years after she was born. What she has left of her father is a very large picture of him in his Giant's uniform. "It really makes me feel good to have this image of him," she said. Her mother was a full-time housewife and homemaker when the children were very young.

A Nurse Anesthetist

In 1931 their mother moved the family to Seattle to join the children's grandmother and their uncle, Sirless Grove, who had migrated to Seattle some years earlier. Frances remembers, "My Uncle Si was quite a business person. He owned two grocery stores, apartments, and a nightclub in the Central Area. One store was located on 24th and Howell Streets; the second store was on 24th and Madison, and the nightclub was on 23rd and Madison. You can get a sense of my Uncle Si's entrepreneurial side by the name he chose for the nightclub, the Social and Educational Club. He was really quite a character. The restaurant in the nightclub was run by my mother, who married Artemus Williams in 1938. Our home was located on 27th and Jefferson Streets, not too far from my uncle's businesses." Her stepfather worked on the railroad for a while and later became a merchant seaman. "He was very good to all of us."

Frances Workcuff in 1937 at age 8.

Artemus and Mabel had two sons, Artemus Jr. (now deceased) and James. For a time, while the three girls and two boys were all together, their mother managed the home and her own businesses, too. For several years, Mabel Grove Williams owned a restaurant on one side of the street and a skating rink on the other.

Home life for Frances consisted of a combination of work and play. She frequently went to the restaurant where her mother spent a significant portion of her time and also got to play at the roller-skating rink. Once she started school, she spent most of her time studying while at home in the afternoon and evening.

Religion was an important aspect of their family life. Her mother was a Methodist and attended First AME Church. As Frances stated, "Mother sang in the choir and she was a member of the usher board. My Uncle Si was Baptist and he insisted that I join Mt. Zion Baptist Church. My mother did not have strong feelings about denominations. All she wanted was to have us attend church on a regular basis. My Uncle began carrying me to church when I was four years old and at age 13, I was baptized. For over half a century my name has been on the roll of Mt. Zion Church."

Frances attended Horace Mann Elementary and Washington Junior High Schools in Seattle. From the time she began going to public school until graduation, all of her teachers were Caucasian. This racial/ethnic difference had no particular meaning for her because the school children reflected the ethnic/racial characteristics of her neighborhood. She did not assign any significance to these ethnic/racial differences. "We lived in a neighborhood where there were Jews, Japanese Americans, Negroes, and Whites. We all got along with our neighbors. We played together outside but we did not go into each other's homes." When she entered Garfield High School, she noticed a sharp difference in the composition of her neighborhood and the behavior of students towards one another. World War II was on and she recalled, "I heard White students calling Japanese students 'Japs.' At Garfield all of our teachers were White. Students tended to stay in their own groups and there really weren't many Negro students there."

The Negro families who were just moving into the region during World War II were young, with young children or no children yet. "It was an experience to see how race relationships changed for the worse with the arrival of these servicemen and their families. Before the war, people really got along with one another. During and after the war, race relations really got pretty bad. The Central Area really changed. As more Negroes moved in, other groups moved out. In a very few years the Central Area was nearly completely Negro." The discrimination which Negro and other students experienced was most evident in school activities. The most glaring example related to yell teams and cheerleaders. When these groups first started, only White boys could be yell-team members. Eventually, White girls were allowed to be cheerleaders. No Negroes or other students of color were allowed to participate in these groups; instead, Frances participated in art and drama. She said, "I spent the rest of my time either studying or working. School was not a particularly pleasant place for me to be."

From the time she was 12 years old, Frances worked in her Uncle Si's grocery store on 24th and Howell with her sisters, earning 25 cents an hour. For three years she never received a raise and at age 15, "I decided that I would not work there any more." From that time until she graduated from high school in 1948, she worked off and on as a coat/hat checker in her uncle's nightclub or in the restaurant area of the club that her mother managed. She was able to keep all of the money she made and worked whenever she was needed.

Working in the nightclub was the most fun; there she saw many different entertainers come and go, such as Quincy Jones, the nationally known musician, a graduate of Garfield High School. "He frequently played at my uncle's club. Tina Turner, the famous singer, was still married to Ike when they appeared at the club too. These were three of the most famous performers that I saw there."

Uncle Si worked hard to have signs indicating that Negroes were not welcomed removed from restaurants where they began to appear in the 1940s. He was thwarted in his efforts because the prohibitive signs were replaced by others that stated, "The management reserves the right not to serve some customers." These signs began to appear as more and more Negroes and other Colored servicemen came to Seattle.

Following graduation, Frances sought employment at Madigan Hospital, in Tacoma because opportunities there to become a civil service employee were open to her. She recalls, "At that time civil service meant a lot to Negroes because we were supposed to have an equal shot at employment just as any other person." She got a job in the message center at Madigan and continued to live at home with her parents.

Marriage and Sickness

In 1950 she met Keith Fraizer, a serviceman at Madigan. Shortly after their meeting, they were married. Two months after their marriage, she was diagnosed with tuberculosis and was sent to Firlands Sanatorium (in Seattle) where she remained for two and one half years. Placed on complete bed rest, she was not allowed out of the sanatorium for 18 months, an absence that created estrangement from her husband. Though they remained married, the marriage essentially ended, even though she was not officially divorced until 1960.

During her illness, she had opportunities to observe how she and other patients were treated, observations that convinced her that she wanted to become a doctor. She had heard that it cost a lot of money to complete medical school and she realized that she did not know of any Negro doctors or women who had graduated from the University of Washington School of Nursing. She quickly abandoned this idea and began to think about becoming a nurse. At Firlands, observing nurses as they delivered a great deal of care to TB patients, she realized that there were some nurses who made her feel much better than others. As she put it, "I decided that I wanted to be one of those skilled nurses who cared."

After a two-year stay in Firlands, her doctor stated that there were no more visible lesions that showed up on x-rays. In spite of this situation, the doctor thought she needed surgery to insure that she was free of TB. She agreed to exploratory surgery and remained in the sanatorium for six additional months until she was officially discharged, free of all symptoms. While in the hospital, Frances was informed that she was eligible for benefits from the Department of Labor and Industries. In order to qualify, there was a good deal of paperwork to be completed. "I just never really had energy enough to do it. So I never received those benefits," she laments.

She began looking for employment shortly after she returned home, finding a job at Pacific Bell Telephone Company. Unfortunately, since she was unable to obtain insurance because she was a former TB patient, she had to resign for lack of insurance. The inability to get insurance motivated her to think about going to school. She had confidence that she could complete the practical nurses' program at Edison Technical School (in Seattle); so, she completed an application. A counselor informed her, however, that she had performed well enough in school that she should apply to the School of Nursing at the University of Washington. She was elated to be given this news.

Entry into a Nursing Program

Frances followed through on the counselor's suggestion, recalling, "This was really the first time in my life when someone at school suggested that I go to a level higher than the one I saw for myself." High school counselors had offered no advice; the Edison counselor, however, "made up for any counseling that I missed in high school." She requested an application from the U.W. School of Nursing. She got a response soon after she completed it and she was admitted in 1953. Among the 25 or so students in the class, Frances and Vivian Lee were the two African Americans admitted at this time to the Virginia Mason Hospital; they later learned that theirs was the first class to have clinical experience at this hospital.

Shortly after she entered the program, her instructors urged her to consider pursuing a degree in education rather than remaining in this nursing program, although she never understood the basis for this suggestion. Instructors continued to make this suggestion to her throughout her time in the nursing program, which she interpreted as a lack of encouragement. While she was disappointed, she decided to ignore their suggestions, knowing that she was passing tests and that her clinical performance was very good. "I was not the smartest student in the class; neither was I the dumbest one," she remembers. She believes she was an average student, as were over half of the other students in the class.

At VMH, Dr. Tate Mason, the son of the founder of the hospital, took a personal and professional interest in the performance and experiences of each student. "I felt that he treated me the same way that he treated all of the other students." Furthermore, she considered her clinical experiences to be quite positive; no patients refused to receive care from her. Throughout the time she was in the program, she took advantage of every available learning opportunity. Although her instructors were never very encouraging to her, their performance evaluations enabled her to complete the program and in 1958 to graduate with her class.

Completion of Training and Employment

Even before graduation, she had sought a paid position as soon as she could, electing first to be a float nurse (one who moves from floor to floor) in order to learn as much as she could on the different services of the hospital. After graduation, she continued as a float nurse until she was eligible to take state board examinations. Passing them, she remained at VMH until she had convinced herself that she had very good nursing skills and that she knew how to use her nursing knowledge to provide high quality care to patients.

In 1960, Group Health Cooperative Hospital was actively recruiting nurses. (At that time GHC was viewed by many people in

African American Registered Nurses in Seattle

Frances Workcuff Fraizer, top row seventh from the left, graduating with the Virginia Mason Division of the University of Washington School of Nursing in 1958.

the community as "communist.") Gertrude Dawson was already working there. "I knew who she was from Mt. Zion Church. I decided to apply and I was hired right away. Once again I applied to be a float nurse. Anyone who knows anything about nursing knows that one of the very best ways to get to know how a hospital really operates is to work on as many different floors as you can and with as many different nurses, doctors and other staff people as possible. That is exactly what I did. Gertrude Dawson welcomed me to the hospital and she also invited me to become a member of Mary Mahoney Nurses Club. I joined in 1960 and I have been a member ever since."

At GHC, she was one of the nurses who helped implement the consulting nurse role. "Patient counseling and patient teaching are activities that I have carried out for many years." Once this service was up and running, she worked in the clinic and outpatient department.

In 1961 she met Werku Demisse and married him shortly thereafter; in 1964 their first and only son, David Demisse, was born. The marriage ended in 1966.

Practice as a Certified Nurse Anesthetist

After having worked at GHC for nearly a decade, she thought she needed a new challenge. One presented itself on an evening when Dr. Patrick Bennett, Chief of Anesthesiology, came to the unit where

A Nurse Anesthetist

she was working. Having known her for some time, he said he would soon be starting a program in anesthesia and planned to start with two or three nurses just to see how the program would progress. Was she interested? His encouragement was all she needed to apply; so, in 1970 she began her study of anesthesia, a two-year program with the two other nurses who were accepted. According to Frances, "It was a real hands-on experience. We started by working directly with another anesthesiologist. In this program I had my very first African American instructor. She was an anesthetist and I identified with her right away. Her name was Loretta Daniel Wasse. She received her training in St. Louis, Missouri. As students we received individualized and group instruction. Loretta and Dr. Bennett were excellent teachers. There were opportunities for significant practice and learning."

Even before she completed the program Frances was certain that she had made the right career choice. Completing the program, taking and passing the anesthesia board exam, she was hired in the role of nurse anesthetist at GHC and practiced full-time from 1972 until 1985. She also joined the Nurse Anesthetist Association and remained a member throughout those years. In her words, "I believe that nurse anesthetists were among the first group of professional nurses to be certified." However, she noticed that, even though GHC doctors were trained much as she and the other two nurse anesthetists were, "Doctors acted superior to nurses. Eventually doctors took over anesthesia. Dr. Bennett was voted out as chief of service and work was just not the same for me."

Frances Demisse is the first African American nurse to enter and complete Group Health Hospital's anesthesia program which began in 1972. She is 3rd from the left in this picture taken of the first graduates.

She had a very successful practice as an anesthetist. After giving anesthesia to her 13,000th patient, she stopped counting. Even this number does not include the patients in obstetrics to whom she administered anesthesia. An important reason for this success was Dr. Bennett, "a former priest from Ireland. He was really interested in developing the most effective program in anesthesia that he could. It just never occurred to him to limit opportunities to me because of my color. Not only did he admit me, he also hired an African American to teach in the program. During the early 1970s opportunities began to open up for African Americans in many fields. That is when the term 'equal opportunity employer' came into vogue. I really benefited from that change."

Following her disappointment with changed policies at GHC, from 1985 to 1991, she practiced as an on-call anesthetist at Shick Shadel Drug and Alcohol Detoxification Center (in Seattle). One of the principal methods of treatment was narco-therapy or narco-analysis—a form of treatment provided to clients when they are in a sleep-like state. "I gave anesthesia for many of these sessions. I loved the work but even there the work became too stressful, so I decided to seek employment in other settings."

Work with the Elderly

Just as Frances was about to retire a second time in 1998, her son died. Always having known that in times of loss, grief, and sorrow caring for others gave her a sense of purpose, as part of her own healing, she began working with the elderly in nursing homes, Branch Villa, Jacobson's, and Sunshine Vista (all in Seattle). She knows that the care she delivers to these patients is appreciated and of high quality. "I go to work when I feel like it and I remain at home when I do not want to work. I have reached a wonderful place and stage in my life." Occasionally, she works as much for herself as for the clients in adult-day-care facilities for the State of Washington, having set up the nursing program for the South East Senior Center in 1996.

Reflections on Her Life

She now feels very satisfied with her career choices. She remains grateful to the counselor at Edison Tech who raised her sights beyond her own view but disappointed that, during her nursing program, she felt unsupported by several of her instructors. During this time, however, she learned to rely on her own judgment of her performance more than on her instructors' judgments. Dr. Patrick Bennett stands out in her mind as the one professional she could always count on to give her support and encouragement and to do so with compassion.

Within her own family, she had the support of her mother until she died in 1996. "My mother let me and my son move in with her while I was studying anesthesia. She was always there for us kids." In April 2000, her sister, Hettie, died, though Viola and her half-brother, James Williams, still live in Seattle.

She has information from the Montana Museum about her grandfather. In addition, she has newspaper clippings and other family records about other family members. She feels compelled to use this information to finish writing her family's history. "I promised my aunt that I would get this story written." Now that she is retired, she plans to use some of her energy working with other people who can help her achieve this goal.

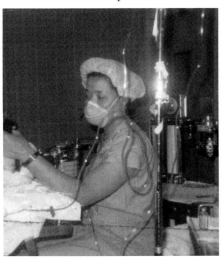

Frances Demisse as a practicing anesthetist. Frances worked at GHC for a total of 25 years, 13 as a nurse anesthetist.

Professionally, Frances is active only in MMPNO. "I let my anesthesia license expire in 1993, although I am still an active RN. Now I look forward to continuing work in church and in community activities of interest to me. After my David's death, I continued going to a congregational church in my neighborhood. My roots are firmly planted in Mt. Zion Church, but for now this very small congregation seems to be most satisfying for me." Frances feels that she will remain active in MMPNO as long as she enjoys sound mental and physical health.

Education: A Pathway to Self-Development and Service to Others

Frances Jefferson Terry

Since early childhood, Frances knew about the importance of education. It was a topic of conversation during family get-togethers and at church gatherings. Told by her parents and grandparents that she should "get a college education and use your education to help others who are less fortunate than you," she took this advice seriously and, at age four, began her educational journey.

Frances Jefferson at 8 months of age.

Formative Childhood Experiences

Frances Jefferson Terry was the second of two children born on January 7, 1930, in Jackson, Mississippi, to Ruth Williams Jefferson and Walter Jefferson. With her older sister, Marie, she spent a good bit of time in the care of their grandmother, a diabetic. The grandmother's health problem first exposed Frances to giving care to someone else in the form of insulin shots. Since the grandmother disliked injecting herself and because Marie didn't want to do it either, Frances learned how to give the injection and liked being able to help her grandmother with this nearly daily task.

The Jeffersons had a family-owned grocery store and barbershop near the family residence. Their father was the barber and their mother was manager of the store. When the father was not busy with

Education: A Pathway to Self-Development

customers at the barbershop, he helped out as needed in the grocery store. Frances' parents were devout Christians raised in different Protestant faiths. Her maternal grandfather was a minister in the African Methodist Episcopal Church and an elementary school teacher in rural areas of Mississippi where children would not have received an education but for her grandfather's efforts. One school year, when Frances was nine months old, her grandmother took delight in caring for the two baby girls while their mother taught school with their grandfather. The next year her father opened the grocery store where her mother worked. Her maternal grandparents lived just across the street from her parents' home; their proximity contributed to a very stable family life for Frances and Marie.

Her paternal grandparents were strong in their Baptist beliefs. She heard it said that her grandfather was very articulate and stronger in mathematics than most Blacks or Whites who lived in their hometown of Madison, Mississippi. He owned his own farm and had the reputation that he would never let anyone cheat him out of a penny. Most of his children and other helpers worked out in the field growing cotton and vegetables while he sat on his porch reading the Bible. On Saturdays, he would help his son in the barbershop.

Their family home was located on a street two or three blocks from a Catholic elementary school. Almost every day, the sisters watched children going to and from school and sometimes followed them to play on the swings and slide. The older children had a volleyball net where they would play until the school bell rang. Then all the children would line up according to their grade level and march into the school. Even before Frances had words to convey her observations, she realized that the school children were Negro and the nuns were Caucasian, whose most striking feature was their clothing, consisting of a long black religious habit with wide sleeves, a cape, a veil, a white cap and a collar. With this garb, they demanded a respect different from that accorded other adults in the neighborhood. But Frances observed another fact about the nuns that impressed her. From their house next door to the school, they often walked about in their neighborhood, visiting the sick and the poor.

As soon as she was old enough, Marie began attending the Catholic school. The younger Frances often walked with her. She liked being at the school so much that she frequently played in the schoolyard before returning home. Her grandmother could see her from the kitchen window; so she didn't worry about her safety. Eventually, the nuns asked Frances if she wanted to attend school, even though she was just four years old. She immediately said, "yes," and, with the family's approval, entered kindergarten, on condition that she could remain in school only if she could keep up with the other children in her class. She met that requirement without difficulty, both in kindergarten and in later grades. She was a very good student and loved by most of her teachers.

At school, Frances saw the nurses check children's eyes and also sometimes give them shots, and she found that she liked watching these procedures. The combination of observing what the nurse did at school and having to give shots to her grandmother at home motivated her to consider becoming a nurse.

At age nine or ten, Frances got her first job counting money in her father's barbershop. In 1939-1940 his haircuts were 25 cents, even then a low price. He was so busy cutting hair and helping in the grocery store that he was often too tired to count his barbering money, which was mostly in either quarters or dollar bills. He gave that job to the sisters, which they continued to do until 1942, when their father decided to visit Seattle with an eye toward moving the family there.

A Move from Mississippi to Seattle

Their mother's half-brother, who lived in Seattle, came to Jackson, Mississippi, to attend a relative's funeral and encouraged Mr. Jefferson to open a barbershop in Seattle. Even though his business was going well in Mississippi, he wanted a better life for his family and himself and decided to explore the idea. Immediately upon arriving, he found "The Welcome Barbershop," at 525 Jackson Street, near the King Street Station. The owner, Mr. Vogel, near retirement, was using only one of the four chairs. When Walter Jefferson introduced himself and told Mr. Vogel that he was interested in relocating his own barbering business to Seattle, Mr. Vogel agreed to rent one of his three unused barber chairs to Walter.

Two days after arriving in Seattle, he began cutting hair in the chair next to Mr. Vogel. The two barbers got along well with each

Education: A Pathway to Self-Development

other. There was plenty of business for both barbers with Pullman porters and service men lined up for service. On some days the barbershop was open for 12 or more hours. The business grew steadily so that soon he could have the family join him. This decision was difficult for Frances, however. At age 12 she was closely tied to her ailing grandmother; yet she wanted to live with both her father and mother. She acceded to her father's wishes, although with considerable emotional distress.

At first the family lived with Uncle Joseph and their five cousins, later finding a house to buy. Meanwhile, the sisters entered school. One day at her mother's suggestion, Frances wore her Girl Scout uniform to school with the hope that this would be the fastest way to get her involved with a troop in Seattle. One White girl in Frances' class did invite her to join her troop, but the next day she informed Frances that her mother said she could not join that troop. The reason was that the girl's mother, a troop leader, did not want to admit a Negro. Mrs. Jefferson called Scout headquarters and learned that there were no "Negro Girl Scout Troops" in Seattle and that Frances should go to the Duwamish Bend Housing Project to see if she could work with a Brownie troop. They never followed up on that suggestion because they both wanted Frances to have the experience of being a Girl Scout with children her own age and at her grade level. Frances never wore her Girl Scout uniform again and remembered years later how sad she felt at seeing the White Girl Scouts in their uniforms when they wore them to school.

Other school experiences were discouraging as well. There were hundreds of students in her school, most of them Caucasian but also Filipinos, Asian Americans, and Hispanics. One of only a few African American students, she "felt very isolated and very alone. One day I saw a White girl spit in the face of a Japanese student. She also called her a 'Jap'. I really wanted to go back to Mississippi." She has replayed this incident over and over in her mind so that it is still vivid and emotionally wrenching.

During the middle of the first school year the Jefferson family moved to a home with an available upstairs apartment west of 12th Ave on Jefferson Street. Fully furnished, it was a big improvement over living with their relatives, but the furniture was not as nice as theirs was in Mississippi. Nevertheless, she was thrilled about the move because she thought this house was located in the Garfield High School attendance area. Unfortunately, the house was one block outside of the boundary line; so, it was necessary for her to attend Broadway High School. Her sister was taking the second half of a course that was offered once a semester; so, she was able to remain at Garfield while Frances had to attend Broadway. For the first time in their lives, the sisters attended separate schools.

One day while Frances was studying, this house caught fire from a cooking accident on the lower level. She managed to get out safely with her mother who was just home from a hospital stay for surgery and her grandmother who was visiting from Mississippi. However, the family lost all their personal belongings except the clothes they were wearing and they were now homeless. The parents found temporary shelter for the children with friends while the adults moved to the downstairs duplex.

Frances' father, during this very difficult period, told one of his customers, a merchant seaman, about his plight. Just about ready to go to sea for six months, he offered his house. Mr. Jefferson accepted. During the six-month period, he found a house to buy at 1100 19th Avenue so that, finally, the Jefferson family could move into their own home. When their furniture arrived from Mississippi, they felt settled and secure.

Following this move, Frances concentrated on performing well in high school, developing excellent typing and shorthand skills. Often she was asked to complete typing tasks for other teachers in the school. Yet, despite her outstanding performance in typing, her teacher told her that she would not give her an A in typing because she was a Negro. After this incident, Frances was never very involved with school-related activities; however, in 1946 she graduated from Broadway High School.

Some months later, her mother suddenly died, creating yet another trauma for the Jefferson family. Her grandmother had come for a visit previously, but her grandfather was in ill health and too old to be able to travel to Seattle for the funeral. So her father decided to have two funerals for his wife, the first in Seattle at the First AME Church, the second in Jackson, Mississippi. Frances and her sister accompanied Mr. Jefferson and their mother's body on the train, returning to Seattle after Mrs. Jefferson's burial.

Education: A Pathway to Self-Development

What should she do then? She decided she needed some time away from school before entering college. Knowing that she had excellent secretarial skills and noticing advertisements for many such jobs, she applied, only to be told, "We cannot hire a Negro." The only job she could find was as dishwasher in a Russian restaurant. But that work was so humiliating that, after one day's work, she quit, not to return even to collect her one day's pay.

Those experiences turned her thoughts toward college, aided by her sister, who was a student at Wilberforce College in Ohio. She encouraged Frances to come join her there, but Frances declined because she knew she wanted to be a nurse and that college had no nursing program.

So, it was back to work. After some months of diligently seeking secretarial employment, Frances got a job working in a restaurant owned by an African American minister and his wife. Located on Sixth and Weller Streets, close to her father's barbershop, it was a good job, where she could use her typing skills to order food and other supplies. She also did bookkeeping tasks and waited table while the minister and his wife did all the cooking and dishwashing. Even though she liked the family atmosphere at this restaurant, she knew she needed to return to school to complete her education.

Acceptance into Professional Nursing School

In 1947, she applied for admission and was accepted into the nursing program at Seattle University. At first she paid little attention to the fact that she had a private room while most other students had roommates. When she inquired about this situation, she was told, "Parents will not tolerate having a Negro girl in a room with their daughters." She found, nevertheless, that most of the students were very accepting of her. Many of them studied with her and were otherwise very friendly. Only a student on affiliation from Idaho was an exception. Ready to return to her home school, this student went about the classroom hugging everyone in the class except Frances when she said goodbye. Everyone observed this behavior, but no one ever discussed it and Frances was too embarrassed to say anything.

The nuns, she thought, were fair in their treatment of her in the classroom and in the clinical setting. However, there were times when she did not feel like involving the nuns in some incidents. For example, she and a practical nurse were on night duty. When this nurse took a patient a bedpan, the patient stated that she wanted a White nurse to take her off the pan when she finished. The practical nurse told the patient, "You will need to remain on this pan until 7:00 am when there will be a White nurse on duty!" The patient quickly changed her mind.

When it was time to complete her pediatric affiliation, she remained at Providence while all of her other classmates went to Children's Orthopedic Hospital. No one ever told her why this happened, but she knew that Children's did not allow Negro nurses to receive their training there. Some months later, for her tuberculosis affiliation she and several classmates went to a hospital in Walla Walla (in Eastern Washington). There, patients and clinical instructors were very accepting of her.

Her psychiatric affiliation was at American Lake Hospital (near Tacoma). There, patients were either intrigued by her or wanted no service from her. On more than one occasion, she was asked by a patient if he or she could just touch her skin. She was really not offended by this request; however, one patient, who was supposed to be quite mentally disabled, told Frances in no uncertain terms, "Don't you talk to me. I don't like Colored people and I don't like Catholics." Frances was both. She thought to herself, "I'm glad I have the keys to the door and he does not!"

While on tuberculosis affiliation in Walla Walla, life was fine until she left the campus. "The campus was a safe haven for me. Once I stepped out into the city, things changed. Even children called me 'nigger' and no restaurants would serve Negroes." It was emotionally painful for Frances to recount these experiences.

Throughout the entire time she was in nursing school, she felt that racism was never far away. What was very encouraging was the fact that at Providence she saw other professional African American nurses, such as Maxine Pitter Haynes and Ernestine Williams, both founding members of MMPNO. "Just seeing both of them gave me the courage to go on."

Even before applying to nursing school, Frances knew that Maxine Pitter Haynes had been denied admission to the School of Nursing at the University of Washington. This information was revealed at a troop meeting of Girl Reserves, sponsored by the local

Education: A Pathway to Self-Development

Phillis Wheatley Young Women's Christian Association (a social organization for young women, whose programs aimed at promoting wholesome social activities with adults who served as role models). The troop leader had referred to Maxine Haynes' denial of admission and called her a "winner against racism" for having gone out of state to complete a nursing program.

Marriage, Motherhood, and Professional Employment

During her Walla Walla affiliation, she met Robert Terry, who came there from Seattle just to meet and visit with her. They learned that most restaurants in Walla Walla, not just those within walking distance of the hospital, said, "We do not serve Colored people." After a third rejection, they decided not to try any other restaurants; she can't remember whether they got any food to eat that day or whether they gave up in disgust and decided not to eat.

Robert had come to Seattle to teach in the public schools, the first African American male to do so. Ms. Thelma De Witty, the first African American female to teach in the Seattle Public Schools, introduced Robert to Frances. And Frances became the first African American to graduate from Seattle University's undergraduate baccalaureate program. In 1951, two weeks after graduation, she married Robert Terry, and between 1951 and 1960 they had five children, Deborah, Robert Jr., Michael, Brian, and Walter. (All their children and 10 grandchildren still live in Seattle.)

After graduation Frances really wanted to work in pediatrics. Applying for a job at Children's Orthopedic Hospital, she learned that she could not be employed there as a nurse "because you are married." Yet the nurse who was conducting the interview wore a wedding ring; she was also Caucasian.

In 1951 Frances received her baccalaureate degree in nursing. She was the first African American to complete the undergraduate program at Seattle University, Seattle, WA.

African American Registered Nurses in Seattle

In 1951 most Negro nurses worked at Harborview or Providence Hospital and were well aware that their employment opportunities were very limited. Members of MMPNO played an important role in providing information to one another when jobs in other hospitals became open to them. They also shared information about how they were responded to and treated by other staff members and patients.

After passing state board examinations, Frances planned to join MMRNC, but, before she had taken the initiative, Gertrude Dawson, one of the founding members of MMRNC, asked her to please attend the next meeting. She accepted and in 1952 joined the organization; thereafter, while raising her family and working part-time at Providence, she could not attend meetings regularly. However, she has supported the organization financially for many years.

Frances' first professional job was at Providence Hospital, where she remained from 1951 to 1961, the decade when all of her children were born. She was able to balance work, usually two days a week, with home responsibilities because the administrators at Providence were very supportive of all nurses, especially those with child-rearing responsibilities.

In 1962, she learned about positions available in the Seattle Public School system. Frances applied for a position, but she was not immediately hired, probably because the district already had one African American nurse. (During the early 60s many organizations felt they had enough African Americans if one was among their employees.) Later, she applied for a position with the Seattle Public Health Department, was hired, and was assigned as a school nurse in the Bellevue School District. Within a few years she was hired by the Seattle Public School District, which had by then evidently changed its employment policies.

Admission to Graduate School

In 1969, Professor Kathryn Barnard, a faculty member at the University of Washington, hired Frances to work at the Northwest Center for the Retarded. Dr. Barnard had a research grant and a clinical affiliation with the center. For the next seven years, Frances directed the Health Services Program for this agency, a job that enabled her to use her skills and knowledge to deliver high quality

Education: A Pathway to Self-Development

care to children and their family members. This work also helped her realize that she wanted to enter graduate school to gain more skills in research and writing. Professor Barnard regularly invited her to attend seminars and lectures at the University. This exposure to academic studies, along with her personal desire to pursue graduate work, prompted her to return to school.

In 1979 she was admitted to the U.W. Department of Psychosocial Nursing (now the Department of Psychosocial and Community Health), an eight-quarter program. She had no difficulty completing the theory courses and was pleased to find two African Americans and one Japanese American on the departmental faculty. Students in her courses were pleasant towards her, which helped her make the necessary adjustments to graduate-school life.

Her entry into graduate studies pleased her father, who had said to her and her sister, "I will use every penny that I make, if I have to, to help you get an education." In 1980, he died; this was a significant event in her life. Since childhood she had realized that her father was a highly respected member of the community, both in Mississippi and in Seattle. She was pleased that he knew before he died that she had returned to graduate school.

One portion of graduate studies was especially challenging for her, a two-quarter internship in Richland (in Eastern Washington). She knew before leaving home that there were few African Americans in Richland, as had been the case during her undergraduate clinical experience in Walla Walla. However, this time it was possible for her to return home to Seattle each weekend. There were no overt racial incidents, but racial tension was just below the surface, making her feel uncomfortable and alone there.

Before moving to Richland, Frances had found a place there to live. A social worker who worked at the local community mental health center rented her a room in her apartment and they got along well. Each respected the other's need for space and quiet; yet at times they had meaningful conversations with one another.

During the six-month experience, Frances learned a great deal about community mental health in a rural setting. The work was demanding but satisfying, the clinic staff helpful and supportive of her. She felt respected for her knowledge and professional judgment. Still, she was more than happy when it was time to return to Seattle.

African American Registered Nurses in Seattle

In 1981 Frances graduated with a master's degree in Psychosocial and Community Mental Health Nursing.

Teaching and Other Challenges

The degree led to several challenging kinds of employment in her field, teaching psych/mental health nursing at Shoreline Community College (in a suburb of Seattle) and clinical instructor at Seattle Central Community College and Seattle University. These experiences she found challenging and extremely rewarding. Also, having passed the American Nurse Association Board examination to become a clinical specialist with prescriptive authority, she worked for a time as a clinical specialist at Harborview Hospital and at Community House Mental Health Agency.

Brief Retirement and Acceptance of a New Challenge

Frances Terry in 1993 as featured in *Harborviews*, No. 143, May 1993.

In 1998 she retired and returned home to enjoy time with her children and grandchildren. Her grandchildren include Tanita Terry Tullis, Timothy Scott Hays, Andrew David Hays, Veronica Terry Hays (adopted into the Hays family at age three, and changed her name to Sakara Rummu-Allah at age 21), Robert Terry II, Kayode Stephens-Terry, Sekou Stephens-Terry, Zawdie Stephens-Terry, Otieno Stephens-Terry, and Obadiah Stephens-Terry.

She has remained active in the Catholic Church, serving as vice-president of the Catholic Caucus, where she works with another member of MMPNO, Elizabeth Thomas, president of the Caucus. She intends to continue working in the church as long as she can, for she feels that Catholicism and nursing have served her well. She desires to be a role model for others who may be experiencing some of the same challenges she faced and continues to face as an African American professional nurse.

Education: A Pathway to Self-Development

Her retirement was brief. In 1999, she decided to accept a part-time position at the local senior citizen center where she is the Health-Enhancement-Program nurse at this agency. The position allows her the opportunity and challenge to develop this into an important program at the center, since the senior citizens in the program, many who are African American, tend to be relatively inactive. She helps them achieve the most relevant health activities for themselves.

Throughout her professional life, Frances has been active in Washington State Nurses Association, King County Nurses Association, and MMPNO. She also organized a Seattle chapter of the National Black Nurses Association, though this chapter is now defunct. Perhaps her greatest honor is her recent induction into the WSNA Hall of Fame as one of the pioneer professional nurses in the Puget Sound area.

In reflecting upon her varied and challenging professional life, Frances states that her patron, Saint Francis of Assisi, gave her words that she deeply believes in: "make me an instrument of thy Peace." She has satisfied her personal desire for success and the family expectations that she work to help others less fortunate than herself. In this process she has been peaceful in her protest against racism and other negative experiences that she has had while pursuing her education and opportunities to serve others. She feels thankful that God "granted me the serenity to accept what cannot be changed; the courage to change what can be changed; and the knowledge to know the difference."

A Sense of Place, Person, and Promise

Lois Price Spratlen

Lois developed a sense of place, personhood, and perseverance early in life. Her most vivid childhood memories are of the stark contrasts in the Negro and White neighborhoods of Charlottesville, Virginia. Her parents were separated and her mother possessed very limited skills. "Mother worked as a domestic, doing washing and ironing at home and walking to White people's homes to pick up dirty laundry. At home, dirty and clean clothes were everywhere. Dirty clothes were placed in the kitchen where the washing machine was located. When there was no more space, some clothes were left on the back porch. Clean clothes were placed on hangers. Often folded clothes were placed on the sofa in the hallway and in the living room. Since this was before the days of electric or gas dryers, during inclement weather, wet clothes were hung in any available space. It was difficult to find a place to sit down without touching other peoples' clothes. The roof of the house often leaked and getting around the wet clothes and the drips from the roof in the upstairs hallway was yet another challenge."

When Lois went with her mother, sister or aunt to pick up dirty clothes, return clean clothes or sometimes remain to clean houses, she saw further contrasts. Most of the homes of White families, several of whom were nurses, were bright and inviting. There were sofas and chairs that appeared to be very comfortable places to sit. Rooms were generally brightly painted and well lit. These were living conditions that Lois did not experience at home.

At age 11, Lois began working outside of the home for pay. Sometimes, she cleaned houses of families for whom her mother and aunt worked. At other times Lois worked as a waitress at parties.

Her father's sister, Aunt Betty, worked as a cook in a residence hall at the University of Virginia where there were frequent teas, receptions and parties.

Beginning in the eighth grade and continuing throughout high school, Lois was active in student government, the choir, the drama club and served as manager of the Jefferson Girls Basketball team. Academically, she was an honor student.

During her junior and senior years of high school, the Principal, Mr. Owen Duncan, selected Lois to serve as the cook for the visiting football team. It was her responsibility to purchase food and prepare the meals for the visiting team members and their coaches. Through very frugal management of the money that she earned, it was possible for Lois to stop cleaning White peoples' houses during the school year, so she was able to concentrate on her studies.

These work experiences enabled her to acquire skills and self-confidence to perform tasks on her own. She truly gained an understanding of place, personhood, and individual performance. Despite being surrounded by domestic workers at home, Lois felt there was a promise of more academic success in her future. She now believes that it was these memorable contrasts that helped her to understand the difference between having and not having and to develop a determination to be in the former group.

Lois' early interest in nursing emanated from her mother's desire to be a registered nurse. "Mother really wanted to be a nurse and she never had the opportunity to do so. When I graduated from high school, she encouraged me to become a nurse. I followed her suggestion and I have never regretted doing so."

Growing Up with Education as a Family Value

Lois was born to Ora Ferguson Price and Madison James Price in Charlottesville, Virginia, on December 31, 1931. She joined an older sister, Violet. Lois never lived with her father, who left while her mother was pregnant with her. Shortly after Lois' birth, her mother returned to her parents' home on Sixth and Commerce Streets, where she remained until she died in 1987 at age 78.

During this growing-up time, 12 people lived in the four-bedroom house, her maternal grandparents, her mother and her mother's sister,

Lois Price at around age 4.

and eight children. She observed her sister's and cousins' departure for school and work in Washington, D.C., Philadelphia, and other cities, and nurtured a desire to create a better life elsewhere. She now feels extremely fortunate to have developed the confidence and to have experienced enough success to begin college and to leave Charlottesville. Lois graduated from high school in 1949 and left for college in September of that same year. Returning for short visits, she has lived away from Charlottesville since that year.

Her mother, Aunt Marie, and a cousin, Pauline Minor, (one of the eight children) were the primary workers in the house, forming a team and sharing the unending burden of washing, starching, and ironing clothes, although all of the children pitched in to help. Their lives consisted largely of very hard physical labor six days a week, 12 to 14 hours each day. Sunday was the only day of the week when no one worked. This day consisted of church services for the adults and Sunday school, church and Baptist Training Union (BTU) for the children. "On a regular basis we visited the cemetery and occasionally, we took a short nap if the weather was rainy or cold. Without a car, we had no diversion other than the radio. Listening to the radio was a family affair when it was possible for everyone to continue working while they listened to programs. Sunday mornings were especially enjoyable family times. We heard singers like Clara Ward, Sister Rosetta Tharpe, Mahalia Jackson and the Harmonizing Four. Once the latter program ended, all the children left home together to walk to Sunday school. There was no television in our home until after I left for college."

The bus system was segregated and Negroes were required to sit in the back of the bus, a requirement her mother resented. Rather than experience that restrictive insult, "mother insisted that we walk. We even walked when there were heavy loads of dirty clothes to

A Sense of Place, Person, and Promise

carry. This was our family's most determined way to preserve our pride. We grew up boycotting the bus long before the Montgomery, Alabama bus boycotts of the 1950s."

Basic needs for food, shelter, and safety were met in the home with the help of her grandfather's railroad-retirement pension. It was only through hard work and participation in church and school activities that their needs for self-esteem and self-actualization were met. They were poor but not deprived.

"My sister, Violet, was the first and only female family member to grow up and work outside of the home in a business. Others did day work in White people's homes. Her first job was with a Negro insurance company that had a branch office there. Later, she became the secretary of Mt. Zion Baptist Church. Our family has belonged to this church since our mother was a little girl. Violet continues to serve in this role. From a family perspective it was a big event for her to move out of our family home and purchase her own home.
This represented greater independence than was customary for a single woman to display in the 1950s. It took a while for Mother to adjust to her absence even though Violet regularly visited our home after she moved away.

"Throughout my entire life, all members of our family valued education. Time was given for everyone to complete their homework and to engage in school-related activities. Mother, Aunt Marie, Violet and Pauline took special pride in my academic accomplishments. As the youngest of eight children who grew up together, I benefited from observing and knowing about the experiences that my sister and cousins had and talked about."

Perceptions of Professionalism

"Growing up in Charlottesville was like living in two separate cities, one Negro, the other White, very separate and very unequal. In my racially segregated neighborhood, professionals and non-professionals lived next door to one another. A medical doctor, two dentists, public elementary and high school teachers lived very near. Workers in a barbershop, beauty salon, and owners of a funeral home also lived in our neighborhood. The segregated public elementary and high schools were just one block from my back door.

"Within this neighborhood my sense of place and person became clear. It was possible to tell who the professionals were because they had fancier homes and some had cars. Their children were very well dressed, too; yet these professionals and many non-professionals attended the same churches in the community and children from these families played together in yards, streets, and at school. Except for the schoolyard, there were few playgrounds for Negro children. Even the city park nearest my home was for 'Whites only', a prohibition so strong and lasting that during the 1990s when a wading pool was developed in this park, the African-American paper carried comments for and against using this pool. The park was desegregated many years earlier, but the historical memory of segregation lingered in the minds of some residents of the city and in my own mind, too."

In academic pursuits Lois often out-performed many of the professionals' children, both in public school and Sunday school. Teachers recognized her for her academic ability, building positively on her sense of person and promise, and helping her to acquire confidence in her ability to succeed.

About three or four miles from Lois' home was the University of Virginia, located in an area where many Whites lived in large, beautiful homes and on streets lined with cars. She considered this area to be off limits, except when she went there to work. She saw White nurses in their white uniforms and blue capes, but African Americans were there only to provide services, like caring for children, pushing baby carriages and cleaning homes. Her memories of cars chauffeured by African-American men are vivid, but less positive than as portrayed in the movie *Driving Miss Daisy*. Before gaining employment on the Chesapeake and Ohio Railroad, her father worked as a chauffeur. Signs in restaurant windows which read "For Whites Only" were among the ever-present Colored and Whites-only signs that put clear restrictions on any Black person's access to public places.

This was a different atmosphere from the one she had experienced in her neighborhood. Instead of being intimidated by or even resentful of these people who looked rich, Lois dreamed of some day being able to attend the University so that she could wear uniforms like the ones her mother washed and ironed for her customers. Although

A Sense of Place, Person, and Promise

she was not seen by Whites to be as good as they were, she perceived herself as capable of attaining professional status.

One experience helped to strengthen that perception. Culminating in frequent reinforcement from teachers and classmates was a gift given to her after elementary school graduation. It was "a treadle Singer sewing machine, my first tangible acknowledgment of academic success." The giver, Mrs. Nannie Cox Jackson, a neighbor and retired high school home-economics teacher, remains an important role model. Much that she taught Lois, from sewing and crocheting to manners and morals, has shaped her life in positive ways. Community leaders and other students must have felt the same influence because, in the 1970s, a public school was named in Mrs. Jackson's honor.

Lois Price at graduation from high school. This 1949 picture of Lois appeared in her high school yearbook. She was one of two valedictorians of her class.

Strong self-confidence sustained Lois through high school, where she continued to perform well. At church and in Sunday school, she was encouraged to serve in leadership roles. The reinforcement that she received in both places, as well as in her home, motivated her to strive for academic excellence. Lois graduated as one of two valedictorians of her high school class.

Completion of Nursing Degree, Marriage, and Early Career

Following graduation from high school, she acted upon the earlier dream and applied to the School of Nursing at the University of Virginia. After several months' delay with no response, she stopped by the school to inquire about her application. The reply: "You will never be admitted to this school." Reporting this news back home, she found that Mrs. Nannie Cox Jackson was willing to call Hampton

Institute (now Hampton University). Within days, Lois was admitted there with a scholarship. Having re-entered her life at the time she graduated from high school, her father accompanied her on the train ride to Hampton and paid college expenses that were not covered by the scholarship. Lois spent the next two and one-half years on the Hampton campus completing pre-nursing courses. The next two years were spent on clinical affiliations at Saint Philip Hospital in Richmond, Virginia, Brooklyn State Hospital in New York, and in public health in Norfolk, Virginia. These rotations were deeply enriching experiences.

At Hampton she received instruction from White teachers for the first time, along with students and faculty who were Africans, American Indians, and East Indians. Adapting well to these new experiences, she continued to succeed academically in the nursing program, which was supposed to take four years but, because of the time needed to complete all clinical work, required nearly five years.

While on a clinical rotation at St. Philip Hospital in Richmond, Virginia, Lois met and married Thaddeus Hayes Spratlen. Following the completion of her nursing program and his discharge from the U.S. Army, they migrated to Columbus, Ohio, where he completed three degrees (B.S., M.A., and Ph.D.) at The Ohio State University. Lois worked at various hospitals in Columbus, where there were limited opportunities for employment and for advancement to leadership positions. Throughout those seven years until 1961, she remained a staff nurse, usually working the evening shift. (It was well known by African-American nurses that the darker the period of the day, the darker the nursing and support staff tended to be!)

In 1961 they moved to Bellingham, Washington, where Thaddeus joined the faculty at Western Washington State College (now Western Washington University). This change in geographical location meant less racial discrimination than before. In the college community they were well accepted. Lois worked part-time in the hospitals as a private duty nurse and enjoyed these nursing experiences. It was possible to manage home life and still remain professionally active too.

In Bellingham the family enjoyed an improved quality of life. Everyone in their family could get on with their lives without the constant reminders and racial barriers generally experienced in most other places they had lived. Their daughters, ages seven, five, and

A Sense of Place, Person, and Promise

four in 1961, received which proved, in effect, the equivalent of a private education because they attended the college's campus laboratory school. Their sons, born in 1961 and 1962, were too young to go to school. Even with these improved conditions, Thaddeus and Lois realized that they needed to expose their children to a broader range of experiences in a multicultural environment, so they decided to leave Bellingham for Los Angeles, California.

Arriving there in 1969, Thaddeus joined the faculty in marketing at UCLA, and Lois, in 1970, entered graduate school in community mental health nursing. It was here that she first encountered questions about her academic ability; she was asked regularly by a few faculty and many students if she were an affirmative-action admission. Considering these questions insulting, she ignored them and within the prescribed two years she completed her course work and thesis, which was accepted with distinction.

The traffic congestion and smog of Los Angeles had begun to exacerbate family members' allergies and other health concerns; so, they decided to relocate to Seattle, moving there in 1972, to join the faculty at the University of Washington. Thaddeus gained an appointment in marketing and international business; Lois gained one in psychosocial nursing.

At the orientation meeting for new faculty in the School of Nursing, Lois met Maxine Pitter Haynes, a faculty member in the Division of Continuing Education and one of the founding members of Mary Mahoney Registered Nurses Club. An invitation to accompany her to a MMRNC meeting led to her joining almost immediately, and, within two years Lois was elected president. She remains very active in the organization.

Completion of Doctoral Studies and Appointment as Ombudsman

During her first six months of teaching in the UW School of Nursing, Department of Psychosocial Nursing, Lois heard the department chair, Oliver H. Osborne, say, "The School of Nursing will have 30 to 40% of its faculty with doctorates by 1990." That was her signal to be in that group of faculty. It was also apparent that she needed to return to school while training grants were still being provided by the federal government so that her family could afford to have both mother and a daughter in college at the same time. Which field would be best for her doctoral work?

She chose a field that might at first seem unrelated to nursing: urban planning. In fact, this field provided the necessary knowledge and skills for designing health programs for large social systems or organizations. As a member of the community mental health board in Bellingham, Washington, Lois had worked alongside urban planners. During graduate school at UCLA she again encountered urban planners who were completing their degrees and also gaining experiences in planning in the Watts area of Los Angeles. She understood what planners do and realized that a degree in planning would complement and extend in positive ways her expertise in community mental health. Receiving a U. S. Housing and Urban Development research award, she began designing preventive health programs in hypertension for public school students and, with the help of Seattle school nurses, implemented preventive programs related to hypertension in one-half of the high schools in Seattle. Completing the Ph.D. in 1976, Lois returned to the U.W. School of Nursing to resume her career.

That career took another turn in 1982 when Lois applied for and was appointed Ombudsman for Sexual Harassment at the University. This position evolved in 1988 to a more comprehensive one; she became University Ombudsman. She is the first nurse to be appointed to these ombuds roles. As such, she has provided a comprehensive preventive health program to address issues of sexual harassment and other forms of workplace misconduct. She believes that her experiences

Lois Price Spratlen in 1988 following her appointment as University Ombudsman at the University of Washington, Seattle, WA. Lois is the first woman and first nurse to serve in this role which was established in 1969. (Mary Levin, photographer)

as an African American woman, nurse, educator, and urban social planner have enhanced her ability to hear, understand, empathize, and communicate. Her focus in particular has been on how to provide relevant services, delivered through education and mediation, to those members of the University community who seek help in resolving conflicts. Further, her background as a board certified psychotherapist has helped her be an effective mediator.

Continuing Attainment of Goals

Throughout her career in professional nursing and, more recently, social planning, Lois has used the skills and knowledge acquired early in life to assist her in achieving professional and personal goals. Role models, reinforcements, and resources needed for success have continued to be available. Whenever she has encountered race and gender bias or other challenges which are highly visible and often very negative experiences, she has marshaled her internal strengths and secured needed help from supportive individuals. They have stimulated her to persevere and succeed wherever she happened to be. She has two recent acknowledgements of that success: being named in 1998 Ombuds of the Year by the California Caucus of College and University Ombuds and induction in 1999 into The American Academy of Nursing. These honors reflect a career of dedication through service delivery to others, and fulfill the promise of a satisfying professional career in nursing.

Lois and Thaddeus are the proud parents of five children and enjoy their seven grandchildren and one great-grandchild. Their children in order of their births are Pamela, Patricia, Paula, Thadd (later changed to Khalfani) and Townsand. Their seven grandchildren include Tuwalole, Dumisani, Janeen, Thaddeus; Martin, Elise, and Emerson. Nizala, Tuwalole's daughter, is their great-grandchild.

In addition to being an active member of MMPNO, Lois is a member of the California Caucus of College and University Ombuds (CCCUO) where she serves as co-editor of the organization's journal. She is also the chair of the King County Board of Ethics (KCBOE). Lois and Thaddeus are active in peace and justice work. These activities are so enjoyable and fulfilling that she will not talk about retirement.

Instead, Lois continues to provide Ombuds services to others at the University and health and social services to residents in the Puget Sound Region.

An Advocate for Children, Families, and Community Change

Elizabeth Moore Thomas

At age 11, Elizabeth Thomas knew she wanted to be a nurse, and since her high school days, she has diligently pursued this goal. She made sure to take classes that would insure her admission to college. Furthermore, even in early life she possessed first-hand knowledge of institutional and organizational barriers that might interfere with or impede her professional development. Later, she encountered obstacles to the maintenance of strong family ties and positive community changes; yet she has always tried to turn obstacles into stepping-stones to success.

Early Assumption of Duties

Born in Mobile, Alabama, on April 15, 1934, she was the fifth of six children born to Earl and Alberta Besteda Moore. Her two older sisters are Earlene and Augusta and her two older brothers are Oscar and Earl; Frances is her youngest sister. During the time that all six children resided at home, a great deal of work was required from everyone to keep things in good order. Their mother never worked outside of the home, "too busy raising the six of us to do much of anything else." Their father was a steady worker at a local automobile tire-recapping station, but he had a drinking problem. According to Elizabeth, "My parents dealt with my dad's drinking by letting mother manage the money. Every week my mother picked up my father's pay check to be sure we had enough money to live on."

Living in the Negro section of Mobile, the family had a small house which made it necessary for the children to share beds with one another. Even though cramped, the house was always clean because their mother taught all of the children how to cook and clean and established a work-rotation schedule, which required them to help one another whether they wanted to or not.

All of the children and their mother attended Mt. Zion Baptist Church, although, once the boys began working, they attended as time permitted. The girls were regularly involved in Sunday school and the Baptist Training Union (Christian education for children and young people), and Elizabeth sang in the youth choir. All church members and staff were Negro, as were the students and teachers in their public school. Miss Maynard, a White missionary, was the only exception.

A Crucial Hospital Experience

In 1945, their mother became ill. She stayed in bed for two or three days with what she said was stomach pain. At that time their father was away in the army, serving in World War II. Finally, she was taken to a hospital for surgery but soon thereafter she died. In later life, Elizabeth learned that her mother had had a ruptured appendix and developed peritonitis, having remained at home too long after the initial pain occurred.

At the time of her mother's death, their Aunts Mattie Kennedy and Carrie Watts, the minister and members of Mt. Zion organized themselves and helped to care for the children until their oldest sister, Earlene, returned home from Spelman College in Atlanta. For several days, there was a whirlwind of activity in their house, some of the helpers coming from outside their immediate neighborhood. When the family learned that their mother would not likely be returning home, Oscar, the oldest son, thought that they should visit their mother in the hospital while she was still alive. Oscar, with Elizabeth and the two older sisters, made the long walk from their home to the hospital. They got all the way to the floor where their mother was, only to be stopped by a hospital staff person, who said to Elizabeth, "You are not old enough to go in." This statement reflected the policy in many hospitals at that time that children under 13 years of age were not allowed to visit. She recalls, "My brother told Augusta to go into the room and stand near the window. He would take me outside and let me stand on his shoulders so that I could look through the window and see Mother." (In some hospitals at that time, Negro

An Advocate for Children, Families, and Community Change

patients were placed in basement floors or separate buildings from White patients and windows in some buildings were easy to see through.) She did see her mother lying in the bed with "tubes in her nose and tubes in her arm," and, although she didn't know what purpose these tubes served, their appearance left a lasting impression on her. It was at that moment that she decided to become a nurse working with children. Still, she says now, "I've never really gotten over not being allowed to see my mother."

The minister, family members, and neighbors came in and out of their home for many days after their mother's death. On one occasion, the minister prayed with them, enabling her to feel "the power of prayer." Since that time, religion has been the centerpiece of her life.

Earlene dropped out of college and stayed home to help raise the children. Once their brothers were through high school, she got married and later returned to college, completing her studies in Mobile. Elizabeth and her sister, Frances, lived in the family home with their father, but Earlene, who lived just up the street, continued to run the affairs of their home, just as her mother had done.

Learning Management and Leadership Skills

Beginning in her freshman year in high school and throughout high school and her first year of college, Elizabeth worked as a maid for a White family and did some of the cooking. Not only was this family very nice to her, but also, through this work experience, she learned how to manage a home, her money, schoolwork, and church activities. Even though she made very little money, she was able to keep all of it for herself. Also active in school, she participated in student government, choir, and drama club, the latter activities more like play than hard work. Since she had a good singing voice, she loved singing at school and at church where she often served as the lead soloist. In school plays she also had several significant roles. Her after-school job was manageable enough that she was able to study and maintain good grades in all of her school subjects. Without doubt, she was a leader in her school, supported by Earlene's running the house and making her and her sister Frances feel secure.

Before Elizabeth had finished high school, her father regularly told her that he wanted her to be a schoolteacher, like her oldest sister, who inspired the pride of everyone in the family. (At the time these children were growing up, teaching and nursing were the most popular professions among Negro women.) Although Elizabeth had decided she wanted to be a nurse, she wanted to please her father; so, after high school graduation in 1951, instead of following her own desire, she enrolled in a branch of Alabama State College in Mobile to become a teacher. After completing the first year with academic success but little personal enjoyment, she decided not to return for a second year. Before the school year had ended, however, she had gone to City Hospital School of Nursing to apply for admission. Her application denied because "Negroes are not admitted to this school," she left without contesting this response and did not tell anyone in her family about it until some time later.

Entry into Nurse's Training

Still determined to be a nurse, Elizabeth decided to speak to Miss Maynard, the missionary who worked at Mt. Zion Church, about her professional aspirations. Miss Maynard was helpful, telling her about the Good Samaritan Hospital in Selma, Alabama, which offered a licensed practical nursing program. After they made necessary arrangements, Miss Maynard gave Elizabeth the $50 needed to enter the program. This was the first time she had ever been away from her family and although she missed seeing her sisters and father, she made a quick adjustment to the new school, developing friendships and feeling comfortable in class with other students.

It was in nursing school that students and teachers began to call Elizabeth "Liz." She has come to like this nickname because she associates it with becoming a nurse and with performing with distinction in the nursing school's 18-month intensive program. She knew within weeks after entering this program that she had really found the right profession. She read many of her assignments two and three times, liked learning the material, and enjoyed being able to answer questions when she was called on in class. Other students and instructors recognized Liz as a good student.

This Catholic school required that all students attend Mass every day. When she first started going, she prayed as she had done at the Baptist Church; however, as she understood more of what was being said, she became more and more interested in Catholicism and

An Advocate for Children, Families, and Community Change

eventually joined the Catholic Church. For some time, she "felt funny attending Mass, and I never told Miss Maynard that I joined the Catholic Church."

Elizabeth completed the nursing program during the allotted 18 months, passed the necessary tests, and became a licensed practical nurse. Even at graduation, Liz told herself that this was just the beginning, she really wanted to be an RN and thought about Grady Hospital School of Nursing in Atlanta, but she needed to work for awhile to earn money before continuing in school.

Employment and a Husband

While in Selma, she met Clarence Thomas, who was in the Air Force, stationed at Gregg Air Force Base. She recalls, "He looked great in his uniform! I met him at the movie theater. We were more interested in getting to know each other than we were in seeing the movie; so, we visited right there in the theater." They began dating and agreed to stay in touch when Liz returned to Mobile in 1954 and applied for a job at City Hospital. Hired immediately, she was promoted within weeks to head nurse of a unit at the same hospital that had denied her admission to their school of nursing and therefore the opportunity to become a registered nurse.

Clarence and Liz stayed in contact with each other and in 1955 they married. Soon after their marriage, they moved to her husband's hometown of St. Louis, Missouri. She soon became pregnant and gave birth in 1956 to Clarence, Jr. Then, when Clarence was on military duty in Korea, she moved to Selma, Alabama, where she worked at Good Samaritan Hospital. She practiced as a licensed practical nurse and remained until 1956-57.

Clarence returned from Korea a changed person. As a result of his being in combat during the war, he experienced what was then called "shell shock," later, "post traumatic stress disorder." The full significance of that problem would emerge later.

The family returned to St. Louis, where Liz worked at St. Mary's infirmary at night and was a student at Saint Mary's Hospital School of Nursing during the day. She also became pregnant again. (Their daughter, Donsetta, was born in 1959.) Clarence's erratic behavior at home was worrisome. Loud noises overhead from planes and the baby's crying provoked strong emotional responses in him. Once, he physically attacked Liz, prompting her to seek help from the Veteran's Administration Hospital. The doctors there recommended that the family move to Washington State where Clarence, Sr. could receive the latest in mental health care. They followed this advice and made plans to move.

In 1961 the family moved to Seattle where Liz and her children could live with Clarence's brother, a teacher at Garfield High School, and his sister, while Clarence, Sr. was temporarily admitted to the Veteran's Hospital in Spokane (in Eastern Washington). Once a bed at American Lake Hospital (near Tacoma) became available, he was transferred there. Nevertheless, even with the best available care, her husband was never able to return home to live for more than short visits with his family. She began to realize she would have to raise their children alone because the doctors had been very candid about the seriousness of her husband's illness. From this point, she was effectively a single mother. Indeed, Clarence would die in 1987.

Further Nursing Training

For 11 years, Liz worked as a practical nurse at Harborview Hospital where she saw Thelma Pegues, a member of Mary Mahoney Registered Nurses Club. That acquaintance helped her sustain her long-held desire to complete a program of study that would enable her to become an RN. Indeed, in 1971, she entered Shoreline Community College (in a suburb of Seattle) to pursue an Associate in Arts degree in nursing, using welfare resources in order to meet all of her expenses. Whereas gaining admission was easy, the learning experience was lonely, with only two other African Americans in the program, Jean Hayes Amos and Annie Jones. They were friendly and

Elizabeth Moore Thomas in 1972 as a student nurse at Shoreline Community College, Seattle, WA.

An Advocate for Children, Families, and Community Change

supportive of one another, but they each had family and work responsibilities that prevented them from spending much time together. Feeling a deep need to be self-reliant, Liz also took courses as a non-matriculated student at Seattle University, along with her community-college courses, completing the two-year degree program right on schedule in 1972. She then made it a point to get off welfare as soon as possible.

At last! Liz took state board examinations and became a registered nurse. Graduation day was one of the happiest days of her life. She was also happy because by this time her youngest sister, Frances, and her family had moved to Seattle. They had always been very close to each other and now that she lived here they could resume that relationship.

Community Nursing Experience and Still More Academic Work

She began working as a Head-Start coordinator for the city of Seattle, assigned as health coordinator at First AME Head Start Program. This job involved assessing children's health status, physical screening and determining whether children had completed the necessary immunizations. Assessing their growth and development and providing health education were integral parts of her responsibilities. Community outreach through organizations and agencies also served as a principal way to access children and their family members as well as putting her into a leadership role in various organizations. This combination of clinical and community practice was especially appealing to her and beneficial for promoting child and community health and wellness. She became well known throughout the Puget Sound area for her work in this program.

As she had before, Liz combined her Head-Start work with studies as a part-time student. This time she matriculated at Seattle University, where she completed requirements for a Bachelor of Science degree in nursing in 1973.

Still another academic experience beckoned, although, by this time, she was tired of going to school, raising two children alone, and working full time. Since many of the children enrolled in the Head Start program went to Virginia Mason Hospital for immunizations and physical examinations, she met Dr. Richard Dion at Virginia Mason Clinic. After a short association, he encouraged her to enter the Pediatric Nurse Practitioner program at the University of Washington. This suggestion reinforced her belief that she should get as much education as possible; so, she called the Maternal/Child Department at the University of Washington and made an appointment with the PNP program director. Even before explaining details of the program, the director said, "There is a five-year waiting list." Liz asked to have her name placed on the list during this brief meeting.

Six months later, when she took another group of children to Virginia Mason, Dr. Dion asked if she had inquired about the PNP program. He greeted the news about a five-year waiting period with surprise, saying that only a few weeks ago he had been asked to recommend someone for the program. He even wondered aloud if there really was such a long waiting list. While Liz was in the office, he called the PNP director and asked if she was still interested in having him recommend a prospective student. He then said, "I have a nurse in my office right now that I want to recommend. When you meet with her, she will have a note from me."

Some days later she returned to the University for a meeting with the director. When Liz entered the office, the director was smoking a cigarillo. So surprised was she to see that Liz was the student recommended by Dr. Dion that she dropped her cigarillo. Regaining her composure, she said, "I was going to call you because an opening has come available." With equal composure, Liz said she would complete the application and all other paperwork required to enter the PNP program. In her own mind, she wondered what had happened to the five-year waiting list.

Once again she endured a lonely learning experience. No other African Americans or other ethnic groups of color were in the PNP program and all instructional staff were Caucasian. However, she made friends with two classmates who supported her and helped her feel welcomed, Bobbie McAbee, who later completed a Ph.D., and Connie Swagel, with whom she shared notes if she missed a class and Xeroxed readings as needed. They continue to maintain contact with one another.

An Advocate for Children, Families, and Community Change

Affiliation with Odessa Brown Clinic in Seattle

After completing the theory courses, students had to find clinical settings for supervised experience. While in church one day, she met Dr. Blanche Lavizzo, an African American physician who was the medical director at Odessa Brown Children's Clinic, located near Liz's home. Some days later, she made an appointment to meet with Dr. Lavizzo to tell her about her need for a clinical practice site; Dr. Lavizzo immediately agreed to allow her to practice at the Clinic.

It turned out to be one of the most positive learning experiences Liz has ever had. Providing care principally to African American children and youth, she received clinical supervision from an African American physician and was allowed to do community-outreach work, using well-established relationships with many agencies, families, and community organizations. So great was the need for aiding residents with accessible health care and so great was her enjoyment in doing this work that she asked, once her student clinical affiliation ended, if there was any possibility that she could be employed. Indeed, she could. Immediately after she had completed all requirements for the PNP in 1975 and thereby becoming the first African American pediatric nurse practitioner in the State of Washington, Liz was hired through the National Health Service Corporation by Children's Hospital for an initial three-year appointment at Odessa Brown Clinic. (Some 25 years later, fewer than five African American nurses have completed the PNP program.) She continued doing clinical practice and community outreach there, now as an independent provider, and has also done a great deal of in-service education for staff and clients at the clinic. Teenage parenting

Pediatric nurse practitioner Elizabeth Thomas with a tiny patient at Odessa Brown Children's Clinic in 1993.

classes, for example, have been extremely effective for the young women and men who are new parents.

Career Achievements

Liz joined Mary Mahoney Professional Nurses Organization in 1973, as soon as she became a registered nurse, and became very active in the organization after she completed her nurse practitioner program, serving as president for four consecutive years. She has been chair of the scholarship committee for over 15 years and has connected MMPNO to special projects that serviced members of the community, such as screening programs, buckle-baby-car-seat programs, and career day outreach to public schools.

As a practicing professional, Liz has had many opportunities to express her thanks to Dr. Richard Dion for his encouragement and support for her professional development. She has kept him informed of her many professional awards and national recognition received for her outstanding work in the field of pediatrics. She had the invaluable opportunity of working with Dr. Lavizzo for nearly a decade before her death in 1985. Other medical directors with whom Liz has successfully worked are Drs. Kenneth Feldman and Ed Marcuse. These individuals made unique contributions to Liz's professional development, and she feels that she has reciprocated with contributions to their careers.

For more than 24 years Liz worked at Odessa Brown, serving as a preceptor to many students from the University of Washington's PNP program. In addition, she was a mentor and clinical supervisor for nursing students from other colleges and universities in the area and has provided in-service seminars for staff at Odessa Brown related to cultural differences in health-seeking and use of health information by African American children, youth, and families. Beyond the clinic, she has served as chairperson of the American Nurses Association Pediatric Nurse Practitioner Certification Committee, a board member of the Washington State Nurses Association and the King County Nurses Association, and a member of numerous community organizations outside of professional nursing. Throughout her professional career, she has been actively involved in her church, serving as president of the National Black Lay Catholic Caucus.

An Advocate for Children, Families, and Community Change

In 1998, before retiring from Odessa Brown Clinic, Liz helped hire another pediatric nurse practitioner to succeed her. Through the hiring practices implemented during her time of employment, she assisted in advancing the role of the nurse practitioner in this setting. This retirement was only partial. She quickly became part-time health coordinator for a new program offered to some students at T.T. Minor School (in Seattle), thus returning to a role similar to the one she had held as Head-Start coordinator at First AME Church. She plans to continue practicing for as long as her health allows. Her part-time work gives her time to enjoy her two children, Clarence and Donsetta, as well as her three grandchildren, Aaron, Anthony, and Jonneice.

Throughout her professional career, Liz has often reflected on the time when she was denied the opportunity to see her mother in her hospital room before she died. In partial compensation for that denial, she has been able to bring children and parents together who were not experiencing physical separation but who were socially and

Elizabeth Thomas in May 2000 receiving the Alvirita Little Award for outstanding community service. Pictured with her are Rear Admiral Kenneth P. Moutsugu, MD, MPH, Deputy Surgeon General of the United States, and Mrs. Alvirita Little.

psychologically separated from one another. During her work with these troubled families, individuals have expressed their gratitude for the extensive help she has provided them.

Among her numerous awards are the Hunthausen Humanitarian Award given annually by the Catholic Community Services to a citizen who has served the community in an exemplary way, especially by working with the poor and the systems that serve them, and induction into the WSNA Hall of Fame for her outstanding contributions to professional nursing. She has also learned from the dean of Shoreline Community College that a scholarship at the college is being established in her name.

In explaining her success she said, "I have always worked very hard. I know how to ask for help and I have faith that help will be received." Help has not always come when she most wanted it, but in time it has. Liz also still believes in the power of prayer. The combination of hard work, directed effort, and fervent prayer has contributed to a successful and committed life. In the process, she has been a valued practitioner for children and families and a positive agent of change in the community.

Seattle's First African American School Nurse

Shirley Williams Ticeson Gilford

Shirley Williams grew up in an extended family that included her maternal grandparents, Nancy and Joseph Robertson. They were among the very few Negroes in Morganza, Louisiana, to own their own farm. It was through the help of their 11 children and their collective blood, sweat, toil, and good fortune that they were successful farmers. Her grandfather took pride in telling Shirley that her mother, Annie Bell, and her mother's sister, Eva, worked alongside their brothers in planting and harvesting their crops.

The two Robertson sisters developed and maintained a very close life-long relationship. Even after they were married and moved to Lemoyen, Louisiana, they lived on the same street just a few houses from one another. There were brothers and relatives there, too, and all of their families remained very close.

A short time before Shirley was born, her mother, who was in poor health, moved in with Eva and Eva's husband, Willie Hawkins, in order to receive needed care. Even so, while giving birth to Shirley on July 29, 1934, her mother nearly died. After the birth, she remained in poor health for some time. Johnny Williams, Shirley's father, remained in their home down the street while her mother was recuperating and frequently visited his wife and newborn child.

Shirley Williams as a young child with her very favorite purse.

Some years later, Shirley's brother, Rechell, was born. Their father, however, was not a significant figure in her life. He was someone she saw once when she was about seven years old, afterward never again. Several years later, after her parents were divorced, her mother married Morris George. They had two sons, Maurice and Wilbert, with whom Shirley spent little time. During her formative years she lived with her Aunt Eva and Uncle Willie. Eva was considerably older than Shirley's mother; so, she was like a surrogate mother to both of them. All three got along very well together.

Learning about Opportunity and Education

Among her striking memories of early childhood were her many uncles and cousins in the neighborhood, who regularly played together and shared Sunday dinners, holidays, and birthdays. One Christmas her Uncle Willie gave her a small blackboard with the alphabet printed at the top. He taught her the alphabet, and she later taught it to her cousins. When Willie died, her Aunt Eva remained sad for sometime, although some years later she remarried.

From Shirley's childhood, her aunt, uncle and mother talked to her about opportunity. The word *opportunity* assumed real meaning for her when her aunt talked to her about attending school. With Shirley standing in front of her, Aunt Eva said, in the presence of Willie and Annie, "Aunt Eva only got a third grade education," holding up three fingers to make her point. Then, turning to look at Annie, she said, "I helped your mother get a sixth grade education," and held up six fingers. She did not tell how many grades in school her Uncle Willie completed. Shirley knew better than to ask. Still solemnly facing her aunt, she absorbed the final comment: "I want things to be better for you than they were for me and your mother. We want you to get a real education." From that day on she thought she had a good understanding of *opportunity*, telling herself that opportunity was education.

Later, she learned that, when her aunt was a child growing up in Morganza, there were no full-time public schools for Negro children. Even Aunt Eva's "third grade education" was really just three months of school during each of three successive years and her mother's "sixth grade education" was a mere 18 months, stretching over six years.

By the time Shirley was five years old and ready to enter school, there were public schools in Lemoyen for Negro children, although public education had always been available for Caucasian children. The segregated schools were perceived by Negro residents to be unequal to the Whites' schools; nevertheless, this was the only school available and Shirley attended it for her first few years.

Church has always occupied an important place in her life. During her childhood, the adults attended church regularly while she and her brother went to Sunday school, church, and Baptist Training Union. At a very early age she began singing in the children's choir and regularly had a leading role in church programs.

At age seven, Shirley made a speech in church that motivated the minister's wife, Mrs. Ruth Crockett, to ask Aunt Eva if she would allow Shirley to attend school in Vidalia, Louisiana. There, she was the principal of the public school, located in Concordia Parish, some 35 miles or more from Lemoyen. That school had more resources than were available in Lemoyen and involved children from many counties. Mrs. Crockett realized that Shirley had demonstrated an aptitude to learn and had leadership skills that needed to be nurtured. She also anticipated that Shirley would make a positive adjustment to living away from home, which she did, performing well in academic work and being liked by classmates. Living with Mrs. Crockett during the school year, she made three or four visits home to Lemoyen from Vidalia, returning in summer to live at her aunt's house, always also visiting with her mother and brother.

Her Aunt's Remarriage and a Family Move to Washington State

In 1944 a dramatic change occurred when her aunt married James Raphael, who worked for the railroad company in Lemoyen. Shortly after their marriage, James responded to a plea from government recruiters who came to town recruiting men and women willing to move to the Pacific Northwest for work in defense plants, shipyards, and other war-related services. He moved without the family to Bremerton, Washington, wanting to test the promise of decent housing and jobs before the entire family's activities were disrupted by a move.

African American Registered Nurses in Seattle

When Eva joined her husband shortly afterward, he had already located a place for them to live, cramped though it was. She was sure that she would find employment in the Bremerton shipyard, and she did. They tolerated these conditions because they knew that soon government housing would be available to them. While Shirley happily continued school and enjoyed living with Mrs. Crockett, the family kept in touch by mail, with the promise that her aunt and step-uncle would return to Lemoyen to get her, which, indeed they did in 1947. Now 12 years old, Shirley was ready to enter junior high school. At the end of the three-day train trip, she saw snow-covered mountains; large, green trees; green grass; and blue sky, scenes still vivid in her memory. Even more surprising was "seeing White people in houses that close to ours. At first I thought there was no segregation, until I learned that the roads and certain streets were used to separate us from Whites." She now knows that some people in Seattle remember that government housing during that period **was** segregated by race. Everyone who had migrated to the Northwest knew that racial segregation was practiced in all areas of life. Many did not bother to comment about housing segregation; rather, they filled their lives with activities that were positive and satisfying.

A New Beginning in School

Since the school year began before Shirley arrived in Bremerton, Aunt Eva went with her to enroll in school the same day she arrived. Forms filled out, they went together to the classroom. Alone, Shirley entered a classroom where initially she thought all of the children were White. While she awaited a desk assignment, her eyes met those of Beulah Smith, another Negro child. They became immediate friends and still remain very close friends.

Bea (as Shirley referred to Beulah) and her family had migrated to Bremerton years earlier, one of the few Negro families to live in a single-family home, rented from another Negro family. In those days, most of the Negroes in Bremerton were associated with the defense industries, working in the Navy yard and living in government housing. Bea had been in the school long enough to have adjusted to being the only Negro student in her classes; however, she was happy to have Shirley join her. Throughout junior high and high school, the girls were in many of the same classes.

Seattle's First African American School Nurse

Most of the students were either kind to her or ignored her. What was most important is that no one ever physically threatened her or Bea during the entire time that they were in school, even on the school bus, although other children kept their distance. "Back then we never felt afraid for our safety," she says.

Schoolteachers varied in their attitudes toward her. She recalls that "it was always possible to feel the way some teachers felt about me. And I was never allowed to forget that I was not one of them."

When they both joined the junior high school glee club, however, they made close friends among others in the group. Later, in the high school choir, the leader, Ralph Manzo, helped all 20 or 30 members to like each other very much, regardless of race. And from that group, another smaller one, which included Shirley and Bea, was chosen because of unusual musical ability. Called the Modernairs, the group traveled about the city, singing in a variety of places, an activity Shirley and Bea very much enjoyed.

These interracial friendships were strictly confined to school and school-related activities with no visits to one another's homes or telephone contact. "This was an experience that we lived and we never talked about it when it was going on. When we returned to our own communities, we socialized with one another. We went to the movies together. We had parties in each other's homes and at the recreation center. Youth activities in our churches were also a significant part of community life. I do not think we [Negroes] were without wholesome things to do," she recalls.

A small incident that occurred in a cooking class remains in her memory as significant. She and her cooking partner, Bea, were preparing a white sauce. While other paired students produced lumpy liquid, Shirley and Bea avoided that mistake because Shirley had thought about how to avoid the problem: by using an eggbeater to mix the flour and water. The cooking teacher, noticing and pleased with this clever thinking, directed the classes' attention to the successful pair and asked Shirley to describe her method to the class. For the first time, other students in the cooking class who had formerly ignored her and Bea, asked Shirley if they could be her cooking partner.

Other Aspects of Life in Bremerton

In several respects, life in Bremerton was similar to that in Louisiana. "The house that we lived in was very similar to ones occupied by White families; yet, we were segregated by roads and streets. Most Negroes and Whites lived very separate lives. There were no racial incidents that I can remember. Negroes and Whites went their separate ways."

Shirley and her relatives attended the Negro Baptist Church with her aunt in a role in the church similar to one she had in Louisiana and Shirley involved in most of the same activities she'd known in Louisiana. However, one important exception was the oratorical groups and contests organized by churches and some social organizations. Those for their church functioned at local, state and regional levels, with contest winners attending the National Baptist Convention and competing with children from other parts of the United States. The winner at the national level received a college scholarship. Shirley qualified for the national competition and traveled to New York where she performed but did not win: "While I did not win the competition, I learned how to speak in public to large audiences without experiencing a lot of fear. This skill has served me very well throughout my entire life." Her church activity and the social life of her community continued until she left for college.

She remembers, "During the 1950s teenage employment was not as readily available as it is today in many areas of the state. While the total number of Negro teenagers was small, when I was growing up in Bremerton, only one Negro teenager got a job in a department store. I never went looking for work because there was nothing available other than babysitting jobs. I worked for my aunt and uncle, doing household chores, and they gave me an allowance." Shirley never really felt deprived because her relatives were "very generous and attentive to my needs."

The Chief Reward of High School Achievement: University Enrollment

No school counselor gave her advice or information about college, nor were there regularly scheduled career days for juniors and seniors; however, visits by representatives from Seattle University made

Seattle's First African American School Nurse

significant impressions upon her and Bea, visits that led to their being admitted to S.U. The path to admission was enhanced by their culminating high school achievements. Of the 400 plus Bremerton High School graduates in 1953, four were African American. Among the six students selected to be commencement speakers, Shirley and Bea were included. "Our oratorical training really paid off and made our parents very happy. Bea actually won the National Elks' oratorical contest and received a four-year scholarship to the college or university of her choice. We both decided to attend Seattle University."

Financing university attendance was the next problem. Although her aunt and uncle were willing to make a big sacrifice to pay her private school tuition, others who knew them well, including friends, Willetta and James Gayton, thought of a way to ease the burden for Shirley's relatives. Seattle residents, the Gaytons had extra space in their home and suggested to Eva and James that Shirley live with them, helping to care for their child. They also knew about Mary Mahoney Registered Nurses Club and encouraged her to apply there for a scholarship which she received in 1955. She was only the second person to receive this award. (The first scholarship was awarded to Viola Davis.) It required, however, that the recipient be enrolled at the University of Washington School of Nursing, not Seattle U; so, she transferred to U.W., spending only one quarter on that campus before being assigned to the Harborview Hospital Division. She also moved from the Gayton home to Harborview Hall.

Shirley Williams in her University of Washington student uniform. She was in the Harborview Division.

The transition from S.U. to the U. W. was smooth. At Harborview, she regularly saw many members of MMRNC. Just seeing these nurses in white, starched uniforms inspired her to work hard. Furthermore, most of her classmates were very accepting of her; they studied together and helped one another complete the program. This acceptance was all the more remarkable because, during those years, it was often true that some White nurses were mean-spirited and treated student nurses poorly, especially Black nurses. Young student nurses like Shirley and her fellow students joined forces across racial lines and helped one another succeed.

Finishing the Degree Program, Marrying, and Finding Employment

Shirley completed the nursing program and in 1958 received a baccalaureate degree. (She had married Clarence Ticeson in 1957.) Before graduation she had also applied for a job in public health with the Seattle/King County Health Department. (A policy change within that department had occurred shortly before, so that in-patient nursing experience was no longer required of applicants.) Assigned to the Central East area of Seattle where many Black people lived, she loved working there, as she had during her student affiliation, although at that time, she recalls, she would have enjoyed being a nurse just about anywhere. This was a time for feeling excited about life for several reasons.

Soon after she passed state board exams and became a registered nurse, Shirley joined MMRNC, as well as the American Nurses Association, Washington State Nurses Association, and King County Nurses Association, becoming an active member of all these organizations and later working even at the national level in ANA.

School Nursing and Community Involvement

During her public health years, she worked as a school nurse because many schools did not have nurses assigned to them. Exposure to this type of nursing led her to seek employment with the Seattle School District where no other African American nurses worked in school nursing. She was also aware of the fact that a friend of hers, Doris Joyner, had applied for a school-nurse position the year before and was not hired. In the face of these conditions, Shirley applied anyway. Once her application reached the district office, she was interviewed by the nursing supervisor, Mrs. Olive Blandau, and the medical director, Dr. Vivian Harlan. As a result she was hired in 1962 by the Seattle School District as the first African American school nurse and assigned to two schools, T.T. Minor and Madrona, both located in the Central District. Shortly thereafter, Verna Hill was hired as a

Seattle's First African American School Nurse

school nurse and was assigned to Meany Junior High, also in the Central District. Word about these hirings passed through the nursing community very fast. This news served as a source of hope for other RNs and student nurses.

Two years later Shirley divorced Clarence Ticeson and directed her energy to working through her associations to improve the status of school nurses. At that time, school nurses were not included in the Seattle Education Association even though most possessed degrees similar to those of teachers. She helped organize nurses to bring down barriers of access to and membership in SEA.

While in nursing school, Shirley realized that members of MMRNC had made it possible for her to pursue her education

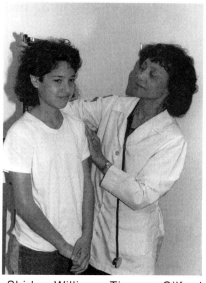

Shirley Williams Ticeson Gilford functioning in her school nurse role. Shirley was the first African American school nurse hired in Seattle, WA in 1962.

without worrying about where money would come from to pay school expenses. Shirley reasoned that one way she could pass on her good fortune to society was by working in professional and community organizations to achieve needed social change. As a child, she had learned from her Aunt Eva that, if you want something to change, you need to work to help make it happen, and, as a member of so many professional associations, she could work with others to carry out that principle.

In addition to membership in her professional associations, she joined community organizations including the Seattle Urban League. During the same time, Shirley served as president of her sorority, Delta Sign Theta, and of MMRNC. In each of these organizations she worked to help other members understand the contributions that nurses, generally, and school nurses, in particular, make to the development of human potential in families, schools, and the larger community.

While working at T.T. Minor and Madrona Schools, she sought broader experience and asked for assignment to Garfield High School in Seattle. While she was there, from 1968 to 1970, grassroots groups in the city were active in such causes as increasing the number of African American administrators and teachers in the Seattle School District and other nearby districts. These efforts resulted in significant hiring efforts. Positions for school nurses began to open, too. Shirley personally encouraged every African American nurse she knew and other nurses of color to apply for jobs. Eventually, Vivian Lee, Muriel Softli, Pat Watts, and Frances Terry became school nurses in the Seattle schools.

Response to Civil Unrest

Another highlight of her public school nursing career was a human sensitivity training program held at Seabeck Conference Center in Seabeck, WA. Small groups of African American and Caucasian students were selected to participate in this program, some of whom would be among the first middle-school students to participate in a busing program aimed at achieving racial desegregation in Seattle's public schools. Since she provided health teaching and services to students and participated in small group discussions, several teachers and staff members confided in Shirley that they did not feel prepared to work with an ethnically diverse student population. She therefore had a role in extending the Seabeck experience by helping Dr. Robert Gary, a Black administrator, to organize programs for students, teachers, staff, and parents that promoted and enhanced skills in multicultural education.

This was a dynamic time to be in school nursing when existing policies, patterns, and practices were being challenged and when militancy among students and community residents was rising. Regularly, she worked with other teachers and administrators to prevent outbursts from spreading to the entire school. On one occasion, a student lost his composure and assaulted a school principal. She intervened directly in this situation and successfully calmed it.

Similarly, when Martin Luther King was assassinated and students demanded that the American flag be flown at half-staff, she participated in administrators' deliberations that led to a decision to honor King in that way at all schools. It was the dynamic combination of students, community residents, and sensitive school administrators that helped to keep the educational process operating while responding to inflammatory external circumstances.

In 1971, Shirley was reassigned again, this time to Hamilton Middle School, outside of the Central Area, the first time she had worked in a predominantly Caucasian community school. Her tenure there lasted only one year, long enough for her to realize that there was still much work to be done in race relations within the Puget Sound region. She said of this experience, "The students and I got along very well. Many of the teachers and staff were also accepting of my presence. However, I ran into problems when I made home visits. It was really a surprise and disappointment to me to observe the reaction of parents to my presence. It was during this year that I realized that I wanted to use my energy working in an environment where I could really be most effective. During this very same period I met and married Lloyd Gilford, an engineer at Boeing in Seattle. We purchased a house in Issaquah and the commute to Hamilton was too far. Once again, I requested a reassignment and my request was granted."

Awards for Contributions

At South Shore Middle School, beginning in 1972, her enthusiasm and love for school nursing returned. She put her heart into her work and within a short time established excellent relationships with teachers, staff, and school administrators, as well as with students. In an environment that was supportive of her many activities, she derived renewed joy from her work. She also received several awards.

In 1970 Shirley was a nominee for Excellence in Education by the Seattle Business Committee for Education. In 1975 she received the Gold Acorn Award for service in the Washington Congress of Parents and Teachers. Reflecting on these awards and others, she said, "It is wonderful to be nominated and given awards by my peers and colleagues. However, the most satisfying recognition that I ever received is when a former student, in a restaurant or in the community, stops to say, 'Mrs. Gilford, I'm so and so. You were my school nurse' (at whichever school they attended), and they tell me I made a difference in their lives." These encounters touch the core of her being. While she appreciates the more public rewards and recognition too, the more direct human relationships are intensely meaningful to her.

In 1981 she was recognized by the King County Nurses Association, which named her "Nurse of the Year," an annual award to a professional nurse who has demonstrated outstanding achievement and contributions to nursing and the community. In the same year, she also served as president of the Seattle School Nurses Association, working with other nurses to develop standards of practice for school nurses. At the national level she was a member of the Executive Committee for the Division of Community Health. At the state level she served the Washington State Nurses Association as the chairperson of the Commission on Nursing Practice and Education. And at the county level she was chairperson of the Subcommittee on School Health in KCNA. In each of these roles she not only saw how her contribution made a real difference but also enjoyed working with her colleagues to achieve objectives.

Retirement from School Nursing

In 1993, after 32 years of service as a school nurse, Shirley retired, although she has continued to receive recognition from the professional associations in which she made such a significant contribution. Most recently she was inducted into the WSNA Hall of Fame. In accepting the honor, she said, "It is truly wonderful to receive this recent recognition along with three other members of Mary Mahoney Professional Nurses Organization, Mary Lee Bell, Muriel Softli, and Elizabeth Thomas. All of us have been very active in WSNA, KCNA, and ANA."

Shirley is now in business with her husband, Lloyd Gilford, who is retired from Boeing. Proud owners of The Gilford Group, a travel agency that provides booking for cruises and other travel-related services, they enjoy good health and plan to continue this work for some time.

Most important, she feels proud to have come from rural Louisiana by way of Bremerton, Washington, to a fulfilling life as Seattle's first African American public school nurse.

Public Health: "The Right Place for Me"

Gwendolyn Harden Browne

Gwen, as she prefers to be called, thinks even now, in retirement, that she always wanted to be a nurse. Her recollection is that she decided to be a community-health nurse when she was about eight or nine years old. Her mother's best friend, Miss Geraldine, a community health nurse, lived a few houses down the street from Gwen's family home in Atlanta, Georgia. She regularly saw Ms. Geraldine going out in the morning to work. Almost daily, Ms. Geraldine stopped in for a short visit with Gwen's mother on her way home from work and told interesting stories about the families she was caring for. Ms. Geraldine was affiliated with Grady Hospital and was well known in the community. Most residents knew that when she requested help, community people responded. Gwen's family was one of those who contributed food, clothing, and other items too.

Miss Geraldine, who appeared to be very happy in doing things for other people and in conveying information about her families that made others want to do something to help, made an indelible impression on Gwen. The combination of her stories and her personal sense of happiness convinced Gwen that community health was the career she wanted to pursue.

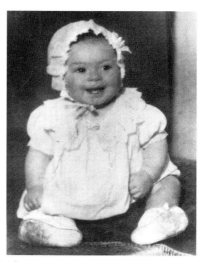

Gwendolyn Harden as a baby.

African American Registered Nurses in Seattle

Early Life in Atlanta and Seattle

Born September 29, 1934, in Atlanta, Gwen was the first and only child of Lucy Williams Harden and Quitman Harden. Very young when they married, her parents had a lot of growing up to do. Lucy worked at the Scripto Pen and Pencil factory, her father at a local paper mill. Based on what her mother told her, she has concluded that these two young people worked hard to save their marriage, but the stresses of life were greater than the strength of their relationship; so, their marriage ended in divorce when Gwen was two or three years old. She has no memory of living with both parents. Following their separation, Gwen's father was not a significant figure in her life; however, she has one vivid and fond memory of him, giving her rides in the cab seat of his motorcycle when he came for visits. She believes that he continued to have some contact with her until she and the whole family left Atlanta several years later.

The immediate void in Gwen's life created by her father's departure was filled by her mother's brother, Uncle George (a Pullman porter on the Southern Pacific Railroad line), his wife, Nancy, and 10 other adults in her mother's family as well as her grandparents. Frugal in managing his financial resources, he had purchased a large house in Atlanta and invited Gwen and her mother to live with this extended family which even included one great grandparent. They accepted his invitation. The only child in this household of adults, Gwen was "surrounded by love" and retains fond memories of the activities that seemed to make her the center of family life.

The family of Baptists, like most of their neighbors, attended Baptist services regularly, taking young Gwen along. She remembers sitting on her uncle's lap and being expected to be quiet during the church service. When she was six or seven years old, she began attending Sunday school. She also received lots of attention from neighbors and other friends in the community.

Uncle George's assigned railroad run, which he made several times a month, was from Atlanta to Seattle. At least every two or three years he obtained passes for all members of the family so that they too could travel to Seattle and spend some time there. They liked its beauty so much that eventually the entire family relocated, having

Public Health: "The Right Place for Me"

looked at areas of the city where they might want to live. At that time, most Negro families were forced by discriminatory practices to live in the Central Area of Seattle.

Before they moved, Gwen's Uncle George bought a restaurant across the street from the King Street Station, an area where, in the early 1940s, several Negro businesses were located, including a record shop, barbershop, dry cleaner, and tavern. Gwen recalls that her uncle told her the merchants met regularly, usually on Mondays, to discuss how business was going and how they could help one another remain in business. He named the restaurant "Nancy's Place" in honor of his wife, and he remained in business in this same location from the early 1940s through the 1970s.

Gwen was never allowed to go near the restaurant until she was about 16 years old, having heard from her uncle, "Some of the men who come to the restaurant are fresh [i.e., flirt with young girls]," and he did not want any of his customers to flirt with her. Whenever she did visit the restaurant, he was there at the end of the counter, never leaving her alone. During short and infrequent visits, she liked ringing up sales on the cash register and, occasionally, serving a customer a soft drink, but her uncle was adamant about not wanting her there too often.

He also bought a house on Fir Street for the family so that Gwen could immediately enroll in Immaculate Conception Elementary School. A sobering experience there was being sent home on two separate occasions by one of the nuns because her skirt was too short. Those incidents led her mother to decide they must follow the standard set forth by the nuns; her skirt hemlines were lowered and she never encountered any other problems while at this school.

The extended family made a smooth adjustment to Seattle, joining Mt. Zion Baptist Church, where Uncle George became a deacon. Serving in that role for the rest of his life, he was respected and admired by members of the congregation. Other family members also assumed active roles in the church.

When Gwen was 10, her mother married James (Jimmy) Hill, a longshoreman. A mature adult by this time, she persisted in her second marriage until the time of her death. After their marriage, Gwen, her mother, and stepfather moved to a house on Beacon Hill where her mother, who had a job at the Cerebral Palsy Center, could bring a few of the children to her home on weekends and some holidays. She usually selected children who did not have parents or close relatives and who, therefore, had few opportunities for outings.

While in junior and senior high school, Gwen did not work outside the home; instead, she cooked, washed dishes, and did the laundry, chores her mother would have had to do after her day job. Gwen wanted to increase her mother's free time to give her opportunities to work in her garden, which was one of her greatest pleasures. Gardening, on the other hand, did not appeal to Gwen.

Acceptance into a University Nursing Program

At the end of four unmemorable years at Seattle's Cleveland High School, Gwen graduated in 1953. During that summer, she and her mother visited Seattle University where they got information about admission. Greeted by a very courteous advisor and without private conversation, they both decided on the spot that this was the appropriate nursing school for Gwen. Although tuition was very high, her mother told her not to worry about the money, saying, "All you have to do is study and get good grades." Accepted for admission for Fall, 1953, she was one of only 10 students in the class. Another was Lois Eason, an African American who still lives in Seattle and is also a member of MMPNO. No African Americans or other persons of color were on the faculty at Seattle University School of Nursing in those days.

She completed the theory courses there and clinical experiences at Providence Hospital, as well as three affiliations, psych/mental health at American Lake (in Eastern Washington), tuberculosis service at Walla Walla (also in Eastern Washington), and public health at Seattle-King County. During these undergraduate experiences, only one professor gave her problems; he wanted nearly verbatim responses to examination questions and in class discussions. After finishing the class, she realized that he just wanted people to have an excellent foundation in anatomy and physiology, but she would have preferred a friendlier approach to instruction. She was not alone in her reaction.

In retrospect Gwen readily acknowledges that she received an excellent education at Seattle University (S.U.), where instructors took a personal interest in all students. Although it was the right

Public Health: "The Right Place for Me"

school for her, she never formed close attachments to any other students; instead, she maintained her ties to her community and family to satisfy her social needs.

While attending S.U. she did not have to work because her mother and Uncle George had saved and planned for her college expenses. She volunteered to be a hostess in the Young Women's Christian Association (YWCA). In this role she and several other volunteers attended social events at Fort Lawton, Fort Lewis, and other army bases in the area where service men were stationed. These events included dances, dinners, and informal receptions, with chaperones present to assure that hostesses were not led astray. At one of these events, during her freshman year, Gwen met Edgar Browne at Fort Lewis. After their first meeting, they continued to see each other frequently. Eventually, he asked Gwen to marry him. When Edgar approached Gwen's mother to ask if they could get married, she answered with an emphatic "No. Gwen has wanted to be a nurse since she was a little girl and I don't want anything to prevent her from reaching this goal."

Marriage, Completion of a Degree, and Motherhood

Gwendolyn Harden Brown in 1957 at graduation from Seattle University with her Bachelor of Science degree. (Gwen is 4th from the left in the front row)

In 1955 Edgar approached her mother again, telling her he'd saved enough money to pay for the remaining two years of Gwen's nursing-school expenses. He showed Mrs. Hill that he'd placed the money in a special account for that purpose. Relenting, she consented to the marriage. As Gwen recalled that incident, she said, "I knew how much it meant to my mother and all of my other family members for me to get my education. I would never have intentionally done anything to disappoint them." In June 1957, Gwen received her baccalaureate degree in nursing. At that time she was seven months pregnant. In August 1957, their son, Brian, was born.

A Public Health Career that Soared

Remaining at home for nearly 18 months, Gwen enjoyed being a full-time mother and housewife; however, in the winter of 1958 she got the urge to do community-health nursing. Never having worked as a professional nurse, she was eager for that experience; so, she went to the Seattle-King County Health Department and applied for a part-time job. Within two days, she was hired as a part-time public health nurse in the South District. Her earlier student experiences in the health department had convinced her that her childhood impressions of community health which were associated with Miss Geraldine, had been accurate. She had no doubt that "community health is the place for me." She found the administrator who conducted the interview to be very encouraging of her aspirations and felt so confident during the interview that she told the administrator, "Public health really needs me."

According to Gwen and other African American nurses who were in the Puget Sound region during the 1940s and 50s, Gwen was the first African American public health nurse in Seattle. (Her baccalaureate education prepared her to engage in community-based practice.) At this time she joined Mary Mahoney Registered Nurses Club, having learned about MMRNC while completing clinical experiences in one of the area hospitals, and she has remained an active member in the organization ever since.

In 1960 Gwen became pregnant with her second child. Her daughter, Melanie, arrived in May. Once, again, Gwen remained at home for about two years, returning in 1962 to the health department.

Public Health: "The Right Place for Me"

After the two-year interruption, she worked as a public health nurse through 1965, providing direct services to clients. At that time, visiting nurse services and public health services were combined. A visiting nurse is a Registered Nurse who provides skilled nursing care to patients under the direction of a doctor. With most having an undergraduate and some having a graduate degree, public health nurses are also Registered Nurses. Their focus is on the community with their efforts aimed at preventing illness and disease. Health education, early detection of individuals at risk of illness, and prompt treatment are hallmarks of preventive services which are provided in schools, community facilities, and public settings where community residents can be reached efficiently. These integrated services enabled Gwen and other nurses to gain valuable experiences in functioning as independent health-care providers. She summarized the challenge by saying, "One has to improvise and think on one's feet in order to give quality care to clients in their homes. It gives nurses a valuable opportunity to test their knowledge and skills on a daily basis."

From 1958 through 1965, Gwen gained experience in working with the diverse ethnic/racial populations in her district. She also acquired an in-depth knowledge of the needs of residents in her community and a sound understanding of the policies and methods of operating in the public health department. All the while, Gwen was being mentored and given opportunities for advancement within the public health system. These combined experiences provided a strong foundation for future roles that she would assume.

She served as an assistant public health nurse supervisor from 1966 through 1968, orienting new public health nurses to their roles and providing them with continuous supervision. Her next promotion in this period was to public health supervisor, a role that included hiring responsibilities and development of policies and programs appropriate for a diverse population of clients.

Then, from 1974 to 1977, she left Seattle and was a public health nurse in the Alameda County Public Health Department in Oakland, California. Upon her return, she was appointed administrator of the North District in January, 1978, where she was once, again, the first African American nurse to serve as district administrator. At a time when a new $2.5 million facility to include personal and environmental health services was being constructed, she met with architects, engineers, builders, interior decorators, and many other personnel. For the first time in her career she was responsible for nurses as well as sanitation engineers, social workers, psychologists, and all other health-care service providers. She remembers the day the building was dedicated. There were smiles and sighs of relief as well as a sense of pride by all who had worked with her to bring the building into service.

It was also in her role as district administrator that Gwen experienced racism and gender bias. She claims to have confronted these challenges head on with her usual sense of confidence and determination, but she did not reveal exactly what steps she took.

Meeting with department heads and staff, Gwen established schedules for regular meetings of all work groups. In her words, "I never worked so hard in my life but it paid off." Within three years the district operations greatly improved. She had gained the respect and cooperation of most of the staff. In addition, she had oral and written confirmation of the quality of her work and service with others.

While Gwen was carrying out this major responsibility as administrator, other managers and supervisors in different districts in King County regularly consulted her. These consultations led her to propose to the chief administrator a rotation plan for all directors, one that would produce more effective evaluation of administrators responsible for delivery of service. Also, those who were ineffective as leaders could be reassigned or given educational opportunities to improve their skills.

After serving at North District for three years, Gwen was assigned to the East District in Bellevue, Washington. While she served as district administrator there, the East District was twice voted the most effectively run district in the department. Once her three-year rotation was up, however, she realized that she wanted to return to direct service delivery. She had found all of her administrative roles very rewarding, but she wanted fewer responsibilities for supervising others, especially those professionals who resented having a woman and nurse supervise them. Returning to direct service, she could once, again, derive joy from designing and delivering programs and services to residents who have the greatest need and the least resources to meet their needs.

Public Health: "The Right Place for Me"

In 1982 she returned to the South District and worked as a public health nurse out of the Rainier office, remaining full-time until 1995, when she retired. During this 13-year period, she developed innovative programs that have been extended to regions throughout the state of Washington.

One of the first of those programs was for adult women incarcerated in the county jail, many of whom were cocaine- and alcohol-dependent. Gwen designed support groups for these residents and extended this program to include education and training for reentry into the community, using a psycho-educational approach that combines social and emotional support with education. Clients decide what topics they desire to learn more about, often serving as group co-leaders. Principal goals of this approach are skill acquisition and competency development.

Gwen learned that many of the women who returned to the community also returned to their mothers' homes and left their infants and children to be cared for by their mothers. Many grandparents were ill prepared to care for infants and young children who were also affected by cocaine and alcohol from their mothers. Working with a social-worker colleague, Abby Moon-Jordan, she created a grandparent parenting program, serving grandparents who are African American, Native American, Japanese American, and Caucasian. This model has been so successful that Gwen and Abby have traveled throughout the State of Washington establishing new programs for grandparents. They have also worked with appropriate agencies and brought into being comprehensive and coordinated services for these cocaine- and alcohol-affected children, many of whom are now healthy teenagers.

Gwen has had a stellar career in public health nursing and she is clear about why she has been so successful. An educational program prepared her to succeed; there was a certainty about her knowledge and skills as a health professional; she had a supportive environment; she had mentors and access to opportunities. Once she was given a chance, she went well beyond what was expected of her. Also, as a public health nurse and as a district administrator, she was known for fairness, openness to new ideas, and a willingness to support those with whom she worked.

African American Registered Nurses in Seattle

Later-life Activity

Since 1994 Gwen has served on the Seattle Mayor's African American Elders Project, which she chaired in 1997. In this role she helped to identify isolated and depressed elderly who were in need of services but were unable to seek them on their own initiative. In addition, she works with a team of health professionals and volunteers to identify and obtain treatment for complex social and health problems for this population group.

Gwen Harden Browne in 1998 after retiring in 1995. In 1978 Gwendolyn was the first public health nurse to be promoted to district administrator.

She was asked in 1999 to serve on the Advisory Board of the School of Public Health Northwest Prevention Effectiveness Center. This program includes researchers and government officials as well as community leaders who are committed to promoting health and healing among elderly at-risk populations. The program is housed at the University of Washington in the School of Public Health and Community Medicine.

Besides actively volunteering for public health activities, Gwen has time to soak up all of the attention that she receives from her two children. Eyeing a certificate on a wall in her home, she stated that her daughter, Melanie, is a 911 [emergency telephone number] supervisor, who in both 1998 and 1999 was voted the King County Employee of the Year. In spite of the demands of work, Melanie and her long-term group of friends check on Gwen nearly every day. Other wall mementos include pictures of her four grandchildren, Bianna, Kiley, and Tegen, children of her son, Brian, and his first wife, Teren; and Taylor, born to Brian's second wife, Shyla. Brian, a baker in Port Townsend, Washington, is quite accomplished in the business and plans to own his own bakery someday.

Public Health: "The Right Place for Me"

Some years ago, Gwen and Edgar were divorced, although they remain good friends. Their shared sense of the importance of family has motivated them to continue to celebrate holidays and special occasions with their children and grandchildren. As she had said of her childhood home, she reiterated, "So you see, I am surrounded by love."

Firmly connected with her family and with a whole range of individuals and organizations, Gwen continues to use her knowledge, skills, and determination to bring services and resources of nursing to residents in several different communities in the Puget Sound Region. Even though she has been retired for nearly five years, she plans to remain active in her grandparents' support group, the African American Elders Project, and Northwest Prevention Effectiveness Center activities. She retired early so that she could engage in such activities and is happy with the balance she has established. All these activities have a community focus, the place where she desires to be. She will continue to give back to the community in important ways because she has enjoyed a level of love and success that enables her to give generously to others. She has found public health the right place to be. When combined with family and community members, Gwen feels rewarded for all that she has achieved.

A Professional Journey: In and Out of Community

Mary Lee Pearson Bell

During the first 15 years of her life, from 1936 to 1951, Mary Lee lived in the South and therefore in a segregated environment. Surrounded by loving family members and caring friends, she learned what it was like to be *in community*.

After age 15, she moved to Washington State, where she has lived ever since. There, in the Puget Sound region (the most populous in the state), she learned what it means to be *out of community*. For example, living for the first time next door to White people on the army base at Fort Lewis (just outside of Tacoma), she felt a dramatic social distance between her family and her neighbors. This was most evident among her parents and the other adults, although even at the high school near the army base some teachers and many of the White students paid no attention to her or were silently hostile. She almost never felt herself to be part of this community. The situation did not change significantly until her college and later adult years in Seattle.

Mary Lee Pearson during high school at age 16.

This tension of being in and out of community has shaped much of Mary Lee's personal and professional life. As she put it, "I emerged from these experiences with a very strong sense of self-confidence

A Professional Journey: In and Out of Community

and self-esteem. Our schoolteachers in the South reinforced what our parents encouraged us to do at home, namely, work hard to succeed." As her story reveals, she used this tension in creative ways.

Childhood Years in Community

Mary Lee was born in Sumter, South Carolina, on October 9, 1936. Segregation by race was pervasive. Without television or any other means for bridging the division, she and others had no way of knowing what life was like in other Negro areas or in White sections of town. Except for Negroes who worked for Whites, Mary Lee remembers almost no contact across racial groups.

From birth to age three, Mary Lee lived with her mother, Susan Johnson Pearson, her father, Ulysses Pearson, and near many of her relatives. Within a month of giving birth to Mary Lee's sister, Bertha, her mother died. Their father, having already made plans to seek work in Virginia, left the two children in the care of his parents. The grandparents provided loving care, to the point that Mary Lee and Bertha viewed them as their mother and father, although the actual father kept in regular touch with the family and sent money for their support. "My father always cared for us." Mary Lee remembers her grandmother reading her father's letters to her; later, when she was older, she read her father's letters to her grandparents.

An aunt and uncle lived on either side of her grandparents' home. They both had children of their own; so, there were cousins and other children their ages to play with, family potlucks where Mary Lee ate some of the most delicious food she ever tasted, and church gatherings. She particularly remembers her Sunday school teachers who were also teachers in the public school and lived in the same neighborhood. Often these teachers knew many of the children in their neighborhood before they started school because they met at other functions in the community. They also knew many of these children's families. While they were generous and sincere in their praise of good performance by a particular child, they could also be quite harsh with children who behaved inappropriately. In those days, many of the teachers demonstrated their approval and disapproval in front of other students, making their expectations very clear. Mary Lee appreciated being complimented by her teachers and worked hard to meet their expectations. She also knew that her grandparents were happy to see their grandchildren perform well.

Even neighbors who were not their blood relatives were referred to as *cousin* or *aunt* or *uncle so-and-so*, making this a very stable time in Mary Lee's life. She definitely felt loved in her community. This very positive foundation in community living helped her and her sister, later, to survive in Washington State.

In 1942, her father was drafted into the U. S. Army. While in service, he met and married Inez Evans, a widow with two children, Alvin and Claudia Darby. As a result of their mother's need to work, they, too, were being raised by their grandparents and were apart from their mother. A few years after Ulysses and Inez married, Ulysses' mother died. Since there were so many other relatives in Sumter, Mary Lee and her sister, Bertha, continued to live with their grandfather for about two years. Their father did not want to disrupt the children's lives by having them move immediately to live with him.

Stationed in Fort Benning, Georgia, Ulysses thought that he would be there long enough to justify having the children from both families come to live with him and Inez. Leaving their grandfather and other relatives, the two girls joined their father, stepmother, stepbrother, and stepsister. Before the families had time to unpack, Ulysses received orders to report to Fort Lewis army base in Washington State; within a year, the four children and Inez joined him there.

The memory of this move and its implications is indelibly etched in Mary Lee's mind. Not only was she working to adjust to being around her parents and siblings, but she was also in an unfamiliar military community. For the first time in all of these children's lives, they were living in a predominantly White community. Each group looked with curiosity toward the other. For Mary Lee, this place was decidedly *out of community*. While her dad "wore the same kind of uniform that the White fathers wore and we lived in nearly identical housing units, the similarity ended there." Adults seemed hostile in their looks at them, leading Mary Lee to comment that, although "we were right next door to one another, I really did not feel like we were members of the same community." Adding to the feeling of estrangement was the fact that the Korean War was on, and families moved in and out so fast that it was really hard for anyone to get to know anyone else.

Critical School Experiences

To assist families in making the adjustment to army life, base personnel offered planned trips to acquaint them with the town. These included tours to the library, parks, and recreational centers in the Tacoma area. One tour took Mary Lee to the school that she would soon be attending, one that appeared huge to her and supposedly accommodating several hundred students.

Since Mary Lee's father had not lived with his new wife before, and the children had never lived with one another, this was a period of major adjustment for the entire family. She recalls not really knowing what to call her father or stepmother. Eventually, she called him *Dad*, as did the other children, and her stepmother, *Mother*.

After the summer of 1951, it was time to enter that huge school. Her memory of that first day is still clear, "a sea of white faces. We did not see one other Negro in the crowd." Reporting first to the office to get room assignments, Mary Lee and her siblings separated, each assigned to a different classroom. Finding her room number without difficulty, she reached the classroom door but hesitated before entering. The teacher, standing in front of the class, saw Mary Lee, but offered no sign of recognition or welcome. Undaunted, Mary Lee spotted an empty desk far across the room and with her "legs feeling like spaghetti," advanced unsteadily toward it. To her surprise, she reached the desk without falling down.

As the day progressed and she went from classroom to classroom, she saw no other Negro students, not even her own siblings. Later she learned that there were never more than 13 Negro students enrolled in the school, four from her own family. On that first day, the strangest school day of her life, no other student said anything to her, nor did she say anything to any other student. She was therefore happy and relieved at the end of the school day to meet her brother and sisters exactly where they had agreed to meet. They hugged one another there on the school ground and had much to talk about as they made their way home.

Mary Lee believes that she and her sister, Bertha, adjusted so quickly to their new stepbrother and stepsister because they needed each other in order to survive in their new school environment. In spite of the fact that the school setting seemed inhospitable, she never experienced physical threats and she does not recall any time when there were altercations at school. Physical safety was not a concern for her.

To help in making them feel a real part of the school, their parents encouraged the children to join some student activity. Mary Lee joined the Genius and the Future Nurses Clubs. In both organizations, she found at least one or two friendly students; her sisters and brother had similar experiences. She recalls that two White female students became so friendly that they agreed to ride with her family to a scheduled school event. The next day these same students told her that their parents said they could not ride with her because it would affect their social standing. By contrast, her brother, Alvin, had a significant number of friends in the school, none of whom, however, ever visited their home.

Mary Lee spent four relatively unhappy years in high school. As an example of those years, she uses two negative incidents and one positive one to make her point. Alvin, her stepbrother, ran for student body president. Before the election, several of her teachers encouraged students in her classes to vote for her brother's opponent, knowing that Mary Lee and Alvin were brother and sister. Fortunately for Alvin, he won the election and served in this leadership role with pleasure and effectiveness.

Another example of poor treatment is the interaction that Mary Lee had with one of the school counselors who called Mary Lee and her sister, Bertha, to her office and told Mary Lee to convince Bertha that she did not need to get a college degree. Mary Lee did not comply with this request. Some time later, Mary Lee's counselor advised Mary Lee to complete a practical nursing program rather than plan to attend college to pursue a professional degree. She and her siblings avoided both counselors thereafter.

Fortunately for Mary Lee, she was a member of the Future Nurses Club. The school nurse, advisor to this group, had college catalogues and other information that she regularly shared with these students. Long before she had finished her senior year, Mary Lee had submitted all of the appropriate paper work for admission to the University of Washington School of Nursing. The school nurse played another important role in Mary Lee's life by creating opportunities for all of the club members to work in the nurse's office during each school week. Mary Lee loved being with the school nurse and other students who were club members, all of whom got along very well and with several of whom she became friends.

Mary Lee remains convinced that her academic performance was not fairly judged by several of her teachers. Occasionally, White students let her see their papers to compare with hers. In at least one case, another female student in her class had received an A for work that appeared identical to hers. When she confronted the teacher about this unfair grade, he said, "What are you complaining about? You received an A-." After that, he refused to talk to her.

In June 1955, Mary Lee, the first Pearson child to do so, graduated from Clover Park High School (Tacoma). As a result of her unhappy memories of the school, she has never returned and never intends to. While the Pearson children were adjusting to high school life, their parents had a son, Christopher Pearson, who became a Muslim and changed his name to Akil Hamadi Azizi. The children were happy to welcome him into the family, but they were really preoccupied with school life much of the time. Each of the other children also graduated, and each has followed her in attending college. Her stepbrother, Alvin, completed his Ph.D. in physics.

Collegiate Experiences

In the fall of 1955, Mary Lee, with another student from her church, Louise Adams, was admitted to the University of Washington. Full of anticipation, they were assigned to different dormitories. Mary Lee did not take many suitcases with her to begin with because she knew she would be returning home on the weekend to tell the family how things were going for her. After picking up her room key at a central office, she made her way to her dorm room. When she arrived there, the door partially open, she found a White student unpacking her things with her mother's help. Seeing Mary Lee, they both sent looks of piercing hostility toward her. Saying nothing, she went in and placed her bags at the foot of the bed opposite the other student's and walked back out, headed for Louise's dormitory. Telling her what she had just experienced, she helped Louise unpack her things. Later, they both walked back to Mary Lee's room in Austin Hall, where they found that the assigned roommate and her mother, along with all of the student's belongings, were gone. During her freshman year, Mary Lee had no other roommate, although the next year an African American student was assigned to be her roommate.

Being at the University of Washington was exciting for Mary Lee. While many of the classes were very large, she met other African American students who provided support for one another. Also, since some instructors did not know her by name or at least she thought they did not, she believed that their evaluation of her work would be more objective if instructors did not associate her name with a face than it would otherwise have been. This assumption has not been proven, but at least this is the way Mary Lee and many other African American students said they felt about being in large classes on the university campus during that period.

Mary Lee successfully completed all prerequisites and entered the School of Nursing on schedule. She knew that a few other African American students had graduated from the school, but she was not personally acquainted with any of them, and there was no other African American in her cohort. It was also well known, but not openly discussed or admitted, that the University of Washington sent clinical nursing students of European descent to Swedish Hospital and all others to Harborview. (Class pictures confirm this fact.) Mary Lee went to Harborview and was happy there, where she saw other African American students, namely, Shirley Williams Ticeson, Florence Martin and Forstine Sharp, who were completing their study there. She also

Mary Lee Pearson in 1959. She was a student at the University of Washington, Harborview Division.

saw a member of the Mary Mahoney Organization, Celestine Thomas. Also, there were African American orderlies and aides who understood the working conditions for African American students and helped out wherever they could. The experiences gave some semblance of community acceptance and support.

It was during Mary Lee's student rotation on the orthopedic floor that she met Rachel Pitts, who worked the evening shift and offered significant support and attention, such as information about churches, hairdressers, good places to eat, and where to meet other African Americans. Many of the other African American nurses worked nights and evenings while student nurses worked mostly days; so, Mary Lee did not see other members of MMRNC.

Even today, Mary Lee has negative feelings towards administrators at the School of Nursing. She feels that they gave "lip service to the idea of racial diversity," yet continued to admit only one or two, and sometimes, no African American students each year, thereby giving little opportunity for students who were admitted to the program to feel a sense of ethnic community. The absence of faculty or staff persons of color further contributed to her sense of being *out of community*.

During Mary Lee's time in the undergraduate nursing program, she never received instruction from an African American or other ethnic racial group member of color; yet, she still thinks she received a superior education at the School of Nursing and that Harborview was a place where students received excellent clinical experiences. While there, she only experienced one racially based incident that caused her to ask for the help of her clinical instructor. Assigned to provide care to a White male patient, she walked into his room and introduced herself to him. He said directly to Mary Lee, "I do not want you to put your black hands on me." Leaving the room immediately, she reported this incident to her clinical instructor and was assigned a different patient. Each incident of this nature and more subtle attitudes that she observed reinforced her perception that she was again *out of community*.

In addition to Harborview, Mary Lee completed affiliations at Doctors Hospital, Firlands, and Western State Hospital, where she noted no blatant racial incidents, although clinical instructors were neutral to mildly negative. By that time in the program, Mary Lee had learned how to survive in a generally inhospitable environment by focusing on the few of her classmates who were friendly towards her; they made the school setting tolerable.

Having completed all requirements by December, 1959, she received her BS degree in nursing. By that time, her grandfather had died, her father was in Korea, and, since no other relatives from Sumter could come to Seattle, she decided not to participate in graduation exercises.

Beginning a Professional Career

Mary Lee had a very good sense of what she needed to do next, look for a job and prepare for state board examinations. She really wanted to work at Harborview in an outpatient clinic; however, she was told that all new graduates needed to start work in the hospital before being assigned to clinics. Instead, she applied to the public health department, where she was offered and accepted a job right away. She took and passed state board examinations and immediately thereafter joined MMPNO, where, welcomed with open arms, she felt she was *in community* for certain. Members of MMPNO were pleased that she had not held a grudge against the organization for not awarding her a scholarship when she applied a year earlier; some apologized for not doing so. But she thought, "Members of Mary Mahoney gave me something better than a scholarship. They really gave me hope and confidence that I could complete this program at a time when few people really knew just how poorly student nurses were treated."

In January 1960, Mary Lee began working as a professional nurse at the Seattle King County Department of Public Health, "the adventure of a lifetime." The agency offered skilled nursing care to patients through the Visiting Nurse Services and preventive healthcare services to the community. All personal health services were provided through the Nursing Division. She found this work exciting and much more fulfilling than her earlier school experiences.

First assigned to the South Office that covered Southeast Seattle, she enjoyed some autonomy, excellent leadership from other nurses, and the opportunity to use her own initiative and creativity in delivering care to clients. It was a great chance to apply the principles of public health she had learned in school to the home environment.

A Professional Journey: In and Out of Community

She had to learn to think quickly, make accurate assessments, and provide care that would positively affect people's lives. It was mainly a White environment, however; so, she had to carry her license when people wanted proof that she had an RN license and was competent to give home care. In addition, she worked in two housing projects where some African Americans lived. She loved giving services to all of her clients, but she especially enjoyed providing services to the residents in these projects.

Mary Lee met Gwendolyn Browne, Lois Eason, and Verna Hill while working at the South office. It was the first time she had worked with other African American nurses and with colleagues who were supportive and congenial. She felt uninhibited in communicating with these nurses, and camaraderie developed that has continued to this time through a public health interest group within MMPNO. That was a good place to get information, plan strategies, and work on projects. This was a very happy time for Mary Lee, when she felt very much a part of a community of nurses and of the larger region as well.

Marriage, Family, and Leadership

Marriage for Mary Lee was the result of a blind date or rather the friend of a blind date, while she was attending the University of Washington. The friend's name was Henry Preston Bell; he had a car and transported her to a dance held by a community organization. That dance led to further dates and finally to marriage on June 23, 1962. (Henry became a public high school teacher in Seattle, retiring after 31 years.) Their first daughter, Valerie, was born a year later, while Henry was still a U.W. student.

Mary Lee returned to work after a short leave. In those days, a public health nurse who went on maternity leave had to return to an office that had a vacancy; no position was held open for anyone. Assigned to Central East office, she became an assistant supervisor with responsibilities including orientation, mentoring, and supervision of new public health nurses, licensed practical nurses, and aides.

A second daughter, Angela, born in 1967, required another leave of about a year, following which she returned to work as a part-time public health nurse. By this time, Mary Lee's ties to the public health community were very strong and she knew this was the right place in the profession for her.

One of her first major assignments was to be the public health nurse for the Teenage Parents Continuation Program, which she served from 1972-1979. This program served pregnant and parenting teens, who were not allowed to continue in regular school during pregnancy. It was unique in that it was a cooperative relationship between the Seattle Public Schools (education), Red Cross (nursery-child care), Medina Children's Services (counseling, support, and/or adoptions), and the Health Department (public health nursing services). She made assessments and referrals for care, health education, home visit follow-up, role modeling, and coordination of care. Since most of these students were African American and brought all of the frustrations of race, poverty, youth, and health problems, better services for teenagers became one of Mary Lee's main concerns, particularly, because adolescent services weren't readily available at that time and many physicians did not tolerate well dealing with teenagers.

In 1978, Mary Lee, along with several other public health and public school nurses, participated in a special summer program offered by the Department of Psychosocial Nursing, now Psychosocial and Community Health, University of Washington, a program that emphasized making social and health systems more responsive than they typically were to the needs of special groups in the community (i.e., the poor, the young, and the elderly). Working with pregnant and parenting teenagers who had many unmet health and social needs, Mary Lee found this summer program perfect for her mission of improved health care for pregnant adolescents.

The summer program led her to pioneer the development of a clinic program in the public schools to meet adolescent students' needs for services, a first for public schools in Seattle. It also motivated her to pursue her master's degree in public administration at Seattle University, an evening-degree program. Continuing to work full-time, she received her master's degree in 1985.

The summer educational experience, furthermore, helped her work through some of her negative feelings about the U.W. School of Nursing because, this time, she was taught by African Americans and other professors of color and she was treated with respect and supported to be successful in this learning program. She gained

A Professional Journey: In and Out of Community

excellent skills of community assessment and program planning, and the theories she learned were relevant to her work in establishing the public school adolescent clinic. All in all, this experience turned her toward being a nurse/scholar and a true member of several professional communities.

With this new confidence and determination, Mary Lee decided that she could better influence future decisions if she became a supervisor. That happened in the fall of 1979, when she became Personal Health Services Supervisor of Columbia Health Center, the former Children and Youth Clinic, which provided comprehensive services to children and youth and was one of 10 sites in the country that was supposedly community based and controlled. Complexities of the job included responding to an influx of refugees, the need for interpretive services, and the need to have personnel who could provide culturally-focused services to these clients.

Another supervisory role came in 1984 when she was reassigned to the Central Public Health Clinic in downtown Seattle. Substance abuse was on the increase and HIV was demanding much attention from all segments of local government. It was evident that this disease was going to be around for awhile

Mary Lee Bell as a nursing supervisor in 1995. In 1979 Mary Lee became the Personal Health Services Supervisor of Columbia Health Center, a role she retained until retirement in 1999.

and needed to be addressed like other chronic diseases. The challenge was to keep the regular (traditional) clinical and field program going and to meet the emergent needs as well. She continued to manage the AIDS-Prevention Screening Clinic and helped to plan, organize, and implement services for pregnant women and children with AIDS. A very discreet service for families in Seattle, it was the only one of its kind in the state and attracted families from elsewhere. Her staff coordinated services in these families' communities. During this time too, almost half of the public-health-nursing referrals were for substance-abusing pregnant women and drug-affected babies and infant mortality and morbidity were increasing. To complicate the treatment problem, hospitals were paying their staffs much better salaries than Public Health; so, it was extremely difficult to hire nurses in public health. In spite of it all, she managed to do some hiring and cross-trained several of the clinic staff to keep things going.

In 1990, the Central Public Health Clinic moved to the Belltown area in downtown Seattle. By this time, one of the laws that gave pregnant teens the right to stay in regular school was showing positive results, but these students needed special services if they were to be successful. Proposition One appropriated funds for these services with the Health Department the designated agency. Mary Lee hired, oriented, and supervised most of the public health nurses who served the Seattle middle and high schools south of Lake Union Ship Canal.

The Health Department had always indicated an interest in racial/ethnic diversity in programming and staffing. Since Mary Lee felt very strongly that the staff providing services should reflect the characteristics of the community they serve, she made it her responsibility to hire as many well-qualified nurses of color as she could. Indeed, she hired more African American nurses than any previous supervisor, at least 12 highly qualified African American nurses. She also played a significant role in assisting many other nurses of color to obtain jobs in public health. Over her 39 years with the department, Mary Lee hired, trained, mentored, and supervised several hundred nurses and other health-care providers.

Her pride in these achievements led her to summarize her career by saying, "Public health provided me with the opportunity to work in many different communities and with many professional nurses who were truly dedicated to diversity and the provision of high quality care to community residents."

Honors and Later Life

Some of her happiest times in working with nurses were in developing articles for publication in professional journals and on a host of other activities. These nurses included members of the Washington State Nurses Association, King County Nurses Association, Sigma Theta

A Professional Journey: In and Out of Community

Tau (a nursing honor society), Service Education Research in Community Health Nursing, Washington State Public Health Association, and many others. In 1981, Mary Lee received the Excellence in Nursing Practice Award from the King County Nurses Association. In 2000, for her dedicated services to members of the county and to the profession, Mary Lee was selected for induction into the Washington State Nurses Hall of Fame.

One reason for her retirement in 1999 was to assist in caring for her stepmother and father, both of whom were 88 years old and in declining health. She felt a special debt of gratitude to her father, who always cared for her and Bertha and other children in their family after he married Inez, providing financial support for them even when he could not be physically present in their lives.

Her stepmother is now in an assisted-care facility, but once each week is brought back to their home in Tacoma, where their father still resides. Her sister, Claudia, makes it possible for her father to remain in the home, living there with him. Both sisters feel that it is their responsibility to be caretakers of their parents for as long as they live, although their brothers help out in their own ways, too.

In retirement, Mary Lee is being selective in her volunteer activities and organizational affiliations. One of her values is sharing meaningful interests in helping others. She remains committed to being active in MMPNO because she wants to help recruit more African Americans and other ethnic groups of students into nursing. She is still in contact with many of the public health nurses that she recruited during her tenure in the health department and wants more of them to pursue graduate studies. "I have my work cut out for me. I intend to continue to promote education just as my parents did. It will continue to be our ticket to a successful future. Our communities need well-prepared people." True to her liking and learning, Mary Lee is contributing to a sense of being *in community* for herself and others.

A Nurse in Public Schools, the U.S. Air Force Reserve, and Overseas Mission Programs

Muriel Grace Softli

During the early 1920s Rudolfo Softli migrated from his home country in Venezuela, South America to Manhattan, New York, coming to America to pursue an education in the field of electronics or engineering. On a different ship but about the same time, Isi Hinds migrated from her home country of Guyana, South America, to the United States in search of the "American Dream." She also settled in Manhattan. By 1926 Rudolfo's and Isi's paths crossed. They met and married and soon began having the first of nine children. Before children began to dominate their lives, though, Rudolfo completed his engineering education at Pratt Institute in Brooklyn but could not find a job in engineering. At that time, Negro engineers were routinely denied employment in many businesses and organizations throughout the United States.

In the face of discrimination, Rudolfo used his engineering knowledge and skills to open a repair business for electrical appliances, radios, and later televisions. In addition, he owned and operated a restaurant a year before moving to the West Coast. From these enterprising endeavors, he earned a decent living for his family. But he never gave up the hope of becoming a practicing engineer and continued to seek employment even when the future looked bleak. The first opportunity came in 1954, when he was hired for a position at Mather Air Force Base in Sacramento, California.

Growing Up in a Large, Cohesive Family

Muriel was born in Manhattan on October 25, 1936, the third child and first girl born into this family. In order of their births, her two older brothers are Cecil and Robert; the younger children in order of their births are Anthony, Edmond, Victor (killed in an automobile accident when he was 16 years old), Linda, David, and Katherine. All of the remaining children are alive and well. All the brothers and their families live in the Seattle area. The two sisters live out of the Seattle area, Linda in Washington, D.C., and Katherine in Vancouver, Washington.

Muriel's mother was a loving, devoted full-time homemaker. Managing the nine children, who were all close enough in ages to be at home together, consumed her adult life through early middle-age. Muriel recalls that "mother was an excellent manager. She kept the house in good shape and attended most of our sports events, parent-teacher association meetings at more than two schools, and coordinated all of our life events." With encouragement throughout their lives to pursue formal education, their mother managed the home so that studying and learning had the highest priority for all the children.

The family was devoutly Christian with the mother, Methodist, and the father, Catholic. Some of the children became either Methodist or Catholic, attending church, Sunday school and other religious activities with their parents. Spirituality and regular church attendance were hallmarks of the Softli's traditions.

Every member of the family had assigned household chores which they accomplished with great gusto in order to go out and play, participate in sports, or attend movies or parties. Muriel and the other girls learned to cook from their mother; traditional dishes from Venezuela or Guyana were the ones she most enjoyed preparing. Holidays, birthdays, and other special occasions that were celebrated here in America or in either of her parents' home countries were also often celebrated in the Softli's home.

There was a fairly large community of immigrants from different parts of South America and the Caribbean Islands in their Manhattan neighborhood. Often, there were block parties, house parties, picnics in the park and other places where neighbors gathered. She loved these large gatherings, for they were real cultural events that often included traditional attire from everyone's country of origin.

A very wide smile covers Muriel's face when she is asked to describe what it was like for her as a child growing up in a large family in New York. She has vivid and fond memories of those early years of her life. The family lived in a large apartment in Manhattan.

Later they moved to East Elmhurst, Queens, to the first family-owned home. The family shared all dinner meals together. After dinner the children did their homework. Most of the boys were in school sports; so, they occasionally missed the dinner meal. During the weekdays there was little time for other activities; however, children were allowed to listen to the radio, and they were among the first families in their area to have television, a set their father had repaired for a customer who didn't come back to claim it. Even then they could only spend a very small amount of time on the weekends watching TV.

Muriel Softli as a child. Her godmother took her to have this photograph taken.

During her elementary school years, Muriel attended PS 127 in East Elmhurst, along with most of the children she played with in the neighborhood. Many ethnic/racial groups were represented among the students. Although most of the teachers were Caucasian, Muriel always got along well with both students and teachers. She loved school and graduated with perfect attendance awards.

For the first two years of high school, Muriel attended Newtown High School in Queens and was active in school life, participating in sports and the Spanish and Latin language clubs. A high school teacher, Miss Bull, who took a great interest in her aspirations toward becoming a nurse, provided her with excellent material about nursing schools in California, as well as in other parts of the United States.

During early childhood and her adolescent years, her life at school, church, and in the community was full of wholesome activities. She had excellent role models in all of these places, all of whom made significant contributions to the person that Muriel is today.

She also enjoyed the attention of her brother's godmother, Mrs. Essie Henry, who, beginning when Muriel was age eight or nine, regularly took her to Carnegie Hall, the theater, and the opera house.

A Nurse in Public Schools

She recalls seeing the opera, *Aida*, for the first time with Mrs. Henry, an exciting experience that was enhanced by later seeing high school students present this same opera at school as an operetta.

Moving from New York to California

Shortly before her junior year of high school, when her father found a job as an engineer in Sacramento, California, the entire family was so happy that their father could finally enjoy working as a professional engineer that they eagerly moved there. The move to California was viewed as a big plus for the entire family. The boys got to play football and other sports; the two younger sisters were cheerleaders. Muriel completed the last two years of high school at Grant Union High School in Sacramento. Her performance had been so outstanding that she received two scholarships for academic achievement, the first African American student in Grant Union High School to receive the Soroptimist International Scholarship. She also received the Iota Phi Lambda Black Business Women's Scholarship.

Muriel knows the exact day when she decided that she would become a nurse. A public health nurse visited their home after the birth of a younger sibling. From that day on she wanted to make home visits and examine babies in people's homes. She remains astonished that her judgment at such an early age yielded more positive personal and professional satisfaction than she ever anticipated.

Entering Nurse's Training

Before graduation, she was accepted in the nursing program at Sacramento Junior College. Deciding whether to enter the program, however, became complicated. Should she accompany her family to Seattle, where her father had been hired by Boeing, or should she enter the SJC program, which had only recently accepted a multiethnic group of students? The decision was affected by her acquaintance with Mrs. May Sanders, an African American nurse whom Muriel's mother had met on a bus. As they conversed, her mother revealed that Muriel had been accepted at SJC in nursing. They arranged a meeting between Muriel and Mrs. Sanders, one in which Muriel learned that Mrs. Sanders, although born in Sacramento, had had to go to New York's Lincoln School of Nursing because no

Negro students were being admitted to SJC when she graduated from high school. Mrs. Sanders also invited Muriel to live in her home between the time her parents moved and her entry into the SJC program. Muriel decided to stay in Sacramento where she began a friendship with Mrs. Sanders that lasted until the latter's death in 1997.

The very strong family traditions that Muriel grew up with made it easy for her to know what her parents expected of her as well as how to perform as a responsible adult. She managed quite well on her own.

At SJC there were more than 50 students in her entering class with only two African Americans, Muriel and Verna Coleman, several Asian Americans and the rest Caucasians. She recalls that all students got along well with one another and that most of the instructors were very supportive; however, one day the Director of Nursing revealed her prejudice. Approaching the two of them as they were walking together in the hallway, she said, "Now let me tell you right now, your boy friends are never to come to the dormitory living quarters." Knowing nothing about these young women's social habits, this director had no basis for giving this admonition. Fortunately for them, they knew better than to show anger toward the director for making such a racially charged statement. Muriel now explains, "The director had great fears of Blacks and Whites mixing in social groups. She was from the Deep South where schools were developed and run without racial mixing. These were the days before Dr. Martin Luther King; affirmative action opened greater opportunities for students regardless of race."

A lifelong studious person, Muriel applied the study habits she had learned in her home to yield, once again, a successful outcome. She received an Associate of Arts degree from SJC in 1958. Between graduation and sitting for state board examinations, she worked briefly in a private general hospital in Sacramento before moving to Seattle to join her family.

Enduring Racial Incidents and Finding Her Nursing Niche

It was during this brief interval that she experienced an incident that left an indelible impression on her, one that helped her become an attentive and more assertive professional. In this small private general hospital, there were only two African American nurses on the staff who were older by many years than Muriel. The Caucasian nurses usually responded to her in positive and supportive ways, but, one evening, she was working with a nurse who had privately been fairly friendly and supportive. Muriel placed a male patient on a bedpan, appropriately raising the head of his bed so that he could be more comfortable using the bedpan. She did not realize that the floor lamp with an exposed light bulb was in direct contact with the bottom sheet on the patient's bed. Stepping out of the patient's room to give him some privacy, she stood near his door in the hallway. The other nurse came down the hall while she was in the hallway and told her to go to dinner. Muriel explained that the patient was on the bedpan and that she wanted to take him off before leaving the floor. This nurse insisted that Muriel should go to dinner, saying that she would take out the bedpan when the patient finished.

Either the patient never turned on his call light when he finished or the nurse forgot to check on the patient. In any case, the sheet and mattress were burned by the exposed light bulb, although neither caught fire. After removing the lamp, caring for the patient, and writing an incident report, Muriel spoke to the nurse in question, who said she did not remember agreeing to help the patient off the bedpan. How could she not remember? Was this a way of embarrassing her African American colleague?

This incident was so frightening for Muriel that she decided to give a month's notice and resign. She would not take a similar chance in the future, especially when a delay of 10 to 15 minutes could have prevented such a risk to the patient and to herself. She was also profoundly disappointed that a professional nurse, who, under non-crisis conditions, agreed to complete a task, failed to do so, and thereby created a crisis for Muriel and possible injury to the patient. Making things worse, the nurse denied agreeing to provide nursing care to a patient on Muriel's behalf. Muriel considered this double jeopardy, and its impact has left the incident still indelibly etched on her mind.

Before migrating to Seattle, she had read in the *American Journal of Nursing*'s classified ads that Harborview Hospital needed nurses. Using this lead, she applied soon after arriving in Seattle and was hired to work in the nursery and post partum ward. She was oriented to the nursery by Mrs. Ira Gordon, a charter member of Mary Mahoney Registered Nurses Club. Shortly thereafter, she also met

African American Registered Nurses in Seattle

Celestine Thomas, Sadie Berrysmith, and Katie Ashford, charter MMRNC members, and, later, Thelma Pegues, a longtime member. Harborview was the first place that Muriel worked where there were several African American nurses employed, although she later realized that it was one of only a few hospitals in the area where African American nurses could find employment.

She joined MMRNC in 1958, as well as the Washington State Nurses Association and King County Nurses Association. She did not merely join but attended organizational meetings. MMRNC nurses met once each month in members' homes. She remembers those meetings fondly: "It was really like a sisterhood. Programs consisted of people sharing information about employment opportunities, educational programs that were opening for African Americans, and how nurses were treated on certain floors of the hospital or clinic. Refreshments were always served and there was time for socializing."

Few African American nurses attended WSNA and KCNA meetings in the late 1950s and early 60s; so, it took some time for her to meet other nurses. Eventually, she developed close relationships with other nurses when she volunteered to serve on committees and task forces. Since 1958 she has been a continuous member of these three professional nursing organizations and frequently attends their meetings. MMRNC was (and is) special: "I saw, for the first time in my professional life, over 10 or 12 African American nurses in the same room at these meetings."

Further Education and Nursing in Africa

In 1959 Muriel was admitted to the baccalaureate program at the School of Nursing at the University of Washington. While she found her instructors were generally very helpful, when it came to assigning grades, she was least likely to be given an A, even when she could show that her performance was as good as that of Caucasian students in her class who were given higher grades. In 1961 she received a BS degree in nursing, an accomplishment that helped her realize that she possessed the necessary credentials to become a public health nurse in New York. By this time, she wanted to return to the East, where her Aunt Mae still lived in her apartment and had room for

A Nurse in Public Schools

Muriel to live as well.

She contacted the New York City Department of Public Health, applied, and, within days, was hired as a public health nurse assigned to Brooklyn, an area that she knew very well. Her adjustment was uneventful. As a public health nurse, she delivered nursing care to children in the public schools. After school hours and summers she worked in the clinics, made home visits, or did special projects. Among the latter was Operation Crossroads Africa which was an outreach program, enabling her to travel to Africa to provide nursing care to people in their own villages and towns. This was the most unaccustomed form of community nursing care in her experience. For three summers she participated in this program, taking many pictures of Africans engaged in their various activities. She treasures these slides and has shown them to many interested groups of people.

Upon her return to New York each fall, she resumed her public health and school-nurse responsibilities. On weekends she worked in the general, private hospital less than 12 or 13 blocks from her home. It was employment that would make it possible for her to raise the funds needed to participate in Operation Crossroads. Also, she wanted to acquire more professional skills for working in acute care settings, anticipating that she would be more inventive than she otherwise might be when she returned to serve patients in foreign countries. She also reasoned that these same skills could be used in a variety of future treatment settings.

She had worked in this small, general hospital for some time before she spoke about her wonderful slide collection, but, once she told others about it, nurses urged her to bring them to work, where they could look at them during lunch hour and after work. One evening she took her slides and projector to the Brooklyn Jewish Hospital, where several nurses stayed after work to watch these nursing travelogues. Excited by their positive response, she decided to walk home, as she had done many times. Unfortunately, this time she was stopped at gunpoint by a man who told her not to yell and to walk into a dark area. She did as she was told. The man searched her purse and inside the projector case. Once he realized that she had nothing that he valued, he instructed her to keep her face turned to the wall and not to move from that spot for half an hour. Disregarding that advice, she continued her walk home, arriving late enough to upset her Aunt May and other relatives living in the other apartment.

This incident was extremely unsettling for Muriel and her Aunt May, but it soon led to their planning for the next five years. She realized that she was very lucky not to have suffered bodily harm. Maybe Seattle was a better place to live which was a view shared by Aunt May. Before leaving Brooklyn, Muriel took time to travel through her old neighborhood schools and was fortunate to run into at least one or two individuals whom she had known earlier. She knew that, once she had resigned, it was highly unlikely that she would ever return to work in or perhaps even visit New York City.

Once settled in Seattle, again, she applied for and gained employment in the outpatient department of King County Hospital, now Harborview, from 1966 to 1968. In 1968 Celestine Thomas called to tell her that a school nurse, Shirley Ticeson (now Shirley Ticeson Gilford), had called to ask if Celestine knew of any nurses who would be interested in school-nursing employment with the Seattle Public Schools. Celestine thought of Muriel and decided to call her. Muriel called Shirley right away to let her know of her Brooklyn experiences in school nursing. Shirley urged her to apply and soon after the job was hers.

Becoming a U.S. Air Force Officer

During this same year, Muriel read in the KCNA newsletter about employment opportunities in the U.S. Air Force Reserves. The ad stated that nurses would need to give only one weekend a month for military nursing. This was such an attractive opportunity that she applied. It took over two years for the review process. During that time, she took a one-year leave of absence from school nursing to complete a master's degree in education at Central Washington University (Ellensburg). Once she received her master's degree in 1970, she was commissioned as a captain in the United States Air Force Reserves. She was assigned to basic flight-nurse training school at Brooks Air Force Base in San Antonio, Texas, where she learned about the physiology of flight nursing and how to provide good airborne nursing care. She also completed requirements to become a school-nurse practitioner in 1974. This array of training helped her feel especially well qualified to provide high quality nursing care to

A Nurse in Public Schools

patients at school, in the air, and in different places around the world.

Called to active duty for the first time during Operation Desert Storm (the 1991 military conflict in the Persian Gulf region), she was stationed in the Raimstein Air Force Base, Germany. Service persons were brought to this hospital directly from the front lines in the Gulf. During this time, Europe experienced one of the coldest winters in many years. Muriel and others stationed at this site worked in an airplane hanger that had been converted nto a medical warehouse. As she remembers it, "The temperature was very cold inside, but replenishing supplies as the C141 planes returned to Germany with the sick and injured servicemen kept us busy and our minds off the cold weather."

Muriel Softli in 1970 at her graduation from Central Washington University where she completed her master's degree in education.

While she was in Germany, school children, teachers, staff members, and some parents from each of the three Seattle schools where she worked sent cards, letters, and notes that now fill several large scrapbooks. These mementos will be kept as fond reminders of the care, respect, and admiration that these people felt for her. When Muriel returned to school nursing after serving in the Desert Storm conflict, she realized that nursing continued to offer her a very rich opportunity to enjoy serving mankind. She wore her military fatigues to school, going from one class to the next until she had been in every classroom to personally thank students, staff, and some parents for the letters, care packages, prayers, and good wishes they had sent. She is convinced that many of these students will remember this military conflict because of their relationship to her. She also received a plaque from the School Nurses of Washington for participating in Operation Desert Storm.

Experiencing the effects of combat and understanding the level of nursing skill needed to provide good care to patients have heightened Muriel's understanding of the meaning of our shared humanity. Having given nursing care to children in schools, to service persons in the air, and to various people in different countries of the world, no matter where she has practiced, she is aware of our shared humanity and the real meaning of life as she defines it: concern, love, and doing something for our fellow man. She has seen service persons who lost body parts; she has provided nursing care to those with mental and emotional disabilities. The most emotionally draining experiences occurred during the Vietnam era when she provided in-flight nursing care between Yokota AFB, Japan, and Travis AFB, California.

For 26 years Muriel Softli served her country as a flight nurse in the U.S. Air Force Reserve. During "Operation Desert Storm" she was stationed at Ramstein Airforce Base in Germany.

Years after entering the Air Force, she observed that there were few if any other African American nurse-officers in the Air Force. (Muriel entered the Air Force during the Vietnam War, an unpopular war, when military service was not viewed positively.) In the mid-1970s she successfully recruited into the Air Force, Rosa Young and Debbie Arnold, African Americans, and Alma Aquino, a Filipina. She wishes she had recruited more nurses, but there just was not time for her to do more than she did.

She remembers the way she was treated by some service persons when she first joined the Air Force. For example, often, when she went to check into her billet (temporary housing) and although she displayed her written orders, the service person would check with the pilot to confirm that she was the officer identified on her papers.

A Nurse in Public Schools

On more than one occasion an enlisted person or a civilian employed on the bases told her, "I have never seen a Black female officer in the Air Force before today." This was just one of the most blatant, racial incidents she experienced.

During her Air Force service, from 1970-1996, she traveled throughout Asia, Europe, Canada, and most states in the United States. These 26 years represent some of her most rewarding nursing experiences. At the time of her retirement, she had logged the third highest number of flight hours of any other nurse in her reserve unit, the 40th Air Medical Evacuation Squadron at McChord Air Force Base, Tacoma. Furthermore, she rose to the rank of Lieutenant Colonel. By whatever measure one uses, military nursing provided her with a wealth of opportunities to serve others and to experience a high level of personal and professional success.

Muriel has worked with the very young, the old, and those in between and finds the profession of nursing to be a human-intensive experience. The more she engages in such interactions, the more aware she becomes of what is truly important in life, that is, treating everyone as important human beings.

Honors and Planning for Retirement

Her plans for her retirement years include missionary nursing in Kenya, where she had earlier been on a medical team that gave meals to the children throughout Kenya. In Nigeria she had taught American-style pediatric nursing, hoping Africans would find some of the skills appropriate for their African hospital setting. She wants to follow up on these earlier efforts. Back in grade school, when she chose nursing as her career, little did she realize that she had chosen a profession that would enable her to work for as long as her health allows. She also expects to travel to new places as soon as she retires.

Nursing has afforded her many rewards. The most recent recognition came in March 2000, when she was inducted into the Washington State Nurses Hall of Fame, along with four other members of Mary Mahoney Professional Nurses Organization and one other member of WSNA. Pleased as she is to have this peer recognition, she knows that most of her happiest moments as a nurse were when she shared a significant moment with a student on the school playground or in the air when she has given nursing care to a service person.

She thanks God for the many blessings of health, family, education, friends, employment, and for being born in the United States. They gave her a firm foundation of human understanding and love, which she has enjoyed throughout her lifetime. "All of these blessings have made it possible for me to see my reason for being and the need to extend myself to help others in this short journey on earth. I wish that all people could experience in their lifetime the peace, joy and happiness I feel and experience daily."

Excellence and Achievement Across Three Generations

Vivian Odell Booker Lee

Throughout her career as nurse, administrator, and parent, Vivian has sought opportunities to serve and to lead. While advancing her own career, she provided creative and relevant programs and services to client groups most in need of such help. In doing so, she followed a model set by her mother and provided a model for her son. Everyone who has associated with her, it seems, has benefited from knowing her.

Strivers for Excellence

The role models provided by her mother, Alvirita Little, and her sister, Verna Booker Hightower, were certainly important during her formative and professional years. While working as a secretary, her mother also did extensive volunteer work that brought her national recognition. For example, she raised money to rebuild churches in Japan after the Second World War and was named one of the 100 most influential women in the United Methodist Church. As a result of her work as founder of Girls Clubs of Puget Sound, now Girls Incorporated, a building on Martin Luther King Way in Seattle is named "The Alvirita Little Center for Girls." Vivian's oldest sister, Verna distinguished herself on the rodeo circuit. Before her untimely death from chronic disease, she was a prizewinning Women's Barrel racer in the Texas/Oklahoma region. She was also a poster model for rodeo events and the first African American woman to ride in the Houston Astrodome rodeo.

Vivian identified with these role models in her home and experienced, through them, the satisfaction of public recognition that each enjoyed. Throughout her childhood and into retirement she has striven for and achieved consistent levels of excellence.

Education, Hard Work, and Racism

Born in Spring, Texas, on January 28, 1938, Vivian is the youngest of five children born to Alvirita and Art Booker. In addition to her sister, Verna, she has three brothers, Art, a retired Air Force Communications specialist, Harold, who earned a masters degree in organic chemistry and a doctorate degree in law, and Alvin a retired Special Forces army officer. These five children spent their early years in Texas. Vivian, the youngest child, was six when her mother decided to leave Texas to marry Frank Little, a career Army service man who brought love and financial security to the family. With Alvirita, he also instilled in all five children the values of education and hard work as pathways for happiness and for contributing to their communities. As they grew to maturity, all five demonstrated that they had internalized these values through their academic achievements and through their active participation in professional, social, and civic organizations in various parts of the United States.

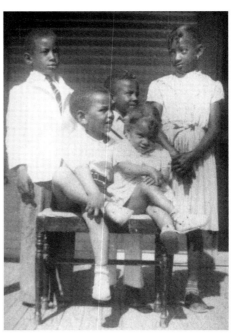

Vivian Booker with her older brothers and sister around 1941 or 1942. She is seated on the bench on the right, and would have been 3 or 4 years old.

The Little family never knew poverty directly, although they were acquainted with numerous African American families who were poor. They did know racism at first hand during Frank Little's army career. All branches of the armed services were segregated until 1948,

Excellence and Achievement Across Three Generations

when President Truman ordered that they be desegregated, an order that needed several years to take effect. Prior to the issuance of this executive order, Frank had served in segregated units on the West Coast and in Japan. This separate and unequal system did not include signs for "Colored" and "Whites," but the mess halls were segregated, as were officers' clubs and service units. While stationed in Japan, Frank observed the mistreatment of Black servicemen by White soldiers and as a Sergeant First Class, often had to intervene on behalf of his Black troops. At home, Frank and Alvirita discussed these problems in the presence of the children. Having analyzed the problem, both parents conveyed their determination to work to bring about better conditions for Blacks living in Japan. They helped their children understand why education and hard work were essential as a means of bringing about changes in social conditions for themselves and other African Americans.

Vivian completed elementary and junior high school in Tokyo and entered Meguro High School there. Her family was in Japan at the beginning of the Korean War and her dad's company was mobilized and shipped to Korea. Within two weeks, many badly wounded soldiers were shipped back to Japan where the army hospital in Tokyo was so full even closets were used to house the wounded. Blood was in such short supply that they allowed adolescents to give a half-pint. According to Vivian, "These were fellows I had known as we were always on the post at the service club and in the mess hall. It was heart wrenching to see them back as amputees. There were not enough staff or enough space or enough blood. I wanted to help. It was at this time that I knew I wanted to become a nurse."

Vivian's schooling was interrupted in her first semester of high school when her stepfather was reassigned in 1951 to Fort Lawton in Seattle. Located in a beautiful section of the city, this army base did not provide on-site housing; so, the family lived in military housing in the south end of Seattle.

The entire family fell in love with Seattle, except for their difficulties with housing. During the early 1950s, overt discrimination in housing and public accommodations prevailed. Vivian recalls the extensive effort and energy which her mother, in particular, and her father, to a lesser degree, expended in trying to find a house to purchase when they were ready to move out of military housing. Some homeowners refused to allow Blacks in to look at their homes when there was a for-sale sign posted in the yard. One family on Beacon Hill, an area that especially appealed to Vivian, told Alvirita, "We will not sell our home to a nigger." Many other potential sellers, though not so blunt, conveyed through their behavior the same sentiment. Eventually, the parents found a home in the Central Area of Seattle where many Blacks had congregated, and Vivian entered Garfield High School.

A Turning Point

Garfield has long been known for its ethnic diversity, at least among students. About half were then and are now African American and Asian American, although the teaching staff is predominantly White. Vivian remembers that most of the teachers and counselors who were members of the staff at Garfield during her high school years were dedicated to teaching all students well. However, it was also apparent that a small minority of White teachers did not attempt to conceal their strong negative attitudes about race. Black students knew which teachers treated them fairly and which appeared to be prejudiced toward them; mostly they tried to avoid those in the latter group. The result was that students tended to cluster in groups according to racial and ethnic identities.

During the 1953-54 school year, Vivian and several other Black students were among the first to enroll in a retail course which prepared students for later work experience. With an excellent teacher, the Black students knew they performed as well in this class as their White peers. Late in the course, the teacher arranged for personnel representatives from local retail stores, such as Sears, J.C. Penney, Rhodes, The Bon Marche, and Frederick & Nelson, to interview students for possible employment. Every White student was accepted for employment; none of the Black students received offers. All the Black students saw this as a blatant example of racism. For Vivian, the experience is indelible; she felt deeply the meaning of racial affiliation and identity and their implications for access to employment. When pressed for an explanation, the store representatives assured the Black students that they had interviewed well but claimed that customers would not want to be served by a Black clerk. That is why these students did not receive job offers.

Eventually, through the interventions of their teacher as advocate, each of the Black students, including Vivian, did get a retailing job. She worked in the basement of the Bon Marche, an experience she recalls as positive. But the negative effects of the initial rejection by the job recruiters remained.

Vivian identifies this experience as a turning point in her life. She recalls how shocked she was when she learned that she was not selected for employment, knowing that she was an excellent student and had performed well during the interviews. And she knew she was well dressed for each interview session. She perceived the treatment given Black students by these recruiters to be a profound injustice and a form of racism. These experiences motivated her to work even harder academically to improve her chances of meeting any criteria for gaining access to educational and employment opportunities.

She still held fast to the goal which she established in elementary school, namely, to become a nurse. Knowing that she wanted to attend college in Seattle, she went, on her own initiative, to see the academic counselor at Garfield to be sure that she had completed all of the appropriate courses to attend college and to meet criteria to enter nursing school. After the experience in the retail class, school life for Vivian was a very serious matter.

Throughout all four years of high school Vivian was a member of the National Honor Society, an unusual achievement in those times for any African American student. The meaning of membership in this society had increased for her after the retail-class experience. As she had discovered, even when academic achievement merited that honor, Black students' names and documentation were often not forwarded so that they might be recognized. She associated such unfair treatment with the segregation and discrimination her stepfather had experienced at an earlier time while in the Army.

As yet another indication of the racial climate in Seattle during her high school years, Vivian recalled an incident that occurred at the time of her senior prom in 1955. A group of Black students had made dinner reservations at Rosellini's 410, an up-scale restaurant in Seattle. When they arrived, dressed in their finest evening attire, the staff refused to let them enter the dining area. Instead, they called the police to escort them out of the restaurant. This practice prevailed in many Seattle restaurants until the early 1960s.

Vivian Odell Booker in 1955 at her graduation with honors from Garfield High School in Seattle. The gold tassel signifies her status as an honor student.

These incidents of discrimination and racism were topics of discussion among all members of the family and served to motivate them to strive for excellence. The irony of racial discrimination was a painful insult for a family with a father serving in the Armed Forces.

In 1955 Vivian graduated with honors from Garfield. She still recalls, with a sense of joy, being seated in her cap and gown, her gold tassel that distinguished honor graduates from others hanging from her cap. She regrets that she was the only African American in her class to have this distinction. In recognition of this honor, she received scholarships from Delta Sigma Theta, an African American sorority, and from the Seattle branch of the Lions Club, a worldwide service organization that provides scholarships and other awards to deserving students.

Professional Nursing Training and Marriage

Even given the unfavorable racial climate during the 1950s, Vivian applied to only one institution, the University of Washington's School of Nursing and was admitted with 19 other students for Fall, 1955. Frances Workcuff was the only other African American student admitted in this class. Previous African American students in nursing, Verna Hill and Shirley Williams Gilford, had paved the way for her, as she fully admits. A new curriculum had just been implemented in the School of Nursing. It included a four-year program which enabled students to complete most clinical components in three years, with the final year allocated for completion of all academic courses leading to a Bachelor of Science degree in nursing. Once the clinical component of the program was finished, students could take a national examination that enabled them to work as registered nurses in

Excellence and Achievement Across Three Generations

hospitals in the area while they completed degree requirements. She passed the National Registered Nurses Examination at the end of her third year and began her professional career as an emergency-room nurse at Virginia Mason and University Hospitals.

These 20 students were grouped together for all clinical courses and lived in Blackford Hall, a dormitory near Virginia Mason Hospital (VMH), where they had clinical instruction and acquired practical clinical skills. She particularly credits Shirley Nash, Bea Olson, and Edith Heinemann, instructors, with contributing greatly to her education and professional development during this time. She was also fortunate in associating with Gloria Henderson, an African American nurse working with an architect to design the emergency-care facility. She assisted in determining the type and placement of equipment and storage of supplies. This first employment experience at VMH prepared Vivian to seek opportunities for later work in nontraditional and expanded roles in nursing and related health services. Indeed, most of her experiences in the U.W. program, she thinks, were very positive and appropriately demanding academically.

Following completion of the degree requirements in the fourth year of her program, she received a BS in nursing and applied for and was hired as the first African American psychiatric nurse at the Veterans Administration Hospital on Seattle's Beacon Hill. She also joined the 50th General Army Nurse Reserve Corps. That was not the only achievement of that period in her life. In 1959 while completing course work for her BS degree, Vivian met and married James Tymony, a political science graduate in his fifth year earning his teaching certificate at the University of Washington. When he completed training in the University of Washington's Reserve Officer Training Corps (ROTC) and became a second lieutenant with the Washington National Guard, he was assigned to weekend active duty status with the Washington National Guard. In 1961, after an elevator accident at the Seattle Armory, Jim died. The impact of his death on Vivian was so devastating that she resigned the VA position.

Continued Education, Return to Nursing, and Remarriage

Refocusing her goals, Vivian decided to return to the University of Washington School of Nursing in 1960 for work on a master's degree in nursing administration. Since academic pursuits had always been a source of satisfaction for her, she hoped that another immersion in the university environment would be an ideal place for working through her grief over the loss of her husband. Finding that she was right in that decision, she completed all course work for the degree with great personal satisfaction and with academic excellence; however, an irreconcilable impasse with her thesis-research advisor led to her decision to leave the university without completing the graduate degree.

She returned to nursing, working in progressively higher levels of responsibility in several different health care facilities, Seattle/King County Public Health Department, Renton School District, and Group Health Cooperative of Puget Sound. She continued her work with the Army Reserve Corps and served as a psychiatric nurse instructor until 1964. During that period she met and married Owen Lee. Successes at work and a new love brought joy back into Vivian's life.

As they celebrated the birth of their son, Anthony, they set about passing on to him the values they had learned during their formative years, education and hard work. To their joy, he internalized these values. At age three he could read. He maintained a 3.8-3.9 GPA through elementary and high school. Upon graduation from Overlake School (a private college-preparatory school), Anthony received two prestigious awards, the Scholastic Award for maintaining the highest GPA during all four years of high school and the Puget Sound Association of Phi Beta Kappa Book Award for highest GPA. He went on to complete a BS degree in mathematics at Brown University and a Ph.D. degree in civil engineering at Massachusetts Institute of Technology. He is currently manager of quantitative analysis for H.E. Butt Food Distributors in San Antonio, TX. Anthony's third-generation academic performance makes his mother proud as he continues to enjoy successes in his current employment. That success is shared by Vivian's mother, her three brothers, and his father, a retired school principal, all still residents of Seattle. (After a brief illness, Owen Lee died on February 14, 2001.) Anthony, knowing the contributions that each of these people has made to community life in Seattle, feels it his responsibility to maintain the tradition.

Excellence and Achievement Across Three Generations

Leadership Roles

While raising her son during the late 1960s and early 1970s, Vivian remained active in nursing as a school nurse. She served in leadership roles of President elect, Secretary, Chairperson of Membership, and Chair of the Fall Conference for the state school-nursing organization. These important roles gave her high visibility among school nurses, resulting in her serving for three years (1966, 1969, and 1970) on the White House Conference on Civil Rights, Food, Nutrition, and Health and Children's Health. Exposure to policy making at this level motivated her to redouble her efforts to work for significant changes in civil rights and family and community health. That work led in 1972 to her becoming the first recipient of the Washington State School Nurse of the Year Award. Numerous other national and regional awards followed.

Known to be very effective in motivating other professionals to identify with organizational goals and for getting things done, Vivian

Vivian O. Lee, Director, Office of Women's Health, PHS (far right) with other attendees at The PHS, Region X, Interpersonal Violence Conference, Seattle, WA, February, 1994: (left to right) Bernard Kelly, Regional Director, HHS; Dr. Joycelyn Elders, Surgeon General of the United States; Riley Hall, Family Planning Consultant (partially hidden in the back); Karen Matsuda, Regional Program Consultant for Family Planning, Office of Women's Health, PHS; Vivian Lee; and Jack Whitney, Regional Health Administrator, PHS.

was invited to apply for an administrative position when the Region X Health Education and Welfare office opened in Seattle (later known as Region X United States Department of Health and Human Services). To prepare for it, she returned to academia at the University of Puget Sound and completed a master's degree in public administration.

During her long and distinguished tenure within the federal system, Vivian is most proud of two programs that she implemented, one for early diagnosis and treatment of chlamydia and the other for the development of a nurse-practitioner training program for obstetrics and gynecology. Both have served as models for other regions of the United States and Canada, resulting in greater efficiency in providing services to clients and enhancement of research and clinical practices by professionals.

During the 1980s, when she was a federal administrator, she was somewhat painfully reminded of her student days by one small but poignant incident. Virginia Mason Hospital had just closed Blackford Hall and gave to students who had been assigned to that facility their school records. Included in them were comments instructors had made about students. Vivian winced when she read that in 1955 she was described as an "attractive Colored girl" and as "an intelligent, personable, Negro woman." What a disappointment to see that her physical appearance had received greater prominence in these instructors' eyes than her academic performance and potential! At the time of our interview, Vivian shared with me the contents of this entire Blackford Hall folder.

The 1980s brought other awards to counteract that disappointment. In 1982 Vivian was the recipient of the Department of Health and Human Service Excellence Award for Administration and she was a member of Washington Governor Evans' Task Force on Equitable Health Care.

Vivian identified her most challenging years as those which occurred during the Reagan/Bush era. According to Vivian, "This was the time when anti-family planning conservatives tried to drastically change federal funding priorities for family planning services. Organized efforts were made to require parental notification for teens in need of services and Congress was pressured to cut funding for planning clinics by 35%. Only by court order were clinicians prevented from implementing the gag rule which would have denied patients full information about options for their pregnancies—adoption, abortion or parenting." Vivian provided effective leadership to agencies throughout Washington, Oregon, Idaho and Alaska to continue to provide comprehensive levels of services to patients. Vivian went on to say that the Black experiences in America are good training for such days of siege. Vivian feels that most African American nurses can thrive and stay the course, even in days of turmoil, because "it's the life." In other words, by virtue of the many disruptive experiences of racism, sexism, and elitism that occur in the normal lifetime of an African American woman, we learn to cope with whatever challenges that occur.

Finally, in 1994, having fulfilled the administrative role with distinction and having completed 22 years of service in Region X Health Services, she retired as the founding director of the Office of Women's Health. The awards continued. In 1993 there was the University of Washington Nursing Alumni Association Distinguished Alumni Award; in 1994 selection by Seattle Mayor, Norm Rice, for the recognition of August 20, 1994 as Vivian Odell Lee Day; in 1996, the University of Washington Alumni Association Volunteer of the Year Award.

Other Roles and Awards for Contributions

Soon after passing state-board examinations in the 50s, Vivian joined the Mary Mahoney Professional Nursing Organization as a result of knowing Verna Hill and Shirley Gilford, graduates of the University of Washington School of Nursing, and Frances Demisse, a VMH classmate. All four were members. Among her many contributions to this organization and others, she is a staunch supporter of the scholarship luncheon, which MMPNO sponsors each year. Soon after she retired, she received the Mary Mahoney Professional Nurses Award for Excellence in Service and Clinical Practice.

In 2000, Vivian received the Charles E. Odegaard Award which was established in April, 1973, to recognize dedicated support of equal opportunity in higher education for minority and economically disadvantaged students. The recipients of this award are individuals from the community or the University whose leadership advances the aims of the Educational Opportunity Program.

Vivian lives through work and gives to others without regard to their racial, ethnic, or gender orientation or any other characteristic they may possess. Her focus is on meeting health needs of individuals, small groups, and communities. She knows that by giving one can truly receive the greatest possible level of personal and professional satisfaction. Vivian's life work, as well as her mother's and her son's, truly reflect excellence and achievement across three generations.

Rising Above Circumstances to Become a Professional Nurse

Rosa Dell Young

Rosa Dell Young grew up with six brothers and sisters in a home where both parents stressed the value of religion and education. Every day of the week the family gathered to recite the 23rd Psalm before going their separate ways into the community to work and attend school. Their father regularly talked to the children about the importance of getting a good education and being a good Christian, instilling in them the idea that the combination of a good education and strong religious values would make them trusted and respected members of their community.

Throughout her entire stay at home, Rosa saw her parents read only the Bible and the local daily newspaper, although the children had school textbooks and magazines such as *Ebony* to read. Whether there was a public library in the Negro section of the town she cannot remember; however, she knows that she never visited any library other than the one at school.

One of Seven

Born September 23, 1943, she is the fourth of seven children born to Beulah Grayson Young and Roosevelt Young. Her siblings were Bessie, Franklin, Ollie, Rosa, Lucinda Maxine, Booker, and Essie. Both brothers are now deceased. Two of her sisters, Bessie Young Jefferson and Ollie Young Madra, live in Cleveland, Ohio; Rosa and Essie Young Brown live in Seattle; and Lucinda Maxine Young lives with their 88-year-old mother in Alexandria, Louisiana. Their mother, still in relatively good health, continues to follow the daily pattern established when the children were growing up, reading the Bible and the local daily newspaper. Rosa visits her mother and sister at least twice each year, also making regular financial contributions, with the hope, shared by all surviving children, of maintaining her mother in the family home for as long as possible.

In 1945, when Rosa was two years old, the family moved from Monroe to Alexandria, Louisiana, because Mr. Young was looking for more opportunities to work than were available to him in Monroe. For several years he worked on the railroad, but Mrs. Young did not like having him away from home for long periods. Eventually, he found a job as a janitor in the public school district and remained in this job until he retired. He died in 1985. For many years her mother worked in a local laundry until the steam press fell on her left hand and caused a crippling burn which prevented her from working outside of the home.

Growing up in a Nourishing Environment

Living in the Negro section of Alexandria, the family knew their neighbors well, and attended neighborhood churches and the racially segregated public schools. Neighbors looked out for one another, and any of the elders in the neighborhood could discipline a child seen misbehaving. Rosa ran errands and performed small chores for elderly neighbors who were sick or who did not have children living in their homes. She recalls making most trips to either the grocery or drugstore and doing some light housework for them.

All members of the Young family attended church and Sunday school regularly where their father was a deacon and a member of the board of trustees of St. Lawrence Baptist Church

Rosa Dell Young during her elementary school days in Louisiana.

Rising Above Circumstances

and their mother was a choir member. In addition to Sunday school, the children belonged to Baptist Training Union, a youth religious education group, sang in the choir, and regularly attended vacation Bible school.

As teenagers the children all worked at odd jobs, the boys as stock clerks in grocery stores and doing yard work and other chores around the house. The girls did babysitting and day work (usually cleaning and household chores in other people's homes) for both Negro and Caucasian families. As a teenager, Rosa worked in White peoples' homes, baby-sitting and doing general housework such as cleaning, washing clothes by machine, and washing dishes by hand. She did not prepare meals. All of the children in her family were allowed to keep and manage the money they earned.

Rosa Dell Young in 1962 at the time of her graduation with honors from high school in Louisiana.

Rosa loved school, where most of her teachers knew her brothers and sisters who had preceded her in each school. In high school she was active in the school choir, drama group, and school band and graduated as an honor student in June 1962. That August she entered Dillard University in New Orleans, always having expected to attend college. She selected Dillard because it had a nursing program and because four or five other students from her high school were also going there.

A Rocky Entry into College and a Restart

During the first weeks of classes, Rosa got the shock of her life, realizing for the first time that she was not well prepared to do the classwork. At first, she was ashamed and afraid to tell anyone she was having a hard time understanding the material; however, before the first month ended, she found out that other students from her school were also having a hard time keeping up with assignments. One of the first things she did was to pray and ask God for help. Soon her instructors were asking her to come in to talk about her performance. With great personal effort and consistent help from instructors, she passed all of her freshman courses; however, she decided to leave college because she and many of her friends were not accepted into the nursing program, their main reason for going to Dillard University.

She left Louisiana for Cleveland, Ohio, where two of her sisters lived, for a short period, staying with them until she found work as a nurses' aide in Highlandview, a county hospital and she was able to have her own place. Most of the registered nurses were Caucasian; licensed practical nurses were mostly Negro; nurses' aides were Negro and Caucasian. While carefully observing how nurses in each category performed their duties, Rosa soon knew definitely that she wanted to be a registered nurse. Being in Cleveland was an education in itself for her, providing her the first chance to interact with people from diverse ethnic and racial groups. She explored activities that she had never before considered, for example, concerts and plays. Yet she missed being in school. When she saw on a bulletin board a notice about opportunities for undergraduate study at Seattle University, she copied down the information in her address book. Shortly thereafter, she applied for and obtained a job in the General Electric plant, where the pay was higher than that for nurses' aides, but the monotony of this job motivated her to write to Seattle University for information about admission to the School of Nursing. When her application was accepted, she came to Seattle to enroll.

She knew no one in Seattle; however, since she was involved with the church at that time, she found Goodwill Baptist Church, very close to Seattle University. She called Reverend Mitchell to introduce herself as a newcomer to the city and to tell him she was a Baptist and would soon join the church. He, in turn, introduced her to the Washington family, A.L. and Willye and their two nieces who took her in and treated her like a family member. She remains a friend of the Washingtons to this day, assisting Mrs. Washington in getting to her clinic appointments and remaining an advocate and friend.

After beginning studies at the university, she learned about Mary Mahoney Registered Nurses Club through Muriel Softli, who was already a member. Through the organization, she received tutorial assistance and a scholarship. Two other Black students in the nursing program, Donna and Gail, as well as Black students in other programs on campus, made her feel comfortable. Being at Seattle University at that time was like being a member of a small community. It was a Jesuit culture that was accepting, supportive, and caring. Though challenged in all her courses, she never felt alone because of the instructors' academic help and MMRNC's financial assistance; other organizations in the community also provided emotional and social support.

After completing the theory courses, she entered clinical affiliations, completing obstetrics and gynecology at Overlake Hospital (in Bellevue, a city near Seattle), where she experienced some racial tension. Some of the nurses were overly protective of her, often carrying babies to their mothers rather than having Rosa perform this very simple task. Another incident that remains in her memory involved a doctor's wife who was her patient and to whom she had given excellent care; yet, when the patient needed to be catheterized, the nurses called in a doctor for this procedure rather than allow Rosa to do it, although she had previously performed many catheterizations. Fearful, she did not complain to the staff about this demeaning treatment.

In 1971 Rosa successfully completed the baccalaureate degree in nursing and took the state board examinations, although she failed the obstetrics/gynecology section. At that time it was necessary to repeat the entire boards rather than just take the portion of the examination that one failed. She recalls her obstetrics/gynecology clinical experiences as so stressful that she believes her education on this service was compromised. Before retaking the examination, she decided to take time for self-study and tutorial assistance.

During the interval, Rosa worked at Harborview Hospital and, some months later, retook and passed the state board test. She is quick to admit that, by failing the examination the first time, she became a more knowledgeable and competent nurse because she realized she had to prove her ability the second time around. A humbling experience, it led to her desire to share it, lest other nurses experience similar difficulties in the future. Such failure is a profound disappointment, but it is one from which it is possible to recover and move on. Passing the examination also led to her becoming a member of MMPNO.

Professional Employment Experiences

For two years, beginning in 1973, Rosa worked as a staff nurse at the Seattle Veteran's Administration Hospital and then for nine and a half years as head nurse. During this period she encountered conditions that she felt included some racial discrimination; her suspicions were confirmed with the help of "one of the White RNs who trusted me enough to tell me that the supervisor had regularly asked her questions about me, which she refused to answer." This incident was so troubling that Rosa decided to leave the hospital to work more than three years as a public health nurse. She loved the autonomy and variety of family health needs; however, asthma, which she acquired as an adult, forced her to return to an inpatient-treatment setting. Many of the families' homes where she provided care had cats and other pets that had caused her debilitating asthma attacks.

Thus, she returned to the Veteran's Hospital Medical Center, where she has remained until the present time, currently serving as night supervisor of nursing and interacting with nurses on all hospital floors. She considers this a position with great potential; however, she really wants to put to better use the Master's Degree in Public Administration that she received from Seattle University in 1980. Just how she will do this she does not know, but with planning she believes she can.

An Interlude in the Air Force Reserves

In 1975 Muriel Softli had encouraged her to join the Air Force Reserves, which she did and for 12 years served as a flight nurse. Eventually, the asthma, which she has suffered from for many years, forced her reassignment to ground duty in the infection-control section, where she knows she has rendered superior service. At the time that she started working in this section, evaluations had consistently been in the marginal range. Through her leadership and

Rising Above Circumstances

the systematic and collaborative efforts of all the nurses in this area, a superlative evaluation resulted. In 1996 she received an award for her outstanding service in managing this area of care.

During her 21 years in the Air Force Reserves, Rosa made every promotion within the expected time, retiring in April 1996 as a lieutenant colonel. Some of her happiest nursing experiences were in the Air Force. "As an officer you are given respect whether people want to give it or not. Military service is steeped in the traditions of rank and respect. Of course there is some discrimination everywhere, but you feel it less in the service."

As a military nurse, she traveled to many parts of the world. During Operation Desert Storm, for example, she was stationed at the Royal Air Force Base in Upper Heyford, England, serving as the officer in charge of the infection-control services. Under stressful conditions, she demonstrated her skills by providing exemplary care to service men and women. She has also traveled with a group of nurses and other civilians to Egypt, the south of France, Italy, New Zealand, and to various parts of Africa.

Rosa Dell Young (seated) is pictured with an Airforce Reserve colleague during her tour of duty in Desert Storm. She served her country for 21 years in the U.S. Airforce Reserve.

A Father's Hopes Come True

She realizes that her father was right. Maintaining her faith in God and diligently and consistently seeking educational opportunities, she has become a trusted and respected member of a large community. "I have been blessed to receive financial support from MMRNC, the Urban League, and Seattle University. Tutoring and emotional support have been provided by members of my church and MMPNO members. As a result of these resources I am motivated to work and give back to my community."

Rosa is an active member now of the First AME Church, having switched from Baptist to Methodist while she was a student at Seattle University. Services were convenient to her schedule and she found the members very friendly. Since her first mentor, Reverend Mitchell, had died, this seemed like an opportune time to change her affiliation. She is a member of the choir and the health unit of the Church.

Among professional organizations, Rosa is active in the Association of Black Health Care Providers and has served for many years as a volunteer for the City of Seattle Head Start Program. The latter service has enabled her to render significant assistance to many children and their family members. At the Veteran's Hospital, she has served as an equal employment officer on several occasions.

During the 1970s, when a Seattle Chapter of the National Black Nurses was established, Rosa had serious conflict with members of MMRNC. Whereas only professional nurses are eligible for membership in MMPNO, the National Black Nurses Association accepts licensed practical nurses as members. Since she had worked as an aide and knew how exposure to registered nurses motivated her to work to become an RN, she thought similar exposure would benefit professional nursing. She was unsuccessful in her effort to obtain a change in MMPNO policy and decreased her participation in the organization. Now that the Black Nurses Organization in Seattle is defunct, she thinks it is time to return to MMPNO as a way of continuing to give back to others.

In reflecting upon her life experiences in attempting to become a nurse, Rosa gives great credit to her parents for giving all of their children the values of religion and education. She recalls, "Dillard University occupies a very special place in my heart. There the instructors encouraged me to continue to work hard to learn the course material. They convinced me that I was capable of doing college work. I developed self-confidence and the determination to succeed." She also acknowledges that Seattle University was the place that took her in and gave her the sense of belonging to the Jesuit family. "The administrators of the University continue to make a place at the table for non-Catholic and different minority groups. I owe them a lot, too," she says.

Rising Above Circumstances

As retirement approaches, Rosa's plans include continuing to work to give back to the community. She also wants to travel to countries that she has not yet visited. Her rise from her Monroe/Alexandria, Lousiana roots and her growing up in a stable laboring family illustrate well what can be achieved through self-determination, family support, and help from many others along the way.

A Vision of Self-Sufficiency Through Service to Others

Wilma Jones Gayden

The birth of Wilma Jones on November 2, 1943, was a big surprise to her parents, Josephine Jackson and Johnny Amos Jones. When their son, Willard, was born on that same day, they expected only one child. The midwife and the parents waited patiently for the afterbirth. The afterbirth was delayed so long that a White neighbor, who had given birth to twins some months earlier, came over to the Jones' house to see the new baby and to see why the afterbirth was taking so long to come. She looked at Wilma's father and said, "Get her to the hospital right away. There is another baby in there!" Once her mother was in the hospital, a second baby started coming. Wilma was delivered by a doctor in that hospital, the first Negro child to be born in that hospital in Tallulah, Louisiana. This story of Wilma and Willard's births has been told so many times that some family members refer to her as the "afterbirth child."

Wilma Jones is the baby on the left, pictured with her twin brother, Willard, in the arms of their mother.

In addition to the twins, there are three other children born to Josephine and Johnny. They are Charles Valey, Tom Jefferson, and

A Vision of Self-Sufficiency Through Service to Others

Josephine. Johnny had two children from his first marriage, Dean Jones Love and James Edward Jones (now deceased). Josephine had two children from her first marriage, Dorothy Hopkins and Earl Hopkins (now deceased), who were many years older than the other children. The children who were reared together included the twins, Charles, Tom, Josephine, and a niece, Joanne.

The Hard Life of Sharecroppers

Following the twins' birth, Josephine and Johnny remained in Tallulah for about one year. In 1944 they relocated to Pascagoula, Mississippi, where Johnny got a job as a laborer in the local shipyard. The family remained in this area for about five or six years before moving to Epps, Louisiana, where the family worked as sharecroppers. (A sharecropper is a tenant farmer who farms the land for the landowner and shares a portion of his crops with the landowner in exchange for rent and other expenses associated with the cost of farming. Often, there are several families, each having a designated number of acres they agree to farm. The plots are typically next to or very near one another.) Families engaged in sharecropping when Wilma was growing up were friendly, supportive, and very busy, everyone working to gain the highest return from their efforts. There was little or no time for any other activities during planting and harvesting seasons.

Josephine and Johnny worked side by side, along with their children, in farming their acres, planting and raising cotton for the landowner. For their family's consumption, they always had a vegetable garden. The workday began with a hearty breakfast of bacon, grits, biscuits, and eggs; then everyone was in the field by 6:00 a.m. with a job to do. The children's first job was carrying water to their parents in the field. Josephine returned from the field by 11:00 a.m. in order to have dinner ready to serve by noon. Everyone returned to the fields at 1:00 and remained until 6:00 p.m.

Before Wilma began working in the field, she helped to manage her younger brothers and sisters and, at a very early age, began helping with the cooking. By age eight, she knew how to prepare most of the food that the family consumed; her greatest challenge was managing the gas stove. Sometimes, when the gas oven did not turn on immediately, she became fearful and turned it off. Finally comfortable with the stove, she felt confident about her cooking and her mother allowed her to prepare several dishes.

Her paternal grandmother came to live with the Jones family after she had had a stroke and, rotating among her children's families, she was sometimes transported on a flatbed truck from one home to another. When it was the Jones's turn to care for Johnny's mother, Wilma fed her, a task she enjoyed doing, except, perhaps, for the times when grandmother had had enough and shut her mouth so tightly that Wilma could not get her to eat any more.

As Wilma recalled these childhood years, she said, "As sharecroppers and children of sharecroppers, we worked hard and sometimes our parents experienced exploitation and injustices. Even so, we often had fun in our individual homes and with other sharecropping families." Sundays were rest days that included going to church and Sunday school. "My dad took us to church and Sunday school, but he would wait outside and talk with other men who did just as he did. These men did not attend church service. My mother and several other mothers taught Sunday school." When she was old enough, Wilma began teaching Sunday school, too, and sang her first solo in Mount Wade Baptist Church in Epps.

"Our family's biggest treat was piling into our father's car on some Saturdays and going to town to get a hotdog and ice-cream cone. Whenever a trip was made into town, all of the family went together. Sometimes, when the workday ended about six o'clock and there was still daylight, we played games. We chased lightning bugs, played hide and seek, jump rope, and ring games like *Little Sally Walker*. Playing house and doll making helped us to dream. The biggest treat of all came when Mr. John McNair's family bought a television. We often gathered at this home to play and watch TV."

During the winter months food came from government commodities. As she says, "We got beans, rice, butter, flour, and meal. This was during the time when sharecroppers were 'laid by' [had limited work to do]." Her mother cared for sick neighbors. "My mother was a very natural caregiver. People regularly called and came to get her to care for their loved ones. Sometimes I went with mother and helped her give care. She would sometimes bathe, feed, and just sit quietly with sick people". Long before Wilma knew

A Vision of Self-Sufficiency Through Service to Others

about the nursing profession, she knew she wanted to give this kind of care to others.

Beginnings of a Love of Learning and a Need for Self-Sufficiency

Wilma is deeply grateful to her mother because she was the one who told their father they needed to move closer to the main road so the children could start school. She wanted more than fieldwork for her children. At age seven, Wilma and Willard entered Adams Elementary School, taken to school on "the yellow school bus that Mr. Willie Jackson drove." All of their teachers were African American: she remembers them as giving love and affection, as well as instruction. It was a supportive educational environment that encouraged her to love learning.

After six years at Adams, the twins went to G. W. Griffith School for 7th through 12th grades. Again, all teachers were African American, as were students. The school White students attended was within walking distance of the Jones's home, but, because schools were segregated by race, the bus traveled 20 miles each way everyday to transport African American children to their school.

As she became more aware and observed the circumstances of life around her, Wilma cherished the caregiving experiences that she shared with her mother as opposed to those of sharecropping, which they also shared. The county school nurse also reinforced Wilma's image of self-sufficiency through nursing and the joys that a career in nursing would provide. Her interest in nursing was heightened when she realized that sharecropping might be very successful one year and less so another year. During successful years they had furniture and a car (a Studebaker sedan that Johnny loved). One year was especially bad. Josephine, Wilma's mother, became very sick and was hospitalized for some time. The children could not visit her because they were under 13 years old, and thus, not allowed into the hospital. Even before her mother was discharged from the hospital, she knew they would lose all of their furniture and the car. Caring neighbors gave them some furniture until they could buy more. Fortunately, they had quilts and blankets that their mother had made some years earlier for them. They served as pallets until they had beds to sleep in again.

The most dramatic and memorable indication of the depth of their economic circumstances was the image etched in Wilma's mind of her father's expressions and responses at that time. He sat with an elbow resting on each knee, his head between his hands, and looked down at the floor. In a loud, mournful, and singsong fashion, he sang, "The Lord will make a way somehow." This posture and his sorrowful singing convinced her that times were hard, a bad year for this family. She could see only one bright spot: her father's sister, Gertha, sent money and clothes to help them.

Things brightened further when their mother returned to health and her parents worked together to pull themselves out of debt. "It was their deep faith in God that gave them the courage and determination to work even harder than before to get back on their feet," she says. Other sharecropping families and many White families in the community also gave help.

In other times crops failed and sharecroppers did not come out of debt. (Sharecroppers usually bought on credit and paid bills when their crops were harvested.) It was during one of these times that her father was stopped on the road when he was walking home by a White store owner who said he wanted to be paid for the food that Johnny Jones had purchased from him. A heated exchange took place. The storeowner, in his truck, reached down as if to get a weapon while saying, "You have already said enough for me to kill you." Her father pulled out a knife to defend himself against this White man and was later jailed for this act. After he was released from jail, one night White people surrounded the family home and threatened them. "The next day some people helped my dad get out of town. Life in Epps was never the same for our family."

Harsh Reminders of Racial Segregation

In 1960 Josephine and Johnny separated; one year later Wilma and Willard were sent ahead of all of the other children to live with their sister, Dorothy, in Houston, Texas. That trip was a stressful learning experience for them. Never having been separated from their family nor having ridden on a bus, they had only their mother's instructions to stay together, not talk to strangers, and sit near the back of the bus. Before taking the children to the bus terminal, their mother

A Vision of Self-Sufficiency Through Service to Others

packed several shoeboxes full of enough fried chicken, teacakes, and other food to last throughout the trip. When the twins boarded the bus, they sat just in front of the long last seat and managed very well until they reached Texarkana, Texas. When the bus stopped, they ran out of the bus and into the bus station to go to the bathroom. In their haste they entered the nearest bathrooms for women and men. Soon Wilma heard over the loudspeaker, "This bathroom is not for you." After she finished using the bathroom, she and her brother were shown the bathrooms for Colored people, their first such experience. This form of racism was now added to their experience of school segregation. From then until they reached Houston, they were careful to read the signs and to enter only the doors labeled "Colored."

In Houston, they joined the New Life Baptist Church right away, which helped them make a successful adjustment to their new home. "Our sister, Dorothy, was a real angel to us," she recalls. Dorothy helped them overcome feelings of loneliness. A short time later, their mother and other sister and brother also moved to Houston.

In Houston's B. C. Elmore High School, Wilma read books about nursing at every opportunity and a school counselor helped her select the appropriate courses for entering nursing. She also worked as a short-order cook at Bailey's Drive-In, where Dorothy worked, and sold Avon products door-to-door in her neighborhood. In 1963 she graduated, knowing well before graduation that, once she had enough money, she would go to nursing school.

PREPARATION FOR A CAREER IN NURSING

During 1963-1965, Wilma attended Texas Southern University in Houston part-time, taking pre-nursing courses while continuing to work on weekends and holidays. She had enough success with each to give her confidence that she was making tangible progress towards becoming self-sufficient. Another opportunity unfolded in Washington State. Her Aunt Gertha Jones, who had helped the family survive, had married J. D. Evans and moved with him to Pasco, Washington, where they owned a grocery store and deli named "The Dew Drop Inn." Although she and her aunt had spent very little time together, after Wilma's high school graduation Gertha invited her to come live with the Evans family where she would be able to attend college.

In 1965 Wilma again took a bus trip. This time, because of all the civil rights activities, Wilma assumed that she would be able to eat in bus station restaurants and sit wherever she wanted to on the bus. Packing food in a shoe box, as her mother had done before, she also had enough money to buy food. When she boarded the bus, she selected a seat near the front, and, when the driver made a stop at a bus station, she went in and sat at the restaurant counter. Other African Americans sat near her. The waitress served all the White patrons and never looked at Wilma and the other African Americans waiting for service. To Wilma's astonishment, none of them received service. Without protest, they left the counter and got back on the bus. No one said anything. With their eyes downcast, everyone sat in silence. Wilma never knew whether people were so angry that they said nothing or too surprised and shocked to know what to do. As for Wilma, she was astonished. Wilma had a full enough shoe box that she did not try to get service in other restaurants along the way, thus avoiding the risk of further humiliation and insult. On her arrival in Pasco, she felt tired and pleased to be with family members who welcomed her with love and food.

After a few days of eating and resting, Wilma started to look for work. With the help of Isabelle Gates Rosenfels, an investigator for the Washington Anti-Discrimination Board and an acquaintance of

Wilma Jones completed her practical nurses program in 1966 and her Associate Arts degree in Nursing in 1968 at the Columbia Basin College in the tri-cities of Pasco, Kennewick and Richland, Washington. She is pictured standing in the back row, third from the left with other classmates.

A Vision of Self-Sufficiency Through Service to Others

Gertha's, she was hired as a clerk in Mrs. Isabelle Gates Rosenfels' office until she found other employment. "I received a tremendous amount of help from Isabelle. She helped me complete my application for employment at Sears Roebuck and she prepared me for the interview. I was hired right away to work part-time evenings and weekends." She continued to work at Sears until the demands of school forced her to stop.

After being in Pasco for a short time, Wilma joined the Morning Star Baptist Church. Since she loves to sing, she joined the choir where she was welcomed with open arms by the members. The love and support she found in this church and in her aunt's home reminded her of experiences in Epps and Houston. The main difference was her "being around more White people, doing the same kind of work that they were doing." With these positive experiences to reinforce her confidence, she was ready to apply for admission to nursing school, Columbia Basin College in the tri-cities of Pasco, Kennewick, and Richland. She entered and completed all requirements for the licensed-practical-nurses program. Through Frances Gleason, director of the LPN program, she learned about Mary Mahoney Registered Nurses Club and got their scholarship information.

Immediately after becoming a LPN, she entered the Associate of Arts Nursing program, using the MMRNC information to apply for a scholarship. Shortly thereafter, she received a letter from the co-chairs of the Scholarship Committee, Celestine Thomas and Thelma Pegues, inviting her to come to Seattle to meet with the committee. She accepted the invitation and stayed in the home of Celestine and Lawrence Thomas during her visit. The committee awarded her a scholarship for the 1967-68 academic year.

That was only a part of the abundant assistance she received in support of her college work. In addition to other scholarships from the Kennewick Altrusa Club and the Kiwanis, "I was also given many other gifts. One year Isabelle and Dick Rosenfels gave me $100. I had never held that much money in my hand before. One Christmas, members of the Morning Star Baptist Choir showered me with gifts that lasted throughout the time I was in school. Cornelius and Doris Walker let me live with them free of charge for one year. Earlene Bynes, my 'Pasco mother,' prepared food for me, gave me clothing, lots of advice, loving care, and encouragement. My Aunt Gertha and her husband helped me buy my first car. I was really poor but many blessings were given to me."

She completed an AA degree and graduated in 1968 which was "the happiest day of my life. My mother came from Texas. Celestine and Lawrence Thomas, Thelma and Piggy Pegues, and Sadie Berrysmith came from Seattle. My Aunt Gertha was there. My dad called the day before graduation to congratulate me. After the ceremony we all went to Ms. Iola James' kitchen and ate some of the best food I ever ate."

Employment as a Nurse

Wilma acknowledged that she received much more from MMRNC than money: "I met friends and families that remain very dear to me." It was the presence of these members of MMRNC, as well as Wilma's desire to practice nursing at a large university hospital, that motivated her to eventually relocate to Seattle. Meanwhile, she decided to remain in Pasco, where she was hired at Kadlec Hospital on the medical unit. "I gained excellent experiences at this hospital. At that time there were no special intensive care or coronary care units on medical floors. Very sick patients were brought directly to the medical floor and staff nurses cared for them. I really learned a lot while working there." Although she did not see other African American nurses at Kadlec, her experiences with the staff, patients, and their family members were positive. (One other Black nurse, Mrs. Ruth Jackson of Pasco, worked in the area.)

After passing state board examinations and having one year of work experience which entitled her to in-state tuition, she felt that she was ready to work in a larger hospital. She also wanted to seek a baccalaureate degree in nursing. With full appreciation for the support and help her aunt and uncle and everyone else had given her, she moved to Seattle in 1969 and found employment at University Hospital on the medical service. On Five South, where Wilma worked, the intensive care unit had not been established. As at Kadlec, patients with very serious illnesses were cared for on the ward and not in a special unit, as they are today. She soon realized that she possessed the knowledge and skills needed to deliver high quality care to patients. Her courses at Columbia Basin College and her Kadlec

A Vision of Self-Sufficiency Through Service to Others

work experiences prepared her well for these new work demands in University Hospital.

Soon after moving to Seattle, Wilma joined the New Hope Baptist Church, founded by the late Dr. C. E. Williams, where she remains a loyal member and Sunday school teacher. She made friends with many people in the congregation and reestablished her friendship with members of MMRNC, joining and actively participating in this organization until 1969.

With Sandra Cravens, an active MMRNC member, she decided to take a chartered tour to Europe. One of the main attractions of this trip was *The Passion Play* that is enacted every 10 years by residents of Oberammergau, Germany. Her decision to make this trip was based partly on the reassurance of Isabelle, her Pasco friend, who had been to Europe and encouraged Wilma to go. She also told the Thomas and Pegues family members that she planned to take her first airplane trip. Both men in these families teased her about plane travel; so, to allay some of her apprehension, Lawrence and Celestine Thomas took her to the airport well in advance of departure time to show her what she needed to pay attention to when she traveled.

During this 1970 trip, they traveled to nine European countries in three weeks. Being able to do this represented for Wilma a new understanding of self-sufficiency. It signified professional success in her dream of becoming a nurse and showed her that she could establish reasonable goals and then find ways to achieve them. She still desired to return to school to complete a BA in nursing; making the trip helped her believe that was still possible.

After returning to Seattle, she learned that Virginia Mason Hospital had a critical care unit, a place she wanted to work. Hired to work nights there, she met some of the nicest, most helpful nurses she ever worked with. Mrs. Hillard, for example, a night supervisor who "could find a vein in any patient," helped her get an IV started when she was having difficulty. Before Wilma left this job, she, too, had developed a high level of proficiency in starting IVs. In this treatment setting, she increased her overall caregiving skills and self-confidence in serving others and enjoyed working at Virginia Mason. While there, she learned that the United States Public Health Hospital, later named Pacific Medical Center (or Pac Med), was hiring nurses. Since their benefit package was more complete than Virginia Mason's, she decided to move to Pac Med, once again working nights in the intensive care units and on the medical floors.

Marriage, Children, and Greater Self-Sufficiency

In 1973 Wilma married Curtis Gayden, whom she had met through Reverend Shelby Tate. From this union have come two daughters, Curiya Suzanne (born in 1975) and Kizuwanda Balayo (in 1977). Curiya Suzanne is married to Damien Webber and they live in Philadelphia, PA. Kizuwanda Balayo is a graduate of Columbia University, NY, with a major in math education. When the children were small, Wilma attended Seattle Pacific University (1974-1977) and completed a B.S. degree in nursing. Achievement of this degree represented one more indication of her progress towards self-sufficiency.

Employed at Pac Med Hospital for 13 years (1973-1987), she worked nights throughout. She considered the staff at Pac Med as one of the most helpful and supportive group of professionals she ever worked with. She left only because the hospital closed its inpatient services. Before the hospital closed, recruiters from Seattle's Providence Hospital came to offer nursing-employment opportunities. Although Wilma completed an application, she was not interviewed since most of the recruitment activities occurred during the day when she was not there. After hearing several of her nurse colleagues say they had been hired at Providence, she called to inquire about the status of her application. Learning that it had not yet been considered, she scheduled an interview appointment and was hired. Once again she began working on the CCU/ICU units.

In the 13 years since 1987 that she has worked on the CCU/ICU night shift at Providence, she is often not considered to be a professional nurse by some patients, their family members, and some staff at the hospital. (Other African American nurses who work in hospitals throughout Puget Sound have had experiences that mirror Wilma's.) She stated, "When I go on duty, I introduce myself to all patients who are awake. Later, when some of these same patients put their call lights on and I respond, they ask to see the nurse." If she replies, "I am the nurse who will be caring for you until 7:00 a.m.," some patients say, "I did not think you were a nurse."

A Vision of Self-Sufficiency Through Service to Others

She currently works on the rehabilitation unit in Providence and plans to continue to work there until some time in the future when she can also carry out her new business venture. This venture is an adult family home where she can care for individuals with health problems that require round-the-clock, skilled nursing care in the home. For many years she has wanted to own such a home and has recently achieved this desire. She and her husband, a Captain in the Seattle Fire Department, have purchased a home where they will soon begin to care for such individuals. Curtis and Wilma will combine their many years of caregiving skills to manage their own business. The home honors the late Mrs. Celestine Thomas, a mentor and Seattle mother to Wilma. The state license, which is needed to establish and run an adult family home, is expected to arrive soon. Wilma is delighted that she has reached this level of professional success; yet, she regrets that Celestine Thomas (because of Alzheimer's disease) did not know about this development during her lifetime.

Wilma Jones Gayden at a recent social function.

She states, with a strong sense of accomplishment, "This is a wonderfully satisfying way to achieve self-sufficiency through service to others".

African American Registered Nurses in Seattle

Afterword

Each of the 26 foregoing stories has its own significance because it depicts an individual life of struggle and achievement. However, that significance may seem all the greater when we expand our context for thinking about each person's efforts with the help of additional information from history and from scholars who have studied the varied influences on human behavior and individual achievement.

Historical Perspective

In 1949, when MMRNC was founded in Seattle, the National Association of Colored Graduate Nurses (NACGN) was dissolving. NACGN served the needs of Negro nurses for 43 years (1908-1951) before being integrated into the American Nurses Association in 1951 (Staupers, 1961). The prevailing thought among NACGN leaders was that, once individual membership in ANA was open to Negroes, NACGN was no longer needed.

Upon hearing the news that NACGN would soon integrate into ANA, Anne Foy Baker asserted that her experiences in trying to gain membership in the Virginia State Nurses Association had convinced her of the continuing need for a Negro nursing organization such as Mary Mahoney Registered Nurses Club. However, she encouraged MMRNC members to also join Washington State Nurses Association. It was not a matter of choosing one group or the other; they needed both organizations. Through participation in the larger organization, Negro nurses could identify their unique needs and priorities and could seek to establish programs to meet those needs. They might also hone their leadership skills for use in other organizations. Maxine Pitter Davis Haynes was the first MMRNC founder to join and actively participate in ANA. Other founders later followed her lead.

These women evidently felt the tug of history that affirmed their perseverance and shared goals. They were able to see themselves as not struggling alone but as a part of a group of women and nurses pursuing common goals.

Human-Needs Perspective

Just as each person's efforts exist within an historical context, so, too, do they arise from and depend on certain universals of human need. Abraham Maslow (1970), a social psychologist, focused on human motivation, proposing that human behavior can be understood within the context of needs which individuals experience. He did not, however, sub-divide his description of a needs hierarchy to allow for cross-cultural differences.

According to him, the presence of a particular need serves as a motivation for action and a direction of the action taken to satisfy a specific need. Needs determine what will be the focus of one's attention and effort and emerge in levels from lowest to highest, with lowest level needs to be satisfied first. His five levels are:

- **physiological:** satisfied with food, air, and water
- **safety:** satisfied by the absence of fear, uncertainty, or harm
- **social:** satisfied through positive interactions with other human beings
- **esteem:** satisfied by one's pride or belief in oneself and by how one is perceived by others or receives respect from others.
- **self-actualization:** satisfied by finding meaning and achieving a defined goal, such as experiencing excellence in some effort through artistic, creative, or intellectual pursuits.

Using Maslow's needs hierarchy in relationship to these 26 stories shows that each of these nurses' basic needs were met for food, shelter, and sustenance, though one nurse's family was threatened with potential harm from a group of White members of the community. Social needs were satisfied through participation in work in and outside the home. School and church served social and religious needs.

Afterword

Through activities which family members enjoyed at church and in their communities, esteem needs were met. Children's participation in school and Sunday school was encouraged by family members, helping them meet esteem and self-actualization needs. In other words, in their early years each of these women was fortunate enough to have reached a fairly high level of needs satisfaction, as defined by Maslow. Adults satisfied these same needs by participating on usher boards, deacon boards, in Bible study, the missionary circle, and Church choirs.

Group-Needs Perspective

Brooks and Nisberg (1974) drew upon their backgrounds in business administration and behavioral sciences to identify dominating interests and motivations among African Americans. They proposed a Black hierarchy that focuses on group characteristics and needs, moving from lowest to highest.

- **survival**: achieved through physiological processes of eating, drinking, and breathing (Having a good, steady job is the anchor for meeting survival needs.)
- **having a good time**: achieved despite experiencing discrimination and deprivation (Black Americans have a zest for life that belies our treatment by the dominant group.)
- **praising God**: satisfied once one survives threats and achieves some measure of happiness (Religious expression of singing, praying, and worshiping together can satisfy this group need. Ministers are significant community leaders, and churches have historically been a source of refuge and strength for the group. Coming together as a group has value. Praying to God together extends this experience.)
- **getting ahead**: satisfied by having a job that provides improved life conditions and better opportunities, along with increases in income that reward improvement. (Gaining access to education and employment for the group is the manner by which this need is satisfied.)
- **up-lifting the race**: satisfied most significantly by moving from slavery to freedom and consistently encouraging and helping others to enhance their life chances for success. (Achieving basic

human rights to life with opportunities to compete, cooperate, compromise, collaborate and succeed are additional ways that Blacks often express an obligation to help other Blacks to improve our condition.)

The Brooks-Nisberg framework has compelling relevance for Black Americans because it represents those needs that have been defined by the group as being important. These needs have been documented through systematic research and reflect dimensions of life where Blacks spend time and to which we give importance. Combined and used with Maslow's hierarchy of needs, they provide a more inclusive set or a system of needs that help explain from a group-focused perspective why we Blacks do what we do.

When the Brooks-Nisberg framework is used as a structure for understanding the actions and activities of these 26 nurses, one observes that the survival needs of each nurse were indeed met in her home. Each nurse's family identified ways to have enjoyment, especially when the workday ended. Sundays had a special character, when few families worked. The freedom to worship was emotionally and socially beneficial to family members. Even in families where some adults worked on Sunday, it was possible for other members, usually women and their female children, to attend church or Sunday school. Church suppers were customary occasions when men in families joined in fellowship with others from the community.

Family members made sacrifices to enable children to go to nursing school. In some families only the female in the family was supported for professional development. Being a nurse was seen by the adults and the child as a way to get ahead.

By joining together in a professional nurses' organization, MMPNO gave service to the community and promoted the entry of new members into the profession. The struggles for acceptance and eventually integration into ANA also served as a mechanism to uplift the race.

Academic Performance Perspective

Claude Steele (1997), a social psychologist, devised a framework that links racial striving to intellectual and academic performance, with four basic components:

Afterword

- **societal scaffolding**: emphasis on the quality of schools and the resources available in the neighborhood (These are significant elements that impact school performance and personal and group identity.)
- **incentives**: availability of role models and family members who recognize, reward, and give importance to academic performance
- **social support**: absence of discrimination and prejudice (An environment where these oppressive factors are not present or are controlled through policies or laws can minimize negative effects of these factors on individual and group performance in academic settings.)
- **individual skills**: achieved when environmental supports for learning exist (Family, friends, and community residents can motivate individuals in their own family and community through participation in community activities that promote individual and group excellence.)

The Steele framework focuses on individual and group characteristics, specifically linking the individual and groups to academic environments where the acquisition of skills can bring personal and group success. The individual and community can be improved, thereby making it possible to advance our group and contribute to the larger society.

While these nurses expressed various influences in their lives in personal terms, they often mentioned out of their experiences some aspects of the Brooks-Nisberg and Steele frameworks. For example, for each of these 26 nurses, the Black church played a central role in their development; for some, it offered both religious guidance and common schooling. The stories reflect academic performance and achievement despite the lack of public support for schooling in some of the small Southern towns where these nurses lived.

The Steele framework is relevant in several other ways. It was common for Colored or Negro children of the era when MMRNC members were growing up to have either no public schools available to them or inferior schools compared to ones attended by White children. Yet through dedication and determination these individuals were able to complete nursing education and pass the same qualifying examinations as White nurses. Family support, peer influences, and the presence of role models in the community helped these MMRNC members to achieve excellence despite segregation and experiences of discrimination. We did not let institutional racism imposed by Whites prevent us from realizing our aspirations to become professional nurses.

What makes any human strive to become the best that she or he can be? Underlying lifetimes of effort are those ultimately enduring qualities of self-confidence, self-determination, persistence, and focus—qualities these women possessed in abundance.

Eugene Smith

"The past is never really past; some things will be with us always."

William Faulkner

References

Adero, M. (Ed.). (1992). *Up South: stories, studies, and letters of this century's African-American migration.* New York: The New Press: Distributed by W.W. Norton.

Brooks, W. C. and Nisberg, J. N. (1974). Effects of Cultural Differences on Motivation. *The Personnel Administrator*, 19(7), October, 28-30.

Carnegie, M. E. (1991). *The Paths We Tread: Blacks in Nursing 1854-1990, 2nd ed.* New York: National League for Nursing Press.

Carnegie, M. E. (1995). *The Paths We Tread: Blacks in Nursing Worldwide, 1854-1994, 3rd ed.* New York: National League for Nursing Press.

Cross-White, A. (1998). *Images of America: Charlottesville, An African-American Community.* Dover, New Hampshire: Arcadia Publishing.

Hine, D. C. (1985). *Black Women in the Nursing Profession: A Documentary History.* New York: Garland Publishing, Inc.

Hine, D. C. (1989). *Black Women in White: Racial Conflict and Cooperation in the Nursing Profession 1890-1950.* Bloomington, Indiana: Indiana University Press.

Katz, W. L. (1995). *Black Women of the Old West.* New York: Ethrac Publications, Inc.

Maslow, A. H. (1970). *Motivation and Personality.* New York: Harper and Rowe Publishers.

References

Miller, H. S. (1986). *America's First Black Professional Nurse.* Atlanta, Georgia: Wright Publishing Co.

Perkins, L. M. (1997). The African-American Elite: The Early History of African American Women in the Seven Sister Colleges, 1880-1960. *Harvard Educational Review,* 67(4), Winter, 718-756.

Staupers, M. K. (1961). *No Time for Prejudice.* New York: The Macmillan Company.

Steele, C. M. (1992). Race and the Schooling of Black Americans. *The Atlantic Monthly,* 269(4), April, 68-78; 680-681.

Steele, C. M. (1997). A Threat in the Air: How Stereotypes Shape Intellectual Identity and Performance. *The American Psychologist,* June, 52(6), 613-630.

Appendix

African American Registered Nurses in Seattle

CONSTITUTION — BY-LAWS
of
Mary Mahoney Registered Nurses Club
Seattle, Washington
1949

NAME:
The name of this Organization shall be the "Mary Mahoney Registered Nurses Club."

PLACE OF BUSINESS:
The principal place of business of this Organization shall be at Seattle, Washington, and at such other places as may be designated by this Organization.

AIMS and OBJECTS:
The aims and objects of this Organization shall be:
1. To keep abreast of modern trends in nursing.
2. To interest more young women in the profession.
3. To participate in civic affairs.
4. To protect our gains we have made so far, professionally, socially, morally, spiritually, and economically.
5. To interest the general public in our problems.

OFFICERS ELECTIVE:
The elective officers of this Organization shall be President, Vice President, Secretary, Assistant Secretary, Treasurer, and Chairman of the legislative boards.

OFFICERS' DUTIES:
President
The President shall preside at all meetings; she shall nominate members of all committees; she shall sign all vouchers properly made out and presented by the secretary. She shall countersign all checks properly made out and presented by the treasurer; she shall do all other things appertaining to her office.

Appendix

Vice President
The Vice President shall act in the absence of the president as presiding officer of the meetings. She shall sign all vouchers and checks in the absence of the president.

Secretary
The Secretary shall keep an accurate record of the proceedings of the Organization; she shall collect all monies coming into the club from every source. She shall issue her vouchers for all monies paid out; she shall turn over to the treasurer all monies collected on behalf of the Organization and take from the treasurer a receipt for the same. She shall receive, read, and answer all correspondence unless otherwise ordered.

Treasurer
The Treasurer shall receive all monies collected by the secretary and give her a receipt for the same, and place said monies in a depository designated by the Organization. She shall issue all checks of the Organization upon receipt of vouchers from the secretary properly made out and countersigned by the president. The treasurer shall be bonded as set forth by the Organization.

The Legislative Committee
It shall be the duty of this committee to assist the president in the orderly procedure during the regular meetings.

THE APPOINTIVE COMMITTEES:
The Appointive Committees shall be as follows:
1. Ways and Means Committee
2. Sick Committee
3. Publicity and Legislative Committee
4. Birthday Committee

COMMITTEE DUTIES:
1. The Ways and Means Committee shall supervise all programs and forms of entertainment.
2. The Sick Committee shall keep the club informed of all illnesses among its members and shall send gifts or cards as directed by the Organization.

3. The Publicity and Legislative Committee shall make all write-ups for newspapers and other forms of publication.

MEMBERSHIP QUALIFICATIONS:
Any Registered Nurse may make application into this Organization. The requirements are:
1. The presentation of her State Board registration number and certificate.
2. She must have a good moral standing in the community.

ANNUAL ELECTION:
The annual election of this Organization shall be held in July of each year.

REGULAR MEETINGS:
The regular meetings of this organization shall be held on the first Saturday of each month.

SPECIAL MEETINGS:
The President or Secretary has the authority to contact members by phone concerning business matters arising between meetings. Special meetings may be called at anytime by the president. Any member may be asked to resign by presenting the written charge to the President and by two-thirds vote of the members present.

DUES:
The dues of this Organization shall be fifty (50) cents per month.

CLUB COLORS:
The club colors shall be yellow and turquoise.

CLUB FLOWER:
The club flower shall be a yellow rose.

AMENDMENTS:
These By-Laws may be amended by presentation of the amendment in writing and a majority vote of the members present at the following meeting, at which time said amendment is presented.

Appendix

Newspaper Ad from *The Northwest Enterprise, April 1950*

MARY MAHONEY REGISTERED NURSE CLUB

The Mary Mahoney Registered Nurses Club, invites you to a musical tea, Sunday, April 23, Y.W.C.A., 4-6 p. m.

We are presenting some of the talented youths of our community, and are making elaborate preparations to serve and entertain you.

We are putting forth these efforts that we may soon announce our readiness to close plans for our scholarship.

We can only be of service, if you the public will be present and support us.

Some worthy girl will profit from your cooperation.

Silver offering.

Watch next week's paper for our program.

Keep off Date
May 8, 1950
Bent Hassan Temple No. 64

Buy where you can work.

African American Registered Nurses in Seattle

June 5, 1955
(From a Seattle newspaper, publication source not available)

Nurses' Club Proud of Its 'First Graduate"

Almost five years ago Viola Wesley, Negro honor graduate of Franklin High School, got a job at Harborview County Hospital as a cashier-typist in the dietary department. Her dream: To become a nurse.

That's where members of the Mary Mahoney Registered Nurses' Club found her—trying to type lessons during lulls in her work. The Negro nurses' organization decided then and there that anyone who wanted to be a nurse that much should be helped.

Saturday Miss Wesley, 23, will be graduated from the University of Washington School of Nursing.

The proudest onlookers will be the 12 nurses of the club who set up a scholarship fund to see to it that her dream became a reality.

The club, named after the first Negro nurse in the United States, sponsored Miss Wesley for four years and two academic quarters of the five-year nurse's course.

Funds Provided

The club provided funds for room and board, tuition, books, uniforms, a $30-a-month charge account and even a monthly appointment at the hairdresser's.

"I can't tell you how much I appreciate it," Miss Wesley said. "More so, because they took a personal interest in me." Miss Wesley's parents died while she was in training.

"We're proud of her for her parents," said Mrs. Juanita Davis, club president.

The club raised the scholarship money by holding an annual St. Patrick's Day dinner at the East Side Y.W.C.A., teas and monthly assessments.

The club will honor its "first graduate" at a reception from 3 to 6 o'clock today in the East Side Y.W.C.A., 2820 E. Cherry St.

Appendix

Further Study Planned

Miss Wesley, 600 24th Ave, N., hopes to work on her master-of-science degree.

Mrs. Mary S. Martyn, chairman of the scholarship fund, explained that the grant totaled $1500. Most of it was spent while Miss Wesley was in her two years of pre-nursing at the university.

"Since she transferred to Harborview we haven't had to pay for room and board—only books, 'lab' fees, uniforms and personal effects," Mrs. Martyn said. Mrs. Davis praised the co-operation of Harborview officials.

The club has grown to 18 members since sponsoring Miss Wesley, and its work isn't over. They'll offer a scholarship to another deserving girl next fall.

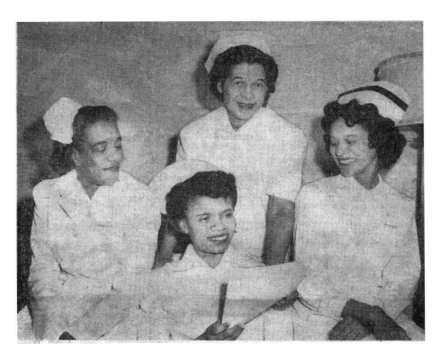

NURSES AID NURSE: Viola Wesley held a picture of the 12 members of the Mary Mahoney Registered Nurses' Club who financed her through almost five years of nurse's training. Club officers looking on were, from left, Mrs. Mary S. Martyn, scholarship-fund chairman, Mrs. Juanita Davis, president, and Mrs. Ernestine Williams, vice-president. Miss Wesley will be graduated Saturday from the University of Washington.

African American Registered Nurses in Seattle

Recipients of the Mary Mahoney Professional Nurses Scholarships and Financial Aid, 1950-2000

Viola Wesley Davis
University of Washington 1955

Shirley Tyson Gilford
University of Washington 1959

Joyce Ray
University of Washington 1962

Ruby Foster
University of Washington 1962

Beulah R. Smith
University of Washington 1963

Patricia Graham Watts
Seattle University 1964

Sandra Cravens
Highline Community College 1965

Wilma Jones Gayden
Columbia Basin Community College 1968

Eleanor Cole Mitchell
Shoreline Community College 1968

Rosa Young
Seattle University 1970

Ozella Rose
University of Washington 1971

Annie P. Jones
University of Washington 1973

Appendix

LaVerne Davis
University of Washington 1974

Johnnie Bairinger
University of Washington 1974

Nettie Fisher
Bellevue Community College 1974

Joyce Ray Rueben
University of Washington 1975

Chere Beaufix
Seattle Pacific College 1978

Luke McCray
Seattle University 1979

Gwen Wilks
University of Washington 1983

Debbie Gray
Seattle Central Community College 1983

Cynthia Hale
Everett Community College 1984

Kathy Marshall
Seattle University 1984-85

Lynn Oliphant
University of Washington 1985

Lisa Hardy
Seattle Central Community College 1985

Enid Moore
Seattle University 1988

African American Registered Nurses in Seattle

Diane Saunders
Tacoma Community College 1989

Jacqueline Hurd
Seattle Central Community College 1990

Jozette Matthews
University of Washington 1990

Morgan Jones
University of Washington 1990

Troy Hudson
Seattle University 1990

Cynthia Smith
Pacific Lutheran University 1990

Robin Nicole Sudduth
University of Washington 1991-92

Desiree Howery
University of Washington 1992-93

Sonia Coleman
Seattle Central Community College
Seattle University 1992-93-94

Rosemary Mukalazi
Seattle Pacific University 1992-93

Lauren Gueno Mathieu
Pacific Lutheran University 1992-93

William V. Randon
Pacific Lutheran University 1992

Shanda Lee Boyd
University of Washington 1992

Appendix

Melodie Bethel
University of Washington 1994

Joanne Hall-Haynes
University of Washington 1994

Wynona Hollins
Seattle University 1994-95

Prisca Ibe
Shoreline Community College 1997

Arthur Lee Davis, Jr.
Pacific Lutheran University 1997

Robin Nicole Sudduth
Seattle University 1997

Angela Lynette Hill
University of Washington 1998

Sabina Dumba
University of Washington 1998

Bianco L. Norman
Seattle Pacific University 1998

Grace Grymes-Chapman
Bellevue Community College 1999

Saibo Twnkara Jawara
Pacific Lutheran University 1999

Aida Jenkins
University of Washington 1999

Angela Lynn Klinedinst
Pacific Lutheran University 1999

African American Registered Nurses in Seattle

Sabina Okeke
Shoreline Community College 1999

Carol V. Dixon
Seattle University 2000

Adaobi Moemenam
Seattle Pacific University 2000

Melissia Yvette Payton
University of Washington 2000

Audrey M. Thomas
Seattle University 2000

Julie L. Vaughn
Seattle Central Community College 2000

Appendix

Members of The Mary Mahoney Registered Nurses Club (MMRNC) in 1959. Standing, left to right: Sadie Berrysmith Wallace, Ira Gordon, Celestine Thomas, Verna Hill, Mary Davis Hooks, Katie Ashford and Mary Martin. Sitting, left to right: Rose McAdory, Mary Lanier, Carrie Davis, Gertrude Dawson, Rachel Pitts, Ernestine Williams, Juanita Davis and Leola Lewis.

African American Registered Nurses in Seattle

Early photo of MMRNC in the 1960s: Standing, left to right: Viola Wesley Davis, Celestine Thomas, Pat Watts, Thelma Pegues, Sandra Craven, Mary Lanier, Eleanor Page Mitchell, Gertrude Dawson, Rachael Pitts, and Verna Hill. Sitting, left to right: Muriel Softli, Sadie Berrysmith Wallace, Mary Lee Bell, and Frances Briscoe.

Founding members 25th anniversary in 1974: Standing left to right: Katie Ashford, Rachel Pitts, Gertrude Dawson, Ernestine Williams, Mary Davis Hooks, Mary Lanier. Sitting, left to right: Celestine Thomas, Juanita Davis, Sadie Berrysmith Wallace, Anne Foy Baker. This was Anne's last trip to Seattle.

Appendix

40th Anniversary in 1989: Standing, left to right: Muriel Softli, Pearl Harris, Maxine Haynes, Lois Price Spratlen, Gertrude Dawson, Verna Hill, Gwendolyn Browne, Frances Demisse, Mary Lee Bell. Sitting, left to right: Celestine Thomas, Thelma Pegues, Sadie Berrysmith Wallace, Izetta Hatcher, Deborah Greenwood, Elizabeth Thomas.

Membership in 1993 at the establishment of the endowment fund: Standing Left to Right: Verna Hills, Betty Jean Sanders Stanton, Gwendolyn Browne, Mary Davis Hooks, Lois Eason, Sadie Berrysmith Wallace, Janice Flemming, Josephine Atteberry, Sharon Carson, Elizabeth Thomas, Pat Burton, Mary Osborne, Elinor Jones, Wilma Gayden, Charlotte Ruff, Gayle Mwamba, Morgan Jones. Sitting Left to Right: Muriel Softli, Celestine Thomas, Mary Lee Bell, Laura Egwautu, Gertrude Dawson, Thelma Pegues, Maxine Haynes, Lois Price Spratlen, Isetta Hatcher, Theresa Lee.

African American Registered Nurses in Seattle

City of Seattle · Office of the Mayor
PROCLAMATION

WHEREAS, the City of Seattle recognizes the vital part nurses play in efficient, compassionate health care delivery -- nursing is fundamental to the provision of quality preventative and curative care; and

WHEREAS, in spite of many challenges and entrenched bigotry, Mary Eliza Mahoney became the first black graduate nurse in the United States, in 1879; and

WHEREAS, the Mary Mahoney Registered Nurse Club of Seattle, was organized in 1949 in her honor, with 13 members, to provide financial assistance to black nursing students and serve as a forum to keep current with modern trends in nursing; and

WHEREAS, individually and collectively, the members of the Mary Mahoney Professional Nurses Association give of themselves in efforts to safeguard the health of the public by providing health education in various settings; and

WHEREAS, the members of the Mary Mahoney Professional Nurses' Organization are holding their 44th Annual Scholarship luncheon to raise funds to continue support for these worthy endeavors;

NOW, THEREFORE, I, NORMAN B. RICE, Mayor of the City of Seattle, do hereby proclaim March 20, 1993, to be

MARY MAHONEY PROFESSIONAL NURSES' ASSOCIATION DAY

in Seattle in honor and recognition of these dedicated professionals.

Norman B. Rice
Mayor

Proclamation from the Office of the Mayor proclaiming March 20, 1993 to be Mary Mahoney Professional Nurses' Association Day.

Appendix

MMPNO members in 1994 in attendance at a meeting. Back row, left to right: Lois Eason, Mary Davis Hooks, Frances Demisse, Gwendolyn Brown, Sadie Berrysmith Wallace. Second row from back, left to right: Gertrude Dawson, Laura Egwuatu, Betty Jean Sanders Stanton, Rachel Pitts, Theresa Lee, Josephine Atteberry. Third row from back, left to right: Pearl Mercadel, Wilma Gayden, Celestine Thomas, Verna Hill. Front tow, left to right: Muriel Softli, Thelma Pegues, Maxine Haynes, Elizabeth Thomas, Lois Price Spratlen, Mary Lee Bell.

MMPNO officers in 1994: Front Row, Left to right: Mary Lee Bell, 1st Vice-President, Celestine Thomas, 2nd Vice-President, Verna Hill, Secretary, Thelma Pegues, Treasurer. Back Row, Left to right: Laura Egwuatu, President, Wilma Gayden, Membership Chair, Rachel Pitts, 3rd Vice-President, Gertrude Dawson, Financial Secretary, Maxine Haynes, Parliamentarian.

African American Registered Nurses in Seattle

Founding Members in 1999 at the time of the 50th anniversary: Back row left to right: Mary Davis Hooks, Rachel Pitts and Gertrude Dawson. Front row left to right: Juanita Davis and Maxine Haynes. Not pictured: Ernestine Williams and Anne Foy Baker.

Appendix

1999 members at the time of the 50th anniversary: Top row, left to right: Doris Boutain, Lynette Wells, Elinor Jones. Second row from top, left to right: Frances Demisse, Verna Hill, Gertrude Dawson, Laura Egwuatu, Lois Eason, Josephine Atteberry. Third row from top, left to right: Charlotte Ruff, Robin Sudduth, Carole Crowder, Monvelia Theresa Blair. Fourth row from top, left to right: Mary Lee Bell, Vanetta Molson Turner, Lois Price Spratlen. Fifth row, left to right: Rachael Pitts, Antwinett Owens Lee, Mary Osborne, Mary Davis Hooks. Front row, left to right: Elizabeth Thomas, Thelma Pegues, Frances Terry, Juanita Davis, Maxine Haynes.

African American Registered Nurses in Seattle

Year 2000 members: Left to Right: Linda LeSuer, Verna Hill, Jean Amos, Josephine Atteberry, Elizabeth Thomas, Muriel Softli, Robin Sudduth, Izetta Hatcher, Gertrude Dawson, Melissia Yvette Peyton, George Sharpe, Lynnette Wells, Charlotte Ruff, Antwinette Lee, Laura Egwuatu, Mary Lee Bell, Mary Davis Hooks, Vanetta Molson-Turner, Diana Benton, Janice Flemming, Rosa Young, Betty Jean Sanders Stanton, Lois Price Spratlen, and Lois Eason.

Year 2000 Officers: Left to right: Verna Hill, Frances Terry, Elizabeth Thomas, Lynnette Wells, Vanetta Molson-Turner, Gertrude Dawson, Antwinett Lee.

Appendix

Year 2000 Inductees into the Washington State Nurses Hall of Fame. Left to right: Frances Terry, Muriel Softli, Shirley Gilford, Mary Lee Bell, Elizabeth Thomas.

Year 2000 Scholarship Recipients with the Scholarship Committee: Left to right: Elizabeth Thomas, Lynnette Wells, Adaobi Moemenam, Julie L. Vaughn, Carol V. Dixon, Audrey M. Thomas, Melissia Yvette Peyton, Jean Amos.